CHILD PARENT RELATIONSHIP
THERAPY (CPRT)
TREATMENT MANUAL

CHILD PARENT RELATIONSHIP THERAPY (CPRT) TREATMENT MANUAL

A 10-Session Filial Therapy Model for Training Parents

Complete Treatment Protocol • Includes CD-Rom of Training Materials, Treatment Outlines, Parent Handouts, Therapist's Guide, and Additional Resources

Sue C. Bratton • Garry L. Landreth
Theresa Kellam • Sandra R. Blackard

Routledge
Taylor & Francis Group
New York   London

Routledge is an imprint of the
Taylor & Francis Group, an informa business

Routledge
Taylor & Francis Group
270 Madison Avenue
New York, NY 10016

Routledge
Taylor & Francis Group
2 Park Square
Milton Park, Abingdon
Oxon OX14 4RN

© 2006 by Taylor and Francis Group, LLC
Routledge is an imprint of Taylor & Francis Group, an Informa business

Printed in the United States of America on acid-free paper
10 9 8 7 6 5 4 3 2

International Standard Book Number-10: 0-415-95212-3 (Hardcover)
International Standard Book Number-13: 978-0-415-95212-5 (Hardcover)
Library of Congress Card Number 2005030590

Library of Congress Cataloging-in-Publication Data

Child parent relationship therapy (CPRT) treatment manual : a 10-session filial therapy model for training parents / Sue Bratton ... [et al.].
    p. ; cm.
  Includes bibliographical references and index.
  ISBN 0-415-95212-3 (pb : alk. paper)
  1. Parent-child interaction therapy--Handbooks, manuals, etc. 2. Play therapy--Handbooks, manuals, etc. 3. Parent and child--Handbooks, manuals, etc.
  [DNLM: 1. Play Therapy--methods--Handbooks. 2. Family Therapy--methods--Handbooks. 3. Parent-Child Relations--Handbooks. WS 39 C5362 2006] I. Bratton, Sue. II. Title.

RJ505.P37C45 2006
618.92'891653--dc22
                                                   2005030590

Visit the Taylor & Francis Web site at
http://www.taylorandfrancis.com

and the Routledge Web site at
http://www.routledgementalhealth.com

Table of Contents

DIRECTIONS FOR USING THE CPRT TREATMENT MANUAL

The ***Child Parent Relationship Therapy (CPRT) Treatment Manual: A 10-Session Filial Therapy Model for Training Parents*** is a companion to the textbook *Child Parent Relationship Therapy (CPRT): A 10-Session Filial Therapy Model* (Landreth & Bratton, 2006), available from the publisher, Routledge. The training materials included in this manual assume the reader is familiar with the information contained in the text. This manual is designed to be helpful to therapists with all levels of experience.

The ***CPRT Treatment Manual*** has three major sections: *Therapist Notebook, Study Guide*, and *Parent Notebook*. The manual also includes a comprehensive resource section and several appendices containing supplemental training materials, clinical forms, organizational tools, assessments, and marketing materials. The accompanying CD-ROM allows the therapist to print the necessary training materials for ease of reproduction. For example, the *Parent Notebook* is designed to be printed from the CD-ROM and then copied double-sided for parents, to ensure correct pagination (to correspond with the page numbers in the *Parent Notebook* that are referred to in the Treatment Outlines in the *Therapist Notebook*). The CD-ROM files also provide the therapist the flexibility to adapt the Treatment Outlines in the *Therapist Notebook* by downloading and adapting the files to accommodate individual or co-leader training styles, therapist level of experience, as well as to adapt content/format to fit specific parent needs. *Note: only Treatment Outlines, client Progress Notes, and marketing materials may be altered, and only by the purchaser of this manual for conducting CPRT with clients.*

The ***Therapist Notebook*** is organized by treatment sessions and contains all materials that the therapist needs to conduct the 10-session CPRT model, including Treatment Outlines for Sessions 1–10 and all corresponding parent handouts, homework, and parent worksheets—with sample answers for the therapist. Sample answers are provided only as an example—there are other responses that could be used that would be consistent with the Child-Centered Play Therapy (CCPT) philosophy. For additional CCPT skills and responses, refer to Chapter 5, "CPRT Skills, Concepts, and Attitudes," in the companion CPRT text (Landreth & Bratton, 2006). The *Therapist Notebook* contains copies of all handouts in the *Parent Notebook*, with a reference to the page number where the handout can be found in the CD-Rom version of the *Parent Notebook*. In preparation for each parent training session, print the Materials Checklist (Appendix A on the accompanying CD-ROM) and review the *Study Guide* for Treatment Outline for that session.

It is recommended that the therapist print out the entire *Therapist Notebook* from the CD-ROM prior to beginning treatment. As noted previously, the CD-ROM files also provide the therapist the flexibility to adapt the Treatment Outlines in the *Therapist Notebook* by downloading and adapting the files to accommodate individual training styles and therapist level of experience. For example, the experienced CPRT/filial therapist may prefer a less detailed outline, while the novice CPRT therapist may prefer to add more detailed explanations of concepts or skills. Outlines can also be altered to accommodate co-leaders. We have found that using a three-ring binder with tabs is an efficient method of organizing and using the materials. These materials are designed to be flexible to help you adapt the training to the developmental needs of parents and children. As noted in the CPRT text (Landreth & Bratton, 2006), the 10-session curriculum presented in this manual can be adapted for use in fewer sessions, as well as extended for a longer number of sessions, depending on parent needs and group size. Although designed for use with groups of parents, the materials are also easily adapted for use with individual parents and couples. As with any treatment/intervention, therapists are expected to exercise clinical judgment in the use of materials and procedures.

The **Study Guide** is designed to be studied prior to each CPRT training session. It is not intended for use during the training sessions. The *Study Guide* is an expanded version of the *Therapist Notebook* and is designed to provide a more in-depth explanation of content for the novice CPRT/filial therapist. This section begins with an overview, *Helpful Hints for Conducting CPRT*. Embedded within each treatment outline are shaded text boxes with additional information and examples for each training concept or activity to aid you in preparing for each session. The material in the shaded text boxes is not meant to be presented in full or memorized. In several cases, the authors have shared personal parenting experiences to illustrate a point, but it is important to use your own stories and metaphors, making teaching points in a way that feels comfortable and congruent. If you are not a parent and have little personal experience with children, do not try to pretend that you do. You can draw on your professional experience as a play therapist, teacher, and so forth, or share stories of friends' or relatives' experiences with children. For the experienced CPRT/filial therapist, the *Study Guide* can serve as a brief review.

We suggest that therapists have the *Therapist Notebook* at hand when reviewing the *Study Guide* in preparation for each session, making any additional notes directly on the session treatment outline for that session (or electronically adapting the outline to fit as needed). Never use the *Study Guide* during treatment sessions; training should not be scripted. The CPRT curriculum is designed to be used by experienced play therapists with prior training and experience in both Child-Centered Play Therapy (CCPT) and group therapy, and who have a solid understanding of CPRT skills, concepts and procedures. This training and experience base is necessary in order to facilitate a lively, spontaneous, and interactive group training process. Reading from the *Study Guide* would interfere with this process and impede the development of a therapeutic connection between the parents and therapist. The therapist should become familiar enough with the material in the *Study Guide* to deliver the training in his or her own unique way of engaging parents in the treatment process. As noted earlier, it is expected that the therapist will exercise clinical judgment in using these materials in order to best meet the specific needs of a particular group of parents. *Note: It is also necessary to refer to the Materials Checklist (See Appendix A on CD-ROM) as you prepare for each training session.*

The **Parent Notebook** includes all of the printed materials that parents will need to complete CPRT training. It is strongly recommended that the entire *Parent Notebook* be printed from the CD-ROM (rather than copied from this manual). The CD-Rom version of the *Parent Notebook* provides for correct pagination (to correspond with the page numbers in the *Parent Notebook* that are referred to in the Treatment Outlines in the *Therapist Notebook*). We suggest organizing the notebook into a three-ring binder to be given to each parent on the first day of training. Providing tabs to identify each session enhances usability of the *Parent Notebook*. However, some therapists may prefer to hand out the materials one section at a time at the beginning of each session. Other useful strategies for the organization of training materials include printing the two most used handouts, *Dos and Don'ts* and *Play Session Procedures Checklist*, on two different colors of paper or using tabs or similar tools to provide an easy method for parents to locate them in their notebooks (both handouts are introduced in Session 3, but referred to in every session thereafter).

Handouts are organized by the CPRT training session they are typically used in. Some flexibility in presenting materials is allowed, depending on the needs of a particular group of parents. Supplemental skill practice worksheets for parents are also included in Appendix C on the accompanying CD-ROM. Although these supplemental worksheets are provided as additional practice for CPRT skills that a particular groups of parents may be having difficulty with, the therapist is cautioned to avoid overwhelming parents with too much information or homework. Again, it is expected that the therapist with exercise clinical judgment in determining when and if to use supplemental materials.

Please note that permission to copy the materials is granted to the therapist in conjunction with the purchase of this training. The copyright statement on the cover page of the *Parent Notebook* should be printed out and included in the notebook handed out to parents.

CPRT Training Resources includes a list of useful CPRT training resources. Resources are organized by videos, books, and manuals. Each of those categories is further divided into recommended and supplemental resources.

Appendix A includes helpful organizational and practical materials for CPRT training. These materials are prepared for ease of reprinting for each new group and include a *Parent Information Form* to complete prior to Session 1 and to note important information about group participants (this form should be brought to every session; therefore we suggest inserting it in the front of the *Therapist Notebook*); the *Materials Checklist* for Sessions 1–10 to help keep track of what the therapist needs to bring to each session (the therapist is advised to bring a few extras of all printed materials that parents will need for each session, in the likely case a parent forgets the notebook); CPRT *Progress Notes* to assess the clinical progress of individual group members throughout Sessions 1–10; and the *Therapist Skills Checklist* for the novice CPRT therapist or student intern to self-assess important CPRT skills. This appendix also contains items for parents that are to be handed out separately from the *Parent Notebook* materials, including *Playtime Appointment Cards, Do Not Disturb Template* and *Certificates of Completion*.

Appendix B includes a poster format of the most frequently used handout, *Play Session Dos and Don'ts*, formatted so that the therapist can print it out on three sheets of 8 ½" x 11" paper, tape it together, and laminate it as a poster to provide a handy visual for referencing these important skills during Sessions 3–10.

Appendix C includes supplemental parent worksheets and therapist versions with example answers. These supplemental handouts provide opportunities for additional practice of CPRT skills and are used at the discretion of the therapist's assessment of the parents' needs. The session numbers on each worksheet corresponds to when that particular skill is generally introduced or practiced. Worksheets include: *Feelings Response Worksheet* for Session 2, *Choice-Giving Worksheet* for Session 6, *Esteem-Building Responses Worksheet* for Session 7, *Encouragement vs. Praise Worksheet* for Session 8, and *Advanced Limit Setting: Giving Choices as Consequences Worksheet* for Session 9. References to these optional worksheets are included in the *Study Guide* in the sessions we recommend their use; however, they may be used flexibly, depending on the needs of a particular group of parents. Although these supplemental worksheets are provided as additional practice for CPRT skills that a particular groups of parents may be having difficulty with, the therapist is cautioned to avoid overwhelming parents with too much information or homework. Again, it is expected that the therapist will exercise clinical judgment in determining when and if to use supplemental materials.

Appendix D includes information for successful marketing of C-P-R Training to parents. A sample brochure, a sample newspaper ad, and two sample flyers are included. These materials may be electronically adapted for therapist use.

Appendix E includes three unpublished assessments that have been used for research in CPRT and filial therapy: *Porter Parental Acceptance Scale* (PPAS), and *Filial Problems Checklist* (FPC), and *Measurement of Empathy in Adult-Child Interaction* (MEACI). All three measures are designed to be administered pre and post treatment. The PPAS and FPC are self-report instruments administered to parents; the PPAS measures parent's attitude of acceptance toward the child of focus, while the FPC measures the parent's perception of the child of focus's behavior. The MEACI is a direct observational measure of parental empathy that requires pre and post videotaping of parents (the use of this instrument requires substantial training and inter-rater reliability). Instruments and scoring are included in separate files for ease of printing. We gratefully acknowledge Dr. Louise Guerney and Dr. Blaine Porter for generously allowing us to include these materials for use by CPRT/filial therapists.

We hope that you find this manual helpful and informative,

Sue, Garry, Theresa, and Sandy

CHILD PARENT RELATIONSHIP THERAPY (CPRT)

THERAPIST NOTEBOOK

Treatment Outlines and Handouts for Sessions 1–10

Using the Therapist Notebook

The ***Therapist Notebook*** is organized by treatment sessions and contains all materials that the therapist needs to conduct the 10-session CPRT model, including Treatment Outlines for Sessions 1–10 and all corresponding parent handouts, homework, and parent worksheets—with sample answers for the therapist. Sample answers are provided only as an example—there are other responses that could be used that would be consistent with the Child-Centered Play Therapy (CCPT) philosophy. For additional CCPT skills and responses, refer to Chapter 5, "CPRT Skills, Concepts, and Attitudes," in the companion CPRT text (Landreth & Bratton, 2006). The *Therapist Notebook* contains copies of all handouts in the *Parent Notebook*, with a reference to the page number where the handout can be found in the CD-Rom version of the *Parent Notebook*. In preparation for each parent training session, print the Materials Checklist (Appendix A on the accompanying CD-ROM) and review the *Study Guide* for the treatment outline for that session.

It is recommended that the therapist print out the entire *Therapist Notebook* from the CD-ROM prior to beginning treatment. As noted previously, the CD-ROM files also provide the therapist the flexibility to adapt the Treatment Outlines in the *Therapist Notebook* by downloading and adapting the files to accommodate individual training styles and therapist level of experience. For example, the experienced CPRT/filial therapist may prefer a less detailed outline, while the novice CPRT therapist may prefer to add more detailed explanations of concepts or skills. Outlines can also be altered to accommodate co-leaders. We have found that using a three-ring binder with tabs for each session is an efficient method of organizing and using the materials.

These materials are designed to be flexible to help you adapt the training to the developmental needs of parents and children. As noted in the CPRT text (Landreth & Bratton, 2006), the 10-session curriculum presented in this manual can be adapted for use in fewer sessions, as well as extended for a longer number of sessions, depending on parent needs and group size. Although designed for use with groups of parents, the materials are also easily adapted for use with individual parents and couples. As with any treatment/intervention, therapists are expected to exercise clinical judgment in the use of materials and procedures.

Child Parent Relationship Therapy (CPRT)

Session 1 – Treatment Outline

⊕ <u>Time</u>
<u>Marker</u>

Note: Print material checklist for this session (CD-Rom, Appendix A – contains list of all materials and where to locate them)

_____ **I.**   **Give Name Tags and *Parent Notebooks* to All Parents as They Arrive**

(Ask parents who need to complete intake information to stay afterward.)

Introduce self/welcome group—have parents briefly share about themselves and why they are here; help them feel supported and that they are not alone in their struggles

_____ **II.**   **Overview of CPRT Training Objectives and Essential Concepts**

☝ **Rule of Thumb: "Focus on the donut, not the hole!"**

CPRT focuses on the relationship, your strengths and your child's strengths, <u>NOT</u> the problem.

- Play is the child's language

- Helps prevent problems because parent becomes aware of child's needs

☝ **Rule of Thumb: "Be a thermostat, not a thermometer!"**

Learn to RESPOND (reflect) rather than REACT. The child's feelings <u>are not</u> your feelings and needn't escalate with him/her.

When your child's feelings and behaviors escalate, you can learn to respond in a helpful way, rather than simply reacting and allowing your feelings and behaviors to escalate, too. Remember: In-control parents are thermostats; out-of-control parents are thermometers.

- You will learn the same basic play therapy skills that graduate students learn in a semester course

<u>These skills will</u>:

  o Return control to you as parent and help child develop self-control

  o Provide closer, happier times with your child—more joy and laughter, warm memories

   Ask parents: *"What do you want your child to remember about you/your relationship 20 years from now?"* (What are parents' best memories from childhood?)

  o Give key to your child's inner world—learn how to really understand your child and how to help your child feel that you understand

- Best of all, you only have to practice these new skills and do something different 30 minutes per week!

- Patience is important in learning a new language

"In 10 weeks, you are going to be different, and your relationship with your child will be different."

_____ III.   **Group Introductions (facilitate sharing and connections between parents)**

- Describe entire family; help pick child of focus if not identified during intake

- Tell concerns about this child (take notes on *Parent Information Form*)

- Facilitate sharing

- Make generalizing/normalizing comments to other parents
  (Example: "Anyone else feel angry with his or her child this week?")

☝ **Rule of Thumb: "What's most important may not be what you do, but what you do after what you did!"**
  We are certain to make mistakes, but we can recover. It is how we handle our mistakes that makes the difference.

_____ IV.   **Reflective Responding**

- Way of following, rather than leading

- Reflect behaviors, thoughts, needs/wishes, and feelings (<u>without asking questions</u>)

- Helps parent understand child <u>and</u> helps child feel understood

"Be With" Attitudes Convey:	Not:
I am here; I <u>hear</u> you	I always agree
I understand	I must make you happy
I care	I will solve your problems

_____ V.   **Optional – Show Video Clips: *Life's First Feelings***

Video clip #1: Discuss

Video clip #2: Discuss reactions (especially difference in mad/sad) as lead-in to *Feelings Response: In-Class Practice Worksheet* (refer parents to page 2 in the *Parent Notebook*)

_____ VI.   **Complete *Feelings Response: In-Class Practice Worksheet***

Complete worksheet together with parents, asking them, <u>as a group</u>, to decide on the feeling word that best describes how the child is feeling and next, <u>as a group</u>, decide on a short response.

___ **VII.**   **Role-Play**

Demonstrate wtih co-leader or ask a parent to tell you about his or her day and simply reflect as the parent talks about it; then pair up parents and have them take turns being the "listener"

____ **VIII.**   **Video Demonstration (optional, if time permits)**

Show demonstration of play session skills of reflection of feeling and allowing the child to lead

____ **IX.**   **Homework Assignments** (refer parents to homework section in their notebook)

1) Notice one physical characteristic about your child you haven't seen before.

_____

2) Practice reflective responding—complete *Feelings Response: Homework Worksheet* and bring next week.

3) Bring your favorite, heart-tugging picture of your child of focus.

4) Practice giving a 30-second Burst of Attention. If you are on the telephone, say, "Can you hold for 30 seconds? I'll be right back." Put the phone aside, bend down, and give your child undivided, focused attention for 30 seconds; then say, "I have to finish talking to _____." Stand back up and continue talking with your friend.

____ **X.**   **Close With Motivational Poem, Story, or Rule of Thumb (optional)**

👍 RULES OF THUMB TO REMEMBER:

1.   **"Focus on the donut, not the hole!"** Focus on the relationship, NOT the problem.

2.   **"Be a thermostat, not a thermometer."** Learn to RESPOND (reflect) rather than REACT.

3.   **"What's most important may not be what you do, but what you do after what you did!"** We all make mistakes, but we can recover. It is how we handle our mistakes that makes the difference.

_____

CHILD-PARENT-RELATIONSHIP (C-P-R) TRAINING
Parent Notes & Homework – Session 1

☝ RULES OF THUMB TO REMEMBER:

1. **"Focus on the donut, not the hole!"** Focus on the Relationship, NOT the Problem.
2. **"Be a thermostat, not a thermometer."** Learn to RESPOND (reflect) rather than REACT.
3. **"What's most important may not be what you do, but what you do after what you did!"** We all make mistakes, but we can recover. It is how we handle our mistakes that makes the difference.

_____

Reflective Responding:

A way of following, rather than leading

Reflect behaviors, thoughts, needs/wishes, and feelings (<u>without asking questions</u>)

Helps parent understand child <u>and</u> helps child feel understood

"Be With" Attitudes Convey:	Not:
I am here; I <u>hear</u> you	I always agree
I understand	I must make you happy
I care	I will solve your problems

Notes (use back for additional notes):

_____
_____
_____
_____
_____
_____
_____
_____

Homework Assignments:

1. Notice one physical characteristic about your child you haven't seen before.

   _____

2. Practice reflective responding (complete **Feeling Response: Homework Worksheet** and bring next week).
3. Bring your favorite, heart-tugging picture of your child of focus.
4. Practice giving a 30-second Burst of Attention. If you are on the telephone, say, "Can you hold for 30 seconds? I'll be right back." Put the phone aside, bend down, and give your child undivided, focused attention for 30 seconds; then say, "I have to finish talking to ____." Stand back up and continue talking with your friend.

CHILD-PARENT-RELATIONSHIP (C-P-R) TRAINING
Feelings Response: In-Class Practice Worksheet – Session 1

Directions: 1) Look into child's eyes for clue to feeling. 2) After you've decided what child is feeling, put the feeling word into a short response, generally beginning with <u>you</u>, "you seem sad," or "you're really mad at me right now." 3) Your facial expression & tone of voice should match your child's (empathy is conveyed more through nonverbals than verbals).

HAPPY

Child: Adam is telling you all the things he's going to show Grandma and Grandpa when they get to your house.

Child Felt: *Excited, Happy, Glad*
Parent Response: *You're excited that Grandma & Grandpa are coming.*

SAD

Child: Sally gets in the car after school and tells you that Bert, the class pet hamster, died—and then tells you about how she was in charge of feeding Bert last week and how he would look at her and then get on his wheel and run.

Child Felt: *Sad, Disappointed*
Parent Response: *You're sad that Bert died.*

MAD

Child: Andy was playing with his friend, Harry, when Harry grabbed Andy's fire truck and wouldn't give it back. Andy tried to get it back and the ladder broke off. Andy comes to you crying and tells you what happened and that it's all Harry's fault.

Child Felt: *Mad, Angry, Upset*
Parent Response: *You're really mad at Harry.*

SCARED

Child: Sarah was playing in the garage while you were cleaning it out, when a big box of books falls off the shelf and hits the floor behind her. She jumps up and runs over to you.

Child Felt: *Scared, Surprised* (depends on child's facial expression)
Parent Response: *1) That (scared, surprised ...) you!*

CHILD-PARENT-RELATIONSHIP (C-P-R) TRAINING
Feelings Response: Homework Worksheet – Session 1

Directions: 1) Look into child's eyes for clue to feeling. 2) After you've decided what child is feeling, put the feeling word into a short response, generally beginning with <u>you</u>, "you seem sad," or "you're really mad at me right now." 3) Remember the importance of your facial expression & tone of voice matching child's (empathy is conveyed more through nonverbals than verbals).

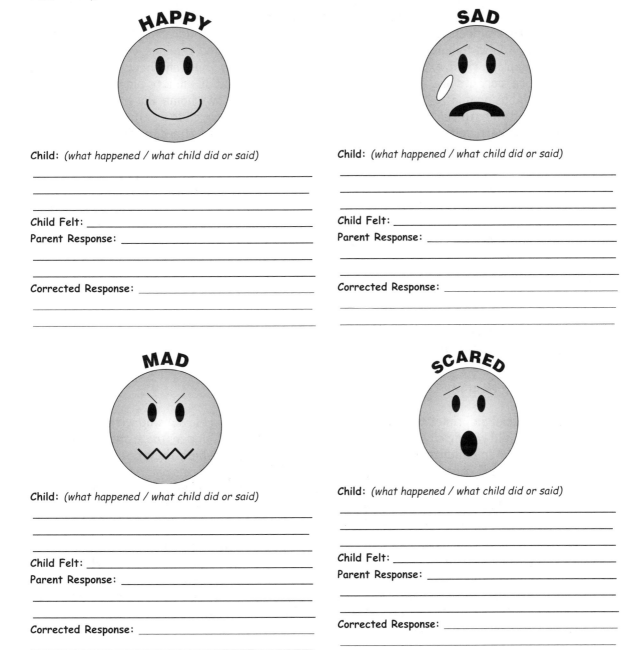

HAPPY

Child: *(what happened / what child did or said)*

_____
_____
_____

Child Felt: _____
Parent Response: _____
_____
_____

Corrected Response: _____
_____
_____

SAD

Child: *(what happened / what child did or said)*

_____
_____
_____

Child Felt: _____
Parent Response: _____
_____
_____

Corrected Response: _____
_____
_____

MAD

Child: *(what happened / what child did or said)*

_____
_____
_____

Child Felt: _____
Parent Response: _____
_____
_____

Corrected Response: _____
_____
_____

SCARED

Child: *(what happened / what child did or said)*

_____
_____
_____

Child Felt: _____
Parent Response: _____
_____
_____

Corrected Response: _____
_____
_____

CHILD-PARENT-RELATIONSHIP (C-P-R) TRAINING
What Is It and How Can It Help?

What Is It?

Child-Parent-Relationship (C-P-R) Training is a special 10-session parent training program to help strengthen the relationship between a parent and a child by using 30-minute playtimes once a week. Play is important to children because it is the most natural way children communicate. Toys are like words for children and play is their language. Adults talk about their experiences, thoughts, and feelings. Children use toys to explore their experiences and express what they think and how they feel. Therefore, parents are taught to have special structured 30-minute playtimes with their child using a kit of carefully selected toys in their own home. Parents learn how to respond empathically to their child's feelings, build their child's self-esteem, help their child learn self-control and self-responsibility, and set therapeutic limits during these special playtimes.

For 30 minutes each week, the child is the center of the parent's universe. In this special playtime, the parent creates an accepting relationship in which a child feels completely safe to express himself through his play—fears, likes, dislikes, wishes, anger, loneliness, joy, or feelings of failure. This is not a typical playtime. It is a special playtime in which the child leads and the parent follows. In this special relationship, there are no:

+ reprimands
+ put-downs
+ evaluations
+ requirements (to draw pictures a certain way, etc.)
+ judgments (about the child or his play as being good or bad, right or wrong)

How Can It Help My Child?

In the special playtimes, you will build a different kind of relationship with your child, and your child will discover that she is capable, important, understood, and accepted as she is. When children experience a play relationship in which they feel accepted, understood, and cared for, they play out many of their problems and, in the process, release tensions, feelings, and burdens. Your child will then feel better about herself and will be able to discover her own strengths and assume greater self-responsibility as she takes charge of play situations.

How your child feels about herself will make a significant difference in her behavior. In the special playtimes where you learn to focus on your child rather than your child's problem, your child will begin to react differently because how your child behaves, how she thinks, and how she performs in school are directly related to how she feels about herself. When your child feels better about herself, she will behave in more self-enhancing ways rather than self-defeating ways.

Child Parent Relationship Therapy (CPRT)

Session 2 – Treatment Outline

⊕ <u>Time</u>
<u>Marker</u>

Note: Print material checklist for this session (CD-Rom, Appendix A – contains list of all materials and where to locate them)

_____ **I.** **Informal Sharing and Review of Homework**

Ask about each parent's week and reflect briefly

Review homework from Session 1:

1. 30-second Burst of Attention

2. *Feelings Response: Homework Worksheet*—refer parents to worksheet for reflecting feelings review and practice

   Remember to reflect parent's experience/model encouragement as parents share

3. Physical characteristic/favorite picture

   Ask questions and reflect answers; ask parents to report a physical characteristic of their child that they hadn't noticed before

_____ **II.** **Handout:** *Basic Principles of Play Sessions* (refer parents to page 6 in the *Parent Notebook*)

1. Parent allows child to lead and parent follows, without asking questions or making suggestions

   • Show keen interest and closely observe

   ☝ **Rule of Thumb: "The parent's toes should follow his/her nose."**
   Body language conveys interest and full attention

   • Actively join in when invited

   • Parent is "dumb" for 30 minutes

2. The parent's major task is to empathize with the child

   • See and experience the child's play through the child's eyes

   • Understand child's needs, feelings, and thoughts expressed through play

3. Parent is then to communicate this understanding to the child

   • Describing what the child is doing/playing

   • Reflecting what the child is saying

   • Reflecting what the child is feeling

4. The parent is to be clear and firm about the few "limits" that are placed on the child's behavior

- Gives child responsibility for behavior

- Limits set on time, for safety, and to prevent breaking toys or damaging play area

- Stated only when needed, but consistently

5. <u>Note:</u> If time allows, briefly review goals of play sessions on handout

_____ **III.   Demonstration of Toys for Play Session Toy Kit**

- Briefly review Toy Categories on *Toy Checklist for Play Sessions* (refer parents to page 7 in the *Parent Notebook*; don't read entire list)

- Demonstrate/show toys and briefly explain rationale—especially for toys that may concern parents (dart gun and baby bottle)

- As toys are shown, briefly provide examples of how you might respond to child playing with that toy (co-leader can role-play with you)

- Discuss finding used, free, and inexpensive toys

- Emphasize the importance of the toys and get commitment that each parent will have over half of the toys by next week—preferably all; if they don't, they likely won't be ready for their first play session

- Discuss pros and cons of involving child in collecting toys for play session kit

_____ **IV.   Choosing a Place and Time for Play Sessions**

- Suggest a room that parent believes will offer the fewest distractions to the child and greatest freedom from worry about breaking things or making a mess
  Kitchen area is ideal if no one else at home; otherwise, need to be able to close a door

- Set aside a regular time in advance
  o   This time is to be undisturbed—no phone calls or interruptions by other children
  o   Most importantly, choose a time when the parent feels most relaxed, rested, and emotionally available to child

Rule of Thumb: "You can't give away that which you don't possess."
(Analogy: oxygen mask on airplane: take care of yourself first, then your child)
You can't extend patience and acceptance to your child if you can't first offer it to yourself. As your child's most significant caregiver, you are asked to give so much of yourself, often when you simply don't have the resources within you to meet the demands of parenting. As parents, you may be deeply aware of your own failures, yet you can't extend patience and acceptance to your child while being impatient and un-accepting of yourself.
  o   <u>Note:</u> Let parents know that you will be asking each of them to report next week on the place and time they have chosen

_____ **V.**   **Role-Play and Demonstration of Basic Play Session Skills (video clip or live)**

Make sure to allow at least 15–20 minutes of demonstration, stopping to answer questions and get reactions, and another 5–10 minutes for paired parent role-plays, followed by 5–10 minutes for therapist to role-play "scenarios" parents had difficulty with in their role-play with parent partners

1. Show video clip that clearly demonstrates the concept of setting the stage, allowing the child to lead (without asking questions), tracking, and conveying the "Be With" Attitudes (or conduct live demo focusing on same attitudes and skills)

   o   Review the "BE WITH" ATTITUDES: I'm here, I hear you, I understand, and I care!

2. Use filial toy kit or toys in playroom for parents to take turns role-playing child and parent in play session, practicing the skills just demonstrated

_____ **VI.**   **Homework Assignments** (refer parents to homework section in their notebook)

1) Priority—Collect toys on *Toy Checklist for Play Sessions.*
   Brainstorm ideas and sources and suggest parents share resources

2) Select a consistent time and an uninterrupted place in the home suitable for the play sessions and report back next week—whatever room you feel offers the fewest distractions to the child and the greatest freedom from worry about breaking things or making a mess. Set aside a regular time in advance. This time is to be undisturbed—no phone calls or interruptions by other children.
   Time _____ Place _____

3) Additional Assignment:

_____ **VII.**   **Close With Motivational Poem, Story, or Rule of Thumb (optional)**

End session with a motivational book, poem, or story, such as "I'll Love You Forever"

👍 RULES OF THUMB TO REMEMBER:

1. **"The parent's toes should follow his/her nose."**

2. **"You can't give away that which you don't possess."** You can't extend patience and acceptance to your child if you can't first offer it to yourself. As your child's most significant caregiver, you are asked to give so much of yourself, often when you simply don't have the resources within you to meet the demands of parenting. As parents, you may be deeply aware of your own failures, yet you can't extend patience and acceptance to your child while being impatient and un-accepting of yourself.

Remember the analogy of the oxygen mask on an airplane!

CHILD-PARENT-RELATIONSHIP (C-P-R) TRAINING
Parent Notes & Homework – Session 2

☞ RULES OF THUMB TO REMEMBER:

1. **"The parent's toes should follow his/her nose."**

2. **"You can't give away that which you don't possess."** You can't extend patience and acceptance to your child if you can't first offer it to yourself. As your child's most significant caregiver, you are asked to give so much of yourself, often when you simply don't have the resources within you to meet the demands of parenting. As parents, you may be deeply aware of your own failures, yet you can't extend patience and acceptance to your child while being impatient and unaccepting of yourself.

Remember the analogy of the oxygen mask on an airplane!

Remember the "BE WITH" ATTITUDES: I'm here, I hear you, I understand, and I care!

Notes (use back for additional notes):

_____
_____
_____
_____
_____
_____
_____
_____
_____
_____
_____
_____
_____
_____
_____
_____

Homework Assignments:

1. Priority—Collect toys on *Toy Checklist for Play Sessions*.

2. Select a consistent time and an uninterrupted place in the home suitable for the play sessions and report back next week—whatever room you feel offers the fewest distractions to the child and the greatest freedom from worry about breaking things or making a mess. Set aside a regular time in advance. This time is to be undisturbed—no phone calls or interruptions by other children.

Time _____ Place _____

3. Additional assignment:

CHILD-PARENT-RELATIONSHIP (C-P-R) TRAINING
Basic Principles of Play Sessions – Session 2

Basic Principles for Play Sessions:

1. The parent sets the stage by structuring an atmosphere in which the **child feels free** to determine how he will use the time during the 30-minute play session. The **child leads** the play and the **parent follows.** The parent follows the child's lead by showing keen interest and carefully observing the child's play, **without making suggestions or asking questions**, and by actively joining in the play when invited by the child. *For 30 minutes, you (parent) are "dumb" and don't have the answers; it is up to your child to make his own decisions and find his own solutions.*

2. The parent's major task is to empathize with the child: to understand the child's thoughts, feelings, and intent expressed in play by working hard to **see and experience the child's play through the child's eyes.** *This task is operationalized by conveying the "Be With" Attitudes below.*

3. The parent is then to **communicate this understanding to the child** by: a) verbally describing what the child is doing/playing, b) verbally reflecting what the child is saying, and c) most importantly, by verbally reflecting the feelings that the child is actively experiencing through his play.

4. The parent is to be clear and firm about the few "limits" that are placed on the child's behavior. Limits are stated in a way that give the child responsibility for his actions and behaviors—helping to foster self-control. Limits to be set are: time limits, not breaking toys or damaging items in the play area, and not physically hurting self or parent. **Limits are to be stated only when needed,** but applied consistently across sessions. *(Specific examples of when and how to set limits will be taught over the next several weeks; you will also have lots of opportunities to practice this very important skill.)*

"Be With" Attitudes:
Your <u>intent</u> in your actions, presence, and responses is what is most important and should convey to your child:
"I am here—I hear/see you—I understand—I care."

Goals of the Play Sessions:

1. To allow the child—through the medium of play—to communicate thoughts, needs, and feelings to his parent, and for the parent to communicate that understanding back to the child.

2. Through feeling accepted, understood, and valued—for the child to experience more positive feelings of self-respect, self-worth, confidence, and competence—and ultimately develop self-control, responsibility for actions, and learn to get needs met in appropriate ways.

3. To strengthen the parent-child relationship and foster a sense of trust, security, and closeness for both parent and child.

4. To increase the level of playfulness and enjoyment between parent and child.

CHILD-PARENT-RELATIONSHIP (C-P-R) TRAINING
Toy Checklist for Play Sessions – Session 2

Note: Obtain sturdy cardboard box with sturdy lid to store toys in (box that copier paper comes in is ideal–the deep lid becomes a dollhouse). Use an old quilt or blanket to spread toys out on and to serve as a boundary for the play area.

Real-Life Toys (also promote imaginative play)
- ☐ Small baby doll: *should not be anything "special"; can be extra one that child does not play with anymore*
- ☐ Nursing bottle: *real one so it can be used by the child to put a drink in during the session*
- ☐ Doctor kit (with stethoscope): *add three Band-Aids for each session (add disposable gloves/Ace bandage, if you have)*
- ☐ Toy phones: *recommend getting two in order to communicate: one cell, one regular*
- ☐ Small dollhouse: *use deep lid of box the toys are stored in–draw room divisions, windows, doors, and so forth inside of lid*
- ☐ Doll family: *bendable mother, father, brother, sister, baby, and so forth (ethnically representative)*
- ☐ Play money: *bills and coins; credit card is optional*
- ☐ Couple of domestic and wild animals: *if you don't have doll family, can substitute an animal family (e.g., horse, cow family)*
- ☐ Car/Truck: *one to two small ones (could make specific to child's needs, e.g., an ambulance)*
- ☐ Kitchen dishes: *couple of plastic dishes, cups, and eating utensils*

Optional
- ☐ Puppets: *one aggressive, one gentle; can be homemade or purchased (animal shaped cooking mittens, etc.)*
- ☐ Doll furniture: *for a bedroom, bathroom, and kitchen*
- ☐ Dress up: *hand mirror, bandana, scarf; small items you already have around the house*

Acting-Out Aggressive Toys (also promote imaginative play)
- ☐ Dart guns with a couple of darts and a target: *parent needs to know how to operate*
- ☐ Rubber knife: *small, bendable, army type*
- ☐ Rope: *prefer soft rope (can cut the ends off jump rope)*
- ☐ Aggressive animal: *(e.g., snake, shark, lion, dinosaurs—strongly suggest hollow shark!)*
- ☐ Small toy soldiers (12–15): *two different colors to specify two teams or good guys/bad guys*
- ☐ Inflatable bop bag (Bobo *clown style preferable*)
- ☐ Mask: *Lone Ranger type*

Optional
- ☐ Toy handcuffs with a key

Toys for Creative/Emotional Expression
- ☐ Playdough: *suggest a cookie sheet to put playdough on to contain mess—also serves as a flat surface for drawing*
- ☐ Crayons: *eight colors, break some and peel paper off (markers are optional for older children but messier)*
- ☐ Plain paper: *provide a few pieces of new paper for each session*
- ☐ Scissors: *not pointed, but cut well (e.g., child Fiskars^μ)*
- ☐ Transparent tape: *remember, child can use up all of this, so buy several of smaller size*
- ☐ Egg carton, styrofoam cup/bowl: *for destroying, breaking, or coloring*
- ☐ Ring toss game
- ☐ Deck of playing cards
- ☐ Soft foam ball
- ☐ Two balloons per play session

Optional
- ☐ Selection of arts/crafts materials in a ziplock bag *(e.g., colored construction paper, glue, yarn, buttons, beads, scraps of fabrics, raw noodles, etc —much of this depends on age of child)*
- ☐ Tinkertoys^μ/small assortment of building blocks
- ☐ Binoculars
- ☐ Tambourine, drum, or other small musical instrument
- ☐ Magic wand

Reminder: *Toys need not be new or expensive. Avoid selecting more toys than will fit in a box—toys should be small. In some cases, additional toys can be added based on child's need and with therapist approval. If unable to get every toy before first play session, obtain several from each category—ask therapist for help in prioritizing.*

Note: Unwrap any new toys or take out of box before play session. Toys should look inviting.

Good Toy Hunting Places: garage sales, attic, friends/relatives, "dollar" stores, toy aisles of grocery and drug stores

Child Parent Relationship Therapy (CPRT)

Session 3 – Treatment Outline

⊕ Time Marker

Note: Print material checklist for this session (CD-Rom, Appendix A – contains list of all materials and where to locate them)

_____ **I.** **Informal Sharing and Review of Homework**

1. Toys collected

2. Time and place for play sessions

   Very important to ask very specific questions about when and where

   Hand out appointment cards—one for parent and one for child to keep

3. Any questions

_____ **II.** **Handout:** *Play Session Do's & Don'ts* (refer parents to page 9 in the *Parent Notebook*)

- Ask parents to refer to *Play Session Do's & Don'ts* handout as you refer to poster and provide examples

- Demonstrate **Play Session Do's** physically with toys as you go over each one (or role-play with co-leader)

<u>**Do:**</u>

1. **Do set the stage (structuring).**

2. **Do let the child lead.**

3. **Do join in the child's play actively, as a follower.**

4. Do verbally track child's play (describe what you see).

5. Do reflect the child's feelings.

6. **Do set firm and consistent limits.**

7. Do salute the child's power and encourage effort.

8. Do be verbally active.

   Note: Emphasize the bolded **Do's** for parents to focus on in first play session

<u>***Don't:***</u>

1. Don't criticize any behavior.

2. Don't praise the child.

3. Don't ask leading questions.

4. Don't allow interruptions of the session.

5. Don't give information or teach.

6. Don't preach.

7. Don't initiate new activities.

8. Don't be passive or quiet.

(Don'ts 1–7 are taken from Guerney, 1972)

_____ **III. View Demonstration Video Clip or Do a Live Demonstration Illustrating the Do's**

Video clip should primarily focus on demonstrating the "Be With" Attitudes and the skill of "allowing the child to lead"

_____ **IV. Handout:** *Play Session Procedures Checklist* (refer parents to page 10 in the *Parent Notebook*)

Briefly go over handout—especially what to do before the session to structure for success. Ask parents to read over carefully at least two days before their play session

Refer parents to photograph in their handouts of toys set up for play session

_____ **V. Parent Partners Role-Play**—focusing on skills they saw you demonstrate, as well as practice beginning and ending the session.

_____ **VI. Discuss With Parents How to Explain the "Special Playtime" to Their Child**

Example explanation: "You may wish to explain to your child that you are having these special playtimes with her because 'I am going to this special play class to learn some special ways to play with you!'"

_____ **VII. Arrange for One to Two Parent(s) to Do Videotaping This Week**

Name/phone number _____ day/time (if taping at clinic)_____
Name/phone number _____ day/time (if taping at clinic)_____

Remind parent(s) who are videotaping this week to make note on their Parent Notes & Homework handout

👍 **Rule of Thumb: "Be a thermostat, not a thermometer."**

Learn to RESPOND (reflect) rather than REACT. The child's feelings <u>are not</u> your feelings and needn't escalate with him/her.

Reflecting/responding to child's thoughts, feelings, and needs creates a comfortable atmosphere of understanding and acceptance for child.

During the 30-minute play session, parents are asked to be a thermostat for their child.

_____ **VIII.   Homework Assignments** (refer parents to homework section in their notebook)

1) Complete play session toy kit—get blanket/tablecloth and other materials (see *Photograph of Toys Set Up for Play Session* in handouts) and confirm that the <u>time and place you chose will work.</u> Make arrangements for other children.

2) Give child appointment card and make "Special Playtime—Do Not Disturb" sign with child one to three days ahead (depending on child's age). See *Template for Do Not Disturb Sign* in handouts.

   The younger the child, the closer to time of play session.

3) Read handouts prior to play session:

   Play Session Do's & Don'ts

   Play Session Procedures Checklist

4) Play sessions begin at home this week—arrange to videotape your session and make notes about problems or questions you have about your sessions.

_____ *I will bring my videotape for next week (if videotaping at clinic: my appt. day/time _____).*

_____ **IX.   Close With Motivational Poem, Story, or Rule of Thumb (optional)**

👍 **RULE OF THUMB TO REMEMBER:**

"Be a thermostat, not a thermometer."

Reflecting/responding to your child's thoughts, feelings, and needs creates a comfortable atmosphere of understanding and acceptance for your child.

CHILD-PARENT-RELATIONSHIP (C-P-R) TRAINING
Parent Notes & Homework – Session 3

☝ RULE OF THUMB TO REMEMBER:

"Be a thermostat, not a thermometer."
Reflecting/responding to your child's thoughts, feelings, and needs
creates a comfortable atmosphere of understanding and acceptance for your child.

Basic Limit Setting:

"Sarah, I know you'd like to shoot the gun at me, but I'm not for shooting. You can choose to shoot at that" (point at something <u>acceptable</u>).

Notes (use back for additional notes):

_____
_____
_____
_____
_____
_____
_____
_____
_____
_____
_____
_____
_____
_____
_____
_____

<u>Note</u>: You may wish to explain to your child that you are having these special playtimes with him or her because "I am going to this special play class to learn some special ways to play with you!"

Homework Assignments:

1. Complete play session toy kit—get blanket/quilt and other materials. (see *Photograph of Toys Set Up for Play Session* in handouts) and confirm that the time and place you chose will work. Make arrangements for other children.

2. Give child appointment card and make "Special Playtime—Do Not Disturb" sign with child one to three days ahead (depending on child's age). See Template for Do Not Disturb Sign in handouts.

3. Read over handouts prior to play session:
   Play Session Do's & Don'ts
   Play Session Procedures Checklist

4. Play sessions begin at home this week—arrange to videotape your session and make notes about problems or questions you have about your sessions.

_____ ***I will bring my videotape for next week (if videotaping at clinic: my appt. day/time _____).***

CHILD-PARENT-RELATIONSHIP (C-P-R) TRAINING
Play Session Do's & Don'ts – Session 3

Parents: *Your major task is to keenly show interest in your child's play and to communicate your interest in, and understanding of, your child's thoughts, feelings, and behavior through your words, actions, and undivided focus on your child.*

Do:

1. Do set the stage.
   a. Prepare play area ahead of time (old blanket can be used to establish a visual boundary of the play area, as well as provide protection for flooring; a cookie sheet under the arts/crafts materials provides a hard surface for playdough, drawing, and gluing, and provides ease of clean up).
   b. Display the toys in a consistent manner around the perimeter of the play area.
   c. Convey freedom of the special playtime through your words: *"During our special playtime, you can play with the toys in lots of the ways you'd like to."*
   d. Allow your child to lead by returning responsibility to your child by responding, *"That's up to you,"* *"You can decide,"* or *"That can be whatever you want it to be."*

2. Do let the child lead.
   Allowing the child to lead during the playtime helps you to better understand your child's world and what your child needs from you. Convey your willingness to follow your child's lead through your responses: *"Show me what you want me to do,"* *"You want me to put that on,"* *"Hmmm…,"* or *"I wonder…."* Use whisper technique (co-conspirators) when child wants you to play a role: *"What should I say?"* or *"What happens next?"* (Modify responses for older kids: use conspiratorial tone, *"What happens now?"* *"What kind of teacher am I?"* etc.)

3. Do join in the child's play actively, as a follower.
   Convey your willingness to follow your child's lead through your responses and your actions, by actively joining in the play (child is the director, parent is the actor): *"So I'm supposed to be the teacher,"* *"You want me to be the robber, and I'm supposed to wear the black mask,"* *"Now I'm supposed to pretend I'm locked up in jail, until you say I can get out,"* or *"You want me to stack these just as high as yours."* Use whisper technique in role-play: *"What should I say?"* *"What happens next?"*

4. Do verbally track the child's play (describe what you see).
   Verbally tracking your child's play is a way of letting your child know that you are paying close attention and that you are interested and involved: *"You're filling that all the way to the top,"* *"You've decided you want to paint next,"* or *"You've got 'em all lined up just how you want them."*

5. Do reflect the child's feelings.
   Verbally reflecting children's feelings helps them feel understood and communicates your acceptance of their feelings and needs: *"You're proud your picture,"* *"That kind'a surprised you,"* *"You really like how that feels on your hands,"* *"You really wish that we could play longer,"* *"You don't like the way that turned out,"* or *"You sound disappointed."* (*Hint: Look closely at your child's face to better identify how your child is feeling.*)

6. Do set firm and consistent limits.
   Consistent limits create a structure for a safe and predictable environment for children. Children should never be permitted to hurt themselves or you. Limit setting provides an opportunity for your child to develop self-control and self-responsibility. Using a calm, patient, yet firm voice, say, *"The floor's not for putting playdough on; you can play with it on the tray"* or *"I know you'd like to shoot the gun at me, but I'm not for shooting. You can choose to shoot at that"* (point to something acceptable).

7. Do salute the child's power and encourage effort.
   Verbally recognizing and encouraging your child's effort builds self-esteem and confidence and promotes self-motivation: *"You worked hard on that!"* *"You did it!"* *"You figured it out!"* *"You've got a plan for how you're gonna set those up,"* *"You know just how you want that to be,"* *"Sounds like you know lots about how to take care of babies."*

8. Do be verbally active.
   Being verbally active communicates to your child that you are interested and involved in her play. If you are silent, your child will feel watched.
   Note: Empathic grunts—"Hmm…"and so forth—also convey interest and involvement, when you are unsure of how to respond.

Don't:
   1. Don't criticize any behavior.
   2. Don't praise the child.
   3. Don't ask leading questions.
   4. Don't allow interruptions of the session.
   5. Don't give information or teach.
   6. Don't preach.
   7. Don't initiate new activities.
   8. Don't be passive or quiet.
      (Don'ts 1–7 are taken from Guerney, 1972)

Remember the "Be With" Attitudes: Your intent in your responses is what is most important. Convey to your child:
"I am here—I hear/see you—I understand—I care."

Reminder: These play session skills (the new skills you are applying) are relatively meaningless if applied mechanically and not as an attempt to be genuinely empathic and truly understanding of your child. **Your Intent & Attitude Are More Important Than Your Words!**

CHILD-PARENT-RELATIONSHIP (C-P-R) TRAINING
Play Session Procedures Checklist – Session 3

Depending on age of child, may need to remind him or her: "Today is the day for our special playtime!"

A. Prior to Session (Remember to "Set the Stage")
- ☐ Make arrangements for other family members (so that there will be no interruptions).
- ☐ Set up toys on old quilt—keep toy placement predictable.
- ☐ Have a clock visible in the room (or wear a watch).
- ☐ Put pets outside or in another room.
- ☐ Let the child use the bathroom prior to the play session.
- ☐ Switch on video recorder.

B. Beginning the Session
- ☐ Child and Parent: Hang "Do Not Disturb" sign (can also "unplug" phone if there is one in play session area). *Message to child: "This is so important that <u>No One</u> is allowed to interrupt this time together."*
- ☐ Tell Child: *"We will have 30 minutes of special playtime, and you can play with the toys in lots of the ways you want to."* (Voice needs to convey that parent is looking forward to this time with child.)
- ☐ <u>From this point, let the child lead.</u>

C. During the Session
- ☐ Sit on the same level as child, close enough to show interest but allowing enough space for child to move freely.
- ☐ Focus your eyes, ears, and body fully on child. (<u>Toes Follow Nose</u>!) *Conveys full attention!*
- ☐ Your voice should mostly be gentle and caring, but vary with the intensity and affect of child's play.
- ☐ Allow the child to identify the toys. [To promote make-believe play (i.e., what looks like a car to you might be a spaceship to your child), try to use nonspecific words ("this," "that," "it") if child hasn't named toy.]
- ☐ Play actively with the child, if the child requests your participation.
- ☐ Verbally reflect what you see and hear (child's play/activity, thoughts, feelings).
- ☐ Set limits on behaviors that make you feel uncomfortable.
- ☐ Give five-minute advance notice for session's end and then a one-minute notice.
  (**"Billy, we have five minutes left in our special playtime."**)

D. Ending the Session
- ☐ At 30 minutes, <u>stand</u> and announce, **"Our playtime is over for today."** Do not exceed time limit by more than two to three minutes.
- ☐ Parent does the cleaning up. If child chooses, child may help. (If child continues to play while "cleaning," set limit below.)
- ☐ <u>If child has difficulty leaving:</u>
  - Open the door or begin to put away toys.
  - Reflect child's feelings about not wanting to leave, but calmly and firmly restate that the playtime is over. (Restate limit as many times as needed—the goal is for child to be able to stop herself.)
    "I know you would like to stay and play with the toys, but our special playtime is over for today."
  - Adding a statement that gives child something to look forward to helps child see that, although she cannot continue to play with the special toys, there is something else she can do that is also enjoyable. For example:
    1. **"You can play with the toys next week during our special playtime."**
    2. **"It's time for snack; would you like grapes or cherries today?"**
    3. **"We can go outside and play on the trampoline."**

<u>Note</u>: *Patience is the order of the day when helping child to leave—OK to repeat limit calmly several times to allow child to struggle with leaving on her own. (Key is showing empathy and understanding in your voice tone and facial expressions as you state the limit). Younger children may need more time to 'hear' limit and respond.*

Never use Special Playtime for a reward or consequence—NO matter the child's behavior that day!

CHILD-PARENT-RELATIONSHIP (C-P-R) TRAINING
Photograph of Toys Set Up for Play Session – Session 3

Child Parent Relationship Therapy (CPRT)

Session 4 – Treatment Outline

Note: Print material checklist for this session (CD-Rom, Appendix A – contains list of all materials and where to locate them)

☝ Rule of Thumb:

When a child is drowning, don't try to teach her to swim.

When a child is feeling upset or out of control, that is not the moment to impart a rule or teach a lesson.

⊕ Time
Marker

_____ **I.** **Informal Sharing, followed by Parent Sharing Highlights of Preparing for and Conducting Home Play Sessions** (parents with video go last)

Be aware of time—keep group process moving!

- Look for something positive to reflect for <u>each</u> parent

- Model encouragement by prizing parents' efforts

- Use parents' sharing to emphasize examples of **Play Session Do's**
  Refer to poster or handout and encourage parents' efforts to recognize the **Play Session Do's**

- Seize opportunities to forge connections between parents with similar struggles

_____ **II.** **Videotaped Play Session Review and Supervision**

- Comment primarily on the positive, taking a few words the parent said or non-verbal behavior and turning that into a **Play Session Do** or another teaching point

  Focus on parent's strengths (remember, the Donut Analogy applies to parents, too)

  o Encourage the parent who videotaped the session to share what it was like to be videotaped knowing that she would have to share it with the class

  o Play videotape until a <u>strength</u> is evident

  o Focus on importance of parent's awareness of self in the play session

  o Ask if the parent has a question about some part of the session or if there is some part he/she would particularly like to show—play that portion of the videotape

      o Identify <u>only one</u> thing the parent might do differently

- Continue to refer to *Play Session Do's & Don'ts* poster or handout, asking parents to try and identify the **Do's** they see demonstrated in videotapped play session

_____ **III.**   **Handout:** *Limit Setting: A-C-T Before It's Too Late* (refer parents to page 13 in the *Parent Notebook*)

(optional) Show video clip on limit setting

- Briefly review the A-C-T model—go over importance of consistency

- Parent is in charge of the structure for the play session: selecting the time and place, establishing necessary limits, and enforcing the limits

- Child is responsible for choices and decisions, within the limits set by parent during playtimes

- Briefly give a few examples of possible limits to set during play sessions

   ☝ **Rule of Thumb: "During play sessions, limits are not needed until they are needed!"**

- Review *Limit Setting: A-C-T Practice Worksheet* (refer parents to page 14 in the *Parent Notebook*)

   Read over and do at least two or three examples together—discuss the rest next week as completed homework; point out question #7, where parents are asked to write down a limit they think they will need to set for their child

- Be prepared for discussion regarding parent concerns about guns (used in limit-setting example)

_____ **IV.**   **Role-Play/Video Clip or Live Demonstration of Play Session Skills and Limit Setting**

- Always allow time for parents to see a demonstration of play session skills that you want them to emulate, focusing on those skills they report the most difficulty with

- After viewing demonstration, ask parents to role-play a few scenarios they believe are most difficult for them, including at least one limit-setting role-play

_____ **V.**   **Arrange for One to Two Parents to Do Videotaping This Week**

Name/phone number _____day/time (if taping at clinic)_____

Name/phone number _____ day/time (if taping at clinic)_____

Remind parent(s) who are videotaping this week to make note on their Parent Notes & Homework handout

_____ **VI.**   **Homework Assignments** (refer parents to homework section in their notebook)

1)   Complete *Limit Setting: A-C-T Practice Worksheet.*

2)   Read over handouts prior to play session:
Limit Setting: A-C-T Before It's Too Late!
Play Session Dos & Don'ts (from Session 3)
Play Session Procedures Checklist (from Session 3)

3)   Conduct play session and complete *Parent Play Session Notes.*

Notice one intense feeling in yourself during your play session this week.

_____ *I will bring my videotape for next week (if videotaping at clinic: my appt. day/time _____).*

_____ **VII.**   **Close With Motivational Poem, Story, or Rule of Thumb (optional)**

✎ RULES OF THUMB TO REMEMBER:

1.   **"When a child is drowning, don't try to teach her to swim."** When a child is feeling upset or out of control, that is not the moment to impart a rule or teach a lesson.

2.   **"During play sessions, limits are not needed until they are needed!"**

CHILD-PARENT-RELATIONSHIP (C-P-R) TRAINING
Parent Notes & Homework – Session 4

☝ RULES OF THUMB TO REMEMBER:

1. **"When a child is drowning, don't try to teach her to swim."** When a child is feeling upset or out of control, that is not the moment to impart a rule or teach a lesson.

2. **"During play sessions, limits are not needed until they are needed!"**

Basic Limit Setting:

Start by saying child's name: *"Sarah,"*
Reflect feeling: *"I know you'd like to shoot the gun at me..."*
Set limit: *"but I'm not for shooting."*
Give acceptable alternative: *"You can choose to shoot at that"* (point at something <u>acceptable</u>).

Notes (use back for additional notes):

_____
_____
_____
_____
_____
_____
_____
_____
_____
_____
_____
_____
_____
_____
_____
_____

Homework Assignments:

1. Complete *Limit Setting: A-C-T Practice Worksheet*.

2. Read over handouts prior to play session:
   Limit Setting: A-C-T Before It's Too Late!
   Play Session Do's & Don'ts
   Play Session Procedures Checklist

3. Conduct play session and complete *Parent Play Session Notes*.
   Notice one intense feeling in yourself during your play session this week.

   _____ I will bring my videotape for next week (if videotaping at clinic: my appt. day/time _____).

CHILD-PARENT-RELATIONSHIP (C-P-R) TRAINING
Limit Setting: A-C-T Before It's Too Late! - Session 4

Acknowledge the feeling
Communicate the limit
Target alternatives

Three Step A-C-T Method of Limit Setting:

Scenario: Billy has been pretending that the bop bag is a bad guy and shooting him with the dart gun; he looks over at you and aims the dart gun at you, then laughs and says, "Now, you're one of the bad guys, too!"

1. **A**cknowledge your child's feeling or desire (*your voice must convey empathy and understanding*).
    "Billy, I know that you think that it would be fun to shoot me, too…"
    Child learns that his feelings, desires, and wishes are valid and accepted by parent (but not all behavior); just empathically reflecting your child's feeling often defuses the intensity of the feeling or need.

2. **C**ommunicate the limit (be specific and clear—and brief).
    "but I'm not for shooting."

3. **T**arget acceptable alternatives (provide one or more choices, depending on age of child).
    "You can pretend that the doll is me (pointing at the doll) and shoot at it."
    The goal is to provide your child with an acceptable outlet for expressing the feeling or the original action, while giving him an opportunity to exercise self-control. Note: Pointing helps redirect child's attention.

When to Set Limits?

  RULE OF THUMB: "During play sessions, limits are not needed until they are needed!"
Limits are set only when the need arises, and for four basic reasons:
*   To protect child from hurting himself or parent
*   To protect valuable property
*   To maintain parent's acceptance of child
*   To provide consistency in the play session by limiting child and toys to play area and ending on time

Before setting a limit in a play session, ask yourself:
*   "Is this limit necessary?"
*   "Can I consistently enforce this limit?"
*   "If I don't' set a limit on this behavior, can I consistently allow this behavior and accept my child?"

Avoid conducting play sessions in areas of the house that require too many limits. Limits set during play sessions should allow for greater freedom of expression than would normally be allowed. The fewer the limits, the easier it is for you to be consistent—**consistency is very important.** Determine a few limits ahead of time (practice A-C-T): no hitting or shooting at parent; no playdough on carpet; no purposefully breaking toys, and so forth. *Hint: Children really do understand that playtimes are "special" and that the rules are different—they will* <u>not</u> *expect the same level of permissiveness during the rest of the week.*

How to Set Limits?

Limits are not punitive and should be stated firmly, but calmly and matter-of-factly. After empathically acknowledging your child's feeling or desire (very important step), you state, "The playdough is not for throwing at the table," just like you would state, "The sky is blue." Don't try to force your child to obey the limit. Remember to provide an acceptable alternative. In this method, it really is up to the child to decide to accept or break the limit; however, **it is your job, as the parent, to consistently enforce the limit.**

Why Establish Consistent Limits?

Providing children with consistent limits helps them feel safe and secure. This method of limiting children's behavior teaches them self-control and responsibility for their own behavior by allowing them to experience the consequences of their choices and decisions. Limits set in play sessions help children practice self-control and begin to learn to stop themselves in the real world.

CONSISTENT LIMITS → PREDICTABLE, SAFE ENVIRONMENT → SENSE OF SECURITY

CHILD-PARENT-RELATIONSHIP (C-P-R) TRAINING
Limit Setting: A-C-T Practice Worksheet - Session 4

<u>A</u>cknowledge the feeling
<u>C</u>ommunicate the limit
<u>T</u>arget alternatives

EXAMPLE # 1

Billy has been playing like the bop bag is the bad guy and hitting him; he picks up the scissors, looks at you, and then laughs and says, "I'm going to stab him because he's bad!"

<u>A</u> **"Billy, I know that you think that it would be fun to stab the bop bag (bobo)..."**

<u>C</u> **"But the bop bag (bobo) isn't for poking with the scissors."**

<u>T</u> **"You can use the rubber knife"**

EXAMPLE # 2

The play session time is up and you have stated the limit two times. Your child becomes angry because you won't give in and let him play longer; he begins to hit you. Hitting is not allowed, so go immediately to second step of A-C-T, then follow with all three steps of A-C-T method of limit setting.

<u>C</u> (firmly) **"Billy, I'm not for hitting."**

<u>A</u> (empathically) **"I know you're mad at me..."**

<u>C</u> (firmly) **"But people aren't for hitting."**

<u>T</u> (neutral tone) **"You can pretend the bop bag is me and hit it (pointing at bop bag)."**

PRACTICE:

1. Your child begins to color on the dollhouse, saying, "It needs some red curtains!"

    (assuming you bought a dollhouse; however, it would be okay to color on a cardboard dollhouse)

<u>A</u> I know you really want to *put curtains on the dollhouse*   .

<u>C</u> But the dollhouse *is not for coloring on*   .

<u>T</u> You can *make red curtains on the paper and tape them on the dollhouse*   .

2. Your child aims a loaded dart gun at you.

<u>A</u> *[Child's name], I know you'd like to shoot the gun at me*   .

<u>C</u> *But I'm not for shooting*   .

<u>T</u> *You can choose to shoot at that (point at something acceptable)*   .

3. After 15 minutes of the play session, your child announces that she wants to leave and go outside to play with her friends.

A   I know you *would like to go play with your friends right now* .

C   *but, we have 15 minutes more in our special playtime* .

T   Then *you can go outside and play* .

4. Your child wants to play doctor and asks you to be the patient. Your child asks you to pull up your shirt so that she/he can listen to your heart.

A   *[Child's name], I know you want me to pull up my shirt like at a real doctor's office* .

C   *But my shirt is not for pulling up* .

T   *You can listen to my heart through my shirt (or you can pretend the doll is me and pull up its shirt)* .

5. Describe a situation in which you think you might need to set a limit during the play session.
   Situation: _____
   _____

A   _____ .

C   _____ .

T   _____ .

CHILD-PARENT-RELATIONSHIP (C-P-R) TRAINING
Parent Play Session Notes - Session 4

Play Session #_____   Date: _____

Significant Happenings:

What I Learned About My Child:

Feelings Expressed:

Play Themes:

What I Learned About Myself:

My feelings during the play session:

What I think I was best at:

What was hardest or most challenging for me:

Questions or Concerns:

Skill I Want to Focus on in the Next Play Session: _____

Child Parent Relationship Therapy (CPRT)

Session 5 – Treatment Outline

⏱ Time
Marker   *Note: Print material checklist for this session (CD-Rom, Appendix A – contains list of all materials and where to locate them)*

_____ **I.**   **Informal Sharing, followed by Review of Homework as Parents Report on Play Sessions (Videotaped parents share last)**

- Parents share an intense feeling they were aware of during their play sessions

    Focus on importance of self-awareness of parents' feelings in the play session; model by reflecting parents' feelings

- Parents share limit-setting attempts <u>during</u> play sessions

    Remember to focus only on play session happenings—redirect limit-setting questions about outside of play sessions to end of session

    Let parents know you will be reviewing limit-setting homework later in the session after videotape review

- Focus on **Play Session Do's** (use poster for parents to refer to)

    Use examples from parents' comments to reinforce **Do's**—Point out difficult situations and spontaneously role-play with parents on how to respond

- Remember the Donut Analogy: Focus on Strengths and Positive Examples

    Find something in <u>each</u> parent's sharing that can be encouraged and supported—facilitate "connecting" among group members; help them see they are not alone in their parenting difficulties

_____ **II.**   **Videotaped Play Session Review and Supervision**

- View one to two parent-child play sessions, following same procedure as last week

- Model encouragement and facilitate peer feedback

- Refer parents to handout, *In-Class Play Session Skills Checklist,* page 19 in the *Parent Notebook* and ask parents to check off skills they see being demonstrated as therapist or other parents point them out

- Continue to refer to *Play Session Do's & Don'ts* poster/handout (from Session 3)

    o Encourage the parent who videotaped to share a bit about the play session before starting video.

> o   Play videotape until a <u>strength</u> is evident
>
> o   Focus on importance of parent's awareness of self in the play session
>
> o   Play portion of videotape that parent has a question about or would particularly like to show
>
> o   Ask what the parent thinks he/she does <u>well</u>
>
> o   Ask what area the parent would like to work on in his/her next play session

_____ **III.   Limit-Setting Review**

(Optional) Show video clip on limit setting

- Review A-C-T Method

  Limit Setting: A-C-T Before It's Too Late! (refer parents to page 13 in the *Parent Notebook*)

  Emphasize importance of using all three steps

  Ask for questions

  Emphasize the importance of stating clear and concise limits

- Review principles of limit setting on *Limit Setting: A-C-T Before It's Too Late!* (refer parents to page 13 in the *Parent Notebook*)

- Review homework worksheet: *Limit Setting: A-C-T Practice Worksheet* (refer parents to page 14 in the *Parent Notebook*)

  Go over any scenarios not covered in Session 4

  Discuss limits parents might need to set and help with ones they generated

  Ask for questions

- Review handout: *Limit Setting: Why Use the Three-Step A-C-T Method?* (refer parents to page 18 in the *Parent Notebook*) if not enough time, ask parents to readover at home

_____ **IV.   Role-Play/Video Clip or Live Demonstration of Play Session Skills and Limit Setting**

- Always allow time for parents to see a demonstration of play session skills that you want them to emulate, focusing on those skills they report the most difficulty with

- After viewing demonstration, ask parents to role-play a few scenarios they believe are most difficult for them, including at least one limit-setting role-play

_____ **V.**   **Arrange for One to Two Parents to Do Videotaping This Week**

Name/phone number _____ day/time (if taping at clinic)_____

Name/phone number _____ day/time (if taping at clinic)_____

Remind parent(s) who are videotaping this week to make note on their Parent Notes & Homework handout

_____ **VI.**   **Homework Assignments** (refer parents to homework section in their notebook)

1)   Give each of your children a Sandwich Hug and Sandwich Kiss.

2)   Read over handouts prior to play session:

Limit Setting: A-C-T Before It's Too Late! (from Session 4)

Play Session Dos & Don'ts (from Session 3)

Play Session Procedures Checklist (from Session 3)

3)   Conduct play session (same time & place):

a.   Complete *Parent Play Session Notes.*

b.   Use *Play Session Skills Checklist* to note what you thought you did well, and select one skill you want to work on in your next play session.

c.   If you needed to set a limit during your playtime, describe on the checklist what happened and what you said or did.

_____ *I will bring my videotape for next week (if videotaping at clinic: my appt. day/time _____).*

4)   Additional Assignment:

_____ **VII.**   **Close With Rule of Thumb**

☞ RULE OF THUMB TO REMEMBER:

"If you can't say it in 10 words or less, don't say it."

As parents, we have a tendency to overexplain to our children, and our message gets lost in the words.

_____

CHILD-PARENT-RELATIONSHIP (C-P-R) TRAINING
Parent Notes & Homework – Session 5

☝ RULE OF THUMB TO REMEMBER:

"If you can't say it in 10 words or less, don't say it."
As parents, we have a tendency to overexplain to our children,
and our message gets lost in the words.

Notes (use back for additional notes):

_____
_____
_____
_____
_____
_____
_____
_____
_____
_____
_____
_____
_____
_____
_____
_____
_____

Homework Assignments:

1. Give each of your children a Sandwich Hug and Sandwich Kiss.

2. Read over handouts prior to play session:
   Limit Setting: A-C-T Before It's Too Late!
   Play Session Dos & Don'ts
   Play Session Procedures Checklist

3. Conduct play session (same time & place).

   a. Complete *Parent Play Session Notes.*

   b. Use *Play Session Skills Checklist* to note what you thought you did well, and select one skill you want to work on in your next play session.

   c. If you needed to set a limit during your playtime, describe on the checklist what happened and what you said or did.

   ____ **I will bring my videotape for next week (if videotaping at clinic: my appt. day/time____).**

4. Additional assignment:

CHILD-PARENT-RELATIONSHIP (C-P-R) TRAINING
Limit Setting: Why Use the Three-Step A-C-T Method - Session 5

<u>A</u>cknowledge the feeling

<u>C</u>ommunicate the limit

<u>T</u>arget alternatives

Discuss the different messages that are implied in the following typical parent responses to unacceptable behavior:

- It's probably not a good idea to paint the wall.

  Message: <u>I'm really not sure whether or not it's okay to paint the wall. It might be okay or it might not.</u>

- You can't paint the walls in here.

  Message: <u>You might be able to paint the walls in the other room.</u>

- I can't let you paint the wall.

  Message: <u>What you do is my responsibility and not your responsibility.</u>

- Maybe you could paint something else other than the wall.

  Message: <u>Maybe you can paint the furniture.</u>

- The rule is you can't paint the wall.

  Message: <u>How you feel about it doesn't matter.</u>

- The wall is not for painting on.

  Message: <u>You're not bad for wanting to, it's just not for anyone to paint on.</u>

CHILD-PARENT-RELATIONSHIP (C-P-R) TRAINING
In-Class Play Session Skills Checklist:
For Review of Videotaped (or Live) Play Session – Session 5

Directions: Indicate ✓ in blank when you observe a play session skill demonstrated in videotaped or live play session

1. ___ Set the Stage/Structured Play Session

2. ___ Conveyed "Be With" Attitudes
   Full attention/interested
   Toes followed nose

3. ___ Allowed Child to Lead
   Avoided giving suggestions
   Avoided asking questions
   Returned responsibility to child

4. ___ Followed Child's Lead
   Physically on child's level
   Moved closer when child was involved in play
   Joined in play when invited—took imaginary/pretend role when appropriate

5. ___ Reflective Responding Skills:

   ___ Reflected child's nonverbal play behavior (Tracking)

   ___ Reflected child's verbalizations (Content)

   ___ Reflected child's feelings/wants/wishes

   ___ Voice tone matched child's intensity/affect

   ___ Responses were brief and interactive

   ___ Facial expressions matched child's affect

6. ___ Used Encouragement/Self-Esteem-Building Responses

7. ___ Set Limits, As Needed, Using A-C-T

CHILD-PARENT-RELATIONSHIP (C-P-R) TRAINING
Parent Play Session Notes – Session 5

Play Session #_____   Date: _____

Significant Happenings:

What I Learned About My Child:

Feelings Expressed:

Play Themes:

What I Learned About Myself:

My feelings during the play session:

What I think I was best at:

What was hardest or most challenging for me:

Questions or Concerns:

Skill I Want to Focus on in the Next Play Session: _____

CHILD-PARENT-RELATIONSHIP (C-P-R) TRAINING
Play Session Skills Checklist - Session 5

Play Session #_____   Date: _____

(Note: Indicate ✓ in column if skill was used; — if skill was not used; and + if skill was a strength)

✓ — +	Skill	Notes/Comments
	Set the Stage/Structured Play Session	
	Conveyed "Be With" Attitudes 　　*Full attention/interested* 　　*Toes followed nose*	
	Allowed Child to Lead 　　*Avoided giving suggestions* 　　*Avoided asking questions* 　　*Returned responsibility to child*	
	Followed Child's Lead 　　*Physically on child's level* 　　*Moved closer when child was involved in play* 　　*Joined in play when invited*	
	Reflective Responding Skills:	
	Reflected child's nonverbal play (Tracking)	
	Reflected child's verbalizations (Content)	
	Reflected child's feelings/wants/wishes	
	Voice tone matched child's intensity/affect	
	Responses were brief and interactive	
	Facial expressions matched child's affect	
	Use of Encouragement/Self-Esteem-Building Responses	
	Set Limits, As Needed, Using A-C-T	

Child Parent Relationship Therapy (CPRT)

Session 6 – Treatment Outline

⏁ Time
Marker
Note: Print material checklist for this session (CD-Rom, Appendix A – contains list of all materials and where to locate them)

_____ **I.**   **Informal Sharing, followed by Review of Homework as Parents Report on Play Sessions (Videotaped parents share last)**

- Parents share experience giving each of their children a Sandwich Hug and Sandwich Kiss

- Parents share limit-setting attempts during play sessions. Review A-C-T Limit Setting as needed (refer to handout from Session 4, page 13 in the parent notebook)

   Remember to focus only on play session happenings—redirect other questions about limit setting by letting parents know you will be focusing on limit setting more later in the session

- Continue debriefing play sessions, focusing on parents' perceived changes in their own behavior (Videotaped parents or last)

   Focus on **Play Session Do's** (use poster for parents to refer to)

   Use examples from parents' comments to reinforce **Do's**

   Point out difficult situations and spontaneously role-play with parents on how to respond

- Remember the Donut Analogy: Focus on the Positive! Find something in each parent's sharing that can be encouraged and supported—facilitate "connecting" among group members.

_____ **II.**   **Videotaped Play Session Review and Supervision**

- View one to two parent-child play sessions, following same procedure as last week

- Model encouragement and facilitate peer feedback

- Refer parents to handout, *In-Class Play Session Skills Checklist,* page 27 in the *Parent Notebook* and ask parents to check off skills they see being demonstrated

- Continue to refer to *Play Session Do's & Don'ts* poster/handout

   Remind parents that, for children,

   parental consistency > predictability > security > child feeling safe and loved!

   ✎ **Rule of Thumb: "Grant in fantasy what you cannot grant in reality."**

In a play session, it is okay to act out feelings and wishes that in reality may require limits.

_____ **III.**   **Choice-Giving**

- Review handout: *Choice-Giving 101: Teaching Responsibility & Decision-Making* (refer parents to page 23 in the *Parent Notebook*)

   ✎ **Rule of Thumb: "Big choices for big kids, little choices for little kids."**

Choices given must be commensurate with child's developmental stage.

- (Optional) Show video: *Choices, Cookies, and Kids* (suggest showing 15–20 minutes and finish video in Session 7)

- As time allows, review second choice-giving handout: *Advanced Choice-Giving: Providing Choices as Consequences* (refer parents to page 24 in the *Parent Notebook*)—*Note: This handout can be deferred to Session 7, or partially covered in this session and completed in Session 7*

_____ **IV.**   **Role-Play/Video Clip or Live Demonstration of Play Session Skills and Choice-Giving**

- Always allow time for parents to see a demonstration of play session skills that you want them to emulate, focusing on those skills they report the most difficulty with

- After viewing demonstration, ask parents to role-play a few scenarios they believe are most difficult for them, including at least one choice-giving role-play

_____ **V.**   **Arrange for One to Two Parents to Do Videotaping This Week**

Name/phone number _____ day/time (if taping at clinic)_____

Name/phone number _____day/time (if taping at clinic)_____

Remind parent(s) who are videotaping this week to make note on their Parent Notes & Homework handout

_____ **VI.**   **Homework Assignments** (refer parents to homework section in their notebook)

1) Read *Choice-Giving 101: Teaching Responsibility & Decision-Making* and *Advanced Choice-Giving: Providing Choices as Consequences*.

2) Read *Common Problems in Play Sessions* and mark the top two to three issues you have questions about or write in an issue you are challenged by that is not on the worksheet.

3) Practice giving at least one kind of choice ("A" or "B") outside of the play session.

A. Provide choices for the sole purpose of <u>empowering your child</u>
   (two positive choices for child, where either choice is acceptable to you and
   either choice is desirable to child)
   What happened _____
   What you said _____
   How child responded _____

B. Practice giving choices as a <u>method of discipline</u> (where choice-giving is used
   to provide a consequence for noncompliance of limit, family rule, or policy)
   What happened _____
   What you said _____
   How child responded _____

4) Conduct play session (same time & place)—review *Play Session Do's & Don'ts &
   Play Session Procedure Checklist*

   a. Complete *Parent Play Session Notes.*

   b. Use *Play Session Skills Checklist* to note what you thought you did well, and
      select one skill you want to work on in your next play session.

____ *I will bring my videotape for next week (if videotaping at clinic: my appt. day/time _____).*

5) Additional assignment:

____ **VII.   Close With Motivational Poem, Story, or Rule of Thumb (optional)**

✎ RULES OF THUMB TO REMEMBER:

1. "Grant in fantasy what you can't grant in reality." In a play session, it is okay to act out feelings
and wishes that in reality may require limits. For example, it's okay for the "baby sister" doll to
be thrown out a window in playtime.

2. "Big choices for big kids, little choices for little kids." Choices given must be commensurate with
child's developmental stage.

👍 RULES OF THUMB TO REMEMBER:

1. **"Grant in fantasy what you can't grant in reality."** In a play session, it is okay to act out feelings and wishes that in reality may require limits. For example, it's okay for the "baby sister" doll to be thrown out a window in playtime.

2. **"Big choices for big kids, little choices for little kids."** Choices given must be commensurate with child's developmental stage.

Notes (use back for additional notes):

_____
_____
_____
_____
_____
_____
_____
_____
_____
_____

Homework Assignments:

1. Read *Choice-Giving 101: Teaching Responsibility & Decision-Making* and *Advanced Choice-Giving: Providing Choices as Consequences*.

2. Read *Common Problems in Play Sessions* and mark the top two to three issues you have questions about or write in an issue you are challenged by that is not on the worksheet.

3. Practice giving at least one kind of choice ("A" or "B") outside of the play session.

   A. Provide choices for the sole purpose of <u>empowering your child</u> (two positive choices for child, where either choice is acceptable to you and either choice is desirable to child)
   What happened _____
   What you said _____
   How child responded _____

   B. Practice giving choices as a <u>method of discipline</u> (where choice-giving is used to provide a consequence for noncompliance of limit, family rule, or policy)
   What happened _____
   What you said _____
   How child responded _____

4. Conduct play session (same time & place)—review Play Session *Do's & Don'ts & Play Session Procedure Checklist*

   a. Complete *Parent Play Session Notes*.

   b. Use *Play Session Skills Checklist* to note what you thought you did well, and select one skill you want to work on in your next play session.
   _____ I will bring my videotape for next week (if videotaping at clinic: my appt. day/time _____).

5. Additional assignment:

CHILD-PARENT-RELATIONSHIP (C-P-R) TRAINING
Choice-Giving 101: Teaching Responsibility & Decision-Making – Session 6

- **Providing children with <u>age-appropriate</u> choices empowers children** by allowing them a measure of control over their circumstances. Children who feel more empowered and "in control" are more capable of regulating their own behavior, a prerequisite for self-control. Choices require that children tap into their inner resources, rather than relying on parents (external resources) to stop their behavior or solve the problem for them. If parents always intervene, the child learns that "Mom or Dad will stop me if I get out of hand" or "Mom or Dad will figure out a solution if I get in a jam."

- **Presenting children with choices provides opportunities for decision-making and problem-solving.** Through practice with choice-making, children learn to accept responsibility for their choices and actions and learn they are competent and capable. Choice-giving facilitates the development of the child's conscience; as children are allowed to learn from their mistakes, they learn to weigh decisions based on possible consequences.

- **Providing children with choices reduces power struggles** between parent and child and, importantly, preserves the child-parent relationship. Both parent and child are empowered; parent is responsible for, or in control of, providing parameters for choices, and the child is responsible for, or in control of, his decision (within parent-determined parameters).

Choice-Giving Strategies

- **Provide age-appropriate choices** that are <u>equally acceptable to the child and to you</u>. Remember that you must be willing to live with the choice the child makes. Do not use choices to try and manipulate the child to do what you want by presenting one choice that you want the child to choose and a second choice that you know the child won't like.

- **Provide little choices to little kids; big choices to big kids**. *Example: A 3-year-old can only handle choosing between two shir or two food items.* **"Sarah, do you want to wear your red dress or your pink dress to school?" "Sarah, do you want an app or orange with your lunch?"**

Choice-Giving to Avoid Potential Problem Behavior and Power Struggles

Choices can be used to avoid a potential problem. Similar to the example above, <u>choices given are equall acceptable to parent and child</u>. In this case, choices are planned in advance by the parent to avoid problems that the child has a history of struggling with. In the example above, if Sarah has trouble getting dressed in the morning, provide a choice of what to wear the evening before (to avoid a struggle the next morning); after she has made the choice, take the dress out of the closet, ready for morning. Children who are given the responsibility for making a decision are more likely to abide by the decision.

In selecting choices to prevent problems, it is very important that parents understand the real problem that their child is struggling with. If your child always comes home hungry and wants something sweet, but you want him to have a healthy snack, plan ahead by having on hand at least two choices of healthy snacks that <u>your child likes.</u> Before he heads for the ice cream, say:

   "Billy, I bought grapes and cherries for snack; which would you like?"
Or, if you made your child's favorite cookies, and it is acceptable for your 5-year-old to have one or two cookies, say:

   "Billy, I made your favorite cookies today; would you like one cookie or two?"

<u>Hint</u>: This is another place where "structuring for success" can be applied by eliminating the majority of unacceptable snack items and stocking up on healthy snack items! Structuring your home environment to minimize conflict allows both you and your child to feel more "in control." Remember: **Be a thermostat!**

Suggested Reading for Parents: "Teaching Your Child to Choose," Parenting, October, 2002.

CHILD-PARENT-RELATIONSHIP (C-P-R) TRAINING
Advance Choice-Giving: Providing Choices as Consequences - Session 6-7

...ldren need parental guidance and discipline. In many instances, parents must make decisions for children—decisions that children are not mature ...ugh to take responsibility for—such as bedtime, other matters of health and safety, and compliance with household policies and rules. However, ...ents can provide their children with some measure of control in the situation by providing choices.

Oreo® Cookie Method of Choice-Giving (from "Choices, Cookies, & Kids" video by Dr. Garry Landreth)

...ample 1: Three-year-old Sarah is clutching a handful of Oreo® cookies, ready to eat them all (it is right before bedtime, and the parent knows it ...uld not be healthy for Sarah to have all the cookies. But Sarah does not know that—she just knows that she wants cookies!): **"Sarah, you can ...oose to keep one of the cookies to eat and put the rest back, or you can put all of the cookies back—which do you choose?"** Or, if it is ...rmissible to the parent for Sarah to have two cookies: **"Sarah, you can have one cookie or two—which do you choose?"**

...ample 2: Three-year-old Sarah does not want to take her medicine and adamantly tells you so! Taking the medicine is ...t a choice—that is a given. But the parent can provide the child with some control over the situation by saying, **"Sarah, ...u can choose to have apple juice or orange juice with your medicine—which do you choose?"**

...ample 3: Seven-year-old Billy is tired and cranky and refuses to get in the car to go home from Grandma and Grandpa's ...use. **"Billy, you can choose to sit in the front seat with Daddy, or you can choose to sit in the back seat with Sarah—which do you choose?"**

Choice-Giving to Enforce Household Policies and Rules

...oice-giving can be used to enforce household policies/rules. <u>Begin by working on one at a time</u>. In general, provide two choices—one is phrased ...itively (consequence for complying with policy), and the other choice (consequence for not complying with policy) is stated as a consequence that ...i believe your child would not prefer (such as giving up favorite TV show). Consequence for noncompliance should be relevant and logical rather ...n punitive, and it must be **enforceable.**

...ample: A household rule has been established that toys in the family room must be picked up off the floor before dinner ...ildren cannot seem to remember without being told repeatedly, and parent is feeling frustrated with constant reminders ...d power struggles).

...e are about to institute a new and significant policy within the confines of this domicile" (big words get children's attention!). **...hen <u>you choose to</u> pick up your toys before dinner, <u>you choose to</u> watch 30 minutes of television after dinner. When <u>you choose not</u> ...ick up your toys before dinner, <u>you choose not to</u> watch television after dinner."** *Note: Be sure to let children know when there are 10–15 ...utes before dinner, so they can have time to pick up their toys.*

...ildren may be able to comply the first time you announce this new policy, because you have just informed them. But ...at is important is that you begin to allow your children to use their internal resources and self-control to <u>remember</u> the ...w policy without constant reminders. (Remember that the new policy was implemented because you were frustrated and ...d of nagging!) So, the second night, parent says, **"Billy and Sarah, dinner will be ready in 10 minutes; it is time to pick up your ...s."** Parent walks out. When it is time for dinner, parent goes back into room to announce dinner:

> The toys have not been picked up—<u>say nothing at that moment</u>. After dinner, go back into family room and announce to children, **"Looks like you decided to not watch television tonight."** Even if children get busy picking up the toys, they have already chosen not to watch TV for this night. **"Oh, you're thinking that if you pick your toys up now that you can watch TV, but the policy is that toys have to be put away before dinner."** After children plead for another chance, *follow through on the consequence,* calmly and empathically stating: **"I know that you wish you would have <u>chosen</u> to put your toys away before dinner, so you could <u>choose</u> to watch TV now. Tomorrow night, you can <u>choose</u> to put your toys away before dinner and choose to watch TV."** *Some children will choose not to watch TV for several nights in a row!*

> The children are busy picking up toys and have put <u>most</u> of them away. Parent says (as she helps with the <u>few</u> remaining toys to demonstrate spirit of cooperation and prevent delay of dinner), **"It's time for dinner—looks like you've chosen to watch TV after dinner tonight."**

Guidelines for Choice-Giving in Relation to Limit Setting and Consequences

...nforce consequence **without fail** and **without anger.**

...Consequence is for "today" only—each day (or play session) should be a chance for a fresh start; a chance to have ...earned from the previous decision and resulting consequence; a chance to use internal resources to control "self" and ...nake a different decision.

> **Reflect** child's choice with empathy, but remain firm. Consistency and follow-through are critical!

> Communicate choices in a matter-of-fact voice—power struggles are likely to result if child hears frustration or anger in parent's voice and believes parent is invested in one choice over another. Child must be free to choose consequence for noncompliance.

...tion: *Once your child has reached the stage of "out of control," your child may not be able to hear and process a choice. Take a step back and focus ...our child's feelings, reflecting her feelings empathically while limiting unacceptable behavior and holding her, if necessary, to prevent her from hurting ...self or you.*

CHILD-PARENT-RELATIONSHIP (C-P-R) TRAINING
Common Problems in Play Sessions – Session 6

Q: My child notices that I talk differently in the play sessions and wants me to talk normally. What should I do?

> **A:** Say, "I sound different to you. That's my way of letting you know I heard what you said. Remember, I'm going to that special class to learn how to play with you." (The child may be: saying he notices the parent is different; having a surprise reaction to the verbal attention; annoyed by too much reflection of words; or saying he notices the difference in the parent's reflective-type responses. The child may also be saying he doesn't want the parent to change, because that will mean he must then change and adjust to the parent's new way of responding.)

Q: My child asks many questions during the play sessions and resents my not answering them. What should I do?

> **A:** We always begin by reflecting the child's feelings. "You're angry at me." Sometimes a child feels insecure when a parent changes typical ways of responding and is angry because he doesn't know how to react. Your child may feel insecure and be trying to get your attention the way he has done in the past. Your objective is to encourage your child's self-reliance and self-acceptance. "In our special playtime, the answer can be anything you want it to be." For example, your child might ask, "What should I draw?" You want your child to know he's in charge of his drawing during the special playtime, so you respond, "You've decided to draw, and in this special playtime, you can draw whatever you decide." Our objective is to empower the child, to enable the child to discover his own strengths.

Q: My child just plays and has fun. What am I doing wrong?

> **A:** Nothing. Your child is supposed to use the time however she wants. The relationship you are building with your child during the special playtimes is more important than whether or not your child is working on a problem. As your relationship with your child is strengthened, your child's problem will diminish. Your child may be working on issues through her play that you are not aware of. Remember the lesson of the Band-Aid. What you are doing in the playtimes is working, even when you don't see any change. Children can change as a result of what they do in play sessions with parents or play therapists, even though we are not aware of what they are working on. Your job during the special playtimes is to follow your child's lead and be nonjudgmental, understanding, and accepting of your child. Your empathic responses will help your child focus on the issues that are important to her.

Q: I'm bored. What's the value of this?

> **A:** Being bored in a playtime is not an unusual happening because parents have busy schedules, are on the go a lot, and are not used to sitting and interacting quietly for 30 minutes. You can increase your interest level and involvement in your child's play by responding to what you see in your child's face and asking yourself questions such as "What is he feeling?" "What is he trying to say in his play?" "What does he need from me?" or "What is so interesting to him about the toy or the play?" and by making more tracking responses and reflective responses. The most important thing you can do is continue to be patient with the process of the play sessions.

Q: My child doesn't respond to my comments. How do I know I'm on target?

> **A:** Usually when you are on target, your child will let you know. If she doesn't respond to a reflection, you may want to explore other feelings she might be having or convey that you're trying to under-stand. For example, if you have reflected "You really are angry!" and your child doesn't respond, you might say, "... Or maybe it's not anger you're feeling, maybe you're just feeling really strong and powerful." If your child still doesn't respond, you might say, "Maybe that's not it either. I wonder what it could be that you're feeling."

Q: When is it okay for me to ask questions, and when is it not okay?

A: Most of the time, questions can be rephrased as statements, for example, "I wonder if that's ever happened to you" instead of "Has that ever happened to you?" The only type of questions that are okay in play sessions are spoken as "stage whispers," as in "What should I say?"

Q: My child hates the play sessions. Should I discontinue them?

A: Communicating understanding is always important. Say, "You don't want to have the special play-time. You would rather do something else. Let's have the special playtime for 10 minutes, then you can decide if you want to have the rest of the special playtime or do something else." This response helps your child to feel understood and to feel in control. A child in that position in a relationship is much more likely to compromise. In most cases, a child will get started playing and will decide to have the rest of the playtime.

Q: My child wants the playtime to be longer. Should I extend the session?

A: Even though your child is having lots of fun, the time limit is adhered to because this promotes consistency, affords you an opportunity to be firm, and provides your child with an opportunity to bring himself under control and end a very desirable playtime. Use A-C-T limit setting, being sure to acknowledge your child's feelings. For example, you can say, "You're really having fun and would like to play a lot longer, but our special playtime is over for today. We will have another special playtime next Tuesday." If your child persists, you could say, "Joey, I wish we had more time, too, but our 30 minutes are up for today. We'll get to have another playtime next Tuesday."

Q: My child wants to play with the toys at other times during the week. Is that OK?

A: Allowing your child to play with these toys only during the 30-minute playtimes helps to convey the message that this is a special time, a time just for the two of you, a fun time. Setting the toys apart makes the playtime unique and more desirable. Another reason is that this time with your child is an emotional relationship time; the toys become a part of that emotional relationship during which your child expresses and explores emotional messages through the toys because of the kinds of empathic responses you make. This same kind of emotional exploration cannot occur during other playtimes because you are not there to communicate understanding of your child's play. Additionally, being allowed to play with these toys only during the special playtimes helps your child learn to delay his need for gratification. If you are having trouble keeping your child from playing with the special toy kit, try storing it out of sight on the top shelf of your closet. If that doesn't work, lock it in the trunk of your car.

Q: My child wants me to shoot at him during the play session. What should I do?

A: Set the limit. If your child says, "I'm the bad guy, shoot me," say, "I know you want me to shoot you, but you're not for shooting; I can pretend you're the bad guy getting away, and I'll catch you, or you can draw a picture of the bad guy getting shot."

Q: _____
_____
_____
_____

CHILD-PARENT-RELATIONSHIP (C-P-R) TRAINING
In-Class Play Session Skills Checklist:
For Review of Videotaped (or Live) Play Session – Session 6

Directions: Indicate ✓ in blank when you observe a play session skill demonstrated in videotaped or live play session

1. ___ Set the Stage/Structured Play Session

2. ___ Conveyed "Be With" Attitudes
   Full attention/interested
   Toes followed nose

3. ___ Allowed Child to Lead
   Avoided giving suggestions
   Avoided asking questions
   Returned responsibility to child

4. ___ Followed Child's Lead
   Physically on child's level
   Moved closer when child was involved in play
   Joined in play when invited—took imaginary/pretend role when appropriate

5. ___ Reflective Responding Skills:

   ___ Reflected child's nonverbal play behavior (Tracking)

   ___ Reflected child's verbalizations (Content)

   ___ Reflected child's feelings/wants/wishes

   ___ Voice tone matched child's intensity/affect

   ___ Responses were brief and interactive

   ___ Facial expressions matched child's affect

6. ___ Used Encouragement/Self-Esteem-Building Responses

7. ___ Set Limits, As Needed, Using A-C-T

CHILD-PARENT-RELATIONSHIP (C-P-R) TRAINING
Parent Play Session Notes – Session 6

Play Session #_____   Date: _____

Significant Happenings:

What I Learned About My Child:

Feelings Expressed:

Play Themes:

What I Learned About Myself:

My feelings during the play session:

What I think I was best at:

What was hardest or most challenging for me:

Questions or Concerns:

Skill I Want to Focus on in the Next Play Session: _____

CHILD-PARENT-RELATIONSHIP (C-P-R) TRAINING
Play Session Skills Checklist - Session 6

Play Session #_____ Date: _____

(Note: Indicate ✓ in column if skill was used; — if skill was not used; and + if skill was a strength)

✓ — +	Skill	Notes/Comments
	Set the Stage/Structured Play Session	
	Conveyed "Be With" Attitudes *Full attention/interested* *Toes followed nose*	
	Allowed Child to Lead *Avoided giving suggestions* *Avoided asking questions* *Returned responsibility to child*	
	Followed Child's Lead *Physically on child's level* *Moved closer when child was involved in play* *Joined in play when invited*	
	Reflective Responding Skills:	
	Reflected child's nonverbal play (Tracking)	
	Reflected child's verbalizations (Content)	
	Reflected child's feelings/wants/wishes	
	Voice tone matched child's intensity/affect	
	Responses were brief and interactive	
	Facial expressions matched child's affect	
	Use of Encouragement/Self-Esteem-Building Responses	
	Set Limits, As Needed, Using A-C-T	

Child Parent Relationship Therapy (CPRT)

Session 7 – Treatment Outline

⊕ Time
Marker

Note: Print material checklist for this session (CD-ROM, Appendix A – contains list of all materials and where to locate them)

_____ **I.** **Informal Sharing, followed by Review of Homework as Parents Report on Play Sessions (Videotaped parents share last)**

- Review *Choice-Giving 101: Teaching Responsibility & Decision Making* (refer parents to page 23 in the *Parent Notebook*)—reinforce basic concepts as parents report on homework assignment to practice giving a choice to their child outside the play session

- (Optional) Complete video, *Choices, Cookies, and Kids,* from Session 6 as needed

- Review and complete as needed: *Advanced Choice-Giving: Providing Choices as Consequences* (refer parents to page 24 in the *Parent Notebook*)

  If parents raise questions about how choices can be used when the child doesn't comply with a limit, briefly discuss the use of choices as consequences. Inform parents that this more advanced skill will be covered in depth in a later session (refer to handout in Session 9: *Advanced Limit Setting: Giving Choices as Consequences for Noncompliance* page 42 in the *Parent Notebook*).

- Briefly review handout: *Common Problems in Play Sessions* (refer parents to pages 25 & 26 in the *Parent Notebook*).

  Use as a chance to review reflective listening, setting limits, giving choices, and so forth.

- Continue debriefing play sessions, focusing on parents' perceived changes in their own behavior

  Focus on **Play Session Do's** (use poster for parents to refer to)

  Use examples from parents' comments to reinforce **Do's**

  Role-play with parents on how to respond to difficult situations

- Remember the Donut Analogy: Encourage…Support…Connect!

  Find something in <u>each</u> parent's sharing that can be encouraged and supported—facilitate "connecting" among group members.

____ II.   **Videotaped Play Session Review and Supervision**

- View one to two parent-child play sessions, following same procedure as last week

- Model encouragement and facilitate peer feedback

- Refer parents to handout, *In-Class Play Session Skills Checklist*, page 33 in the *Parent Notebook* and ask parents to check off skills they see being demonstrated

- Continue to refer to *Play Session Do's & Don'ts* poster/handout

    o Play videotape until a <u>strength</u> is evident

    o Focus on importance of parent's awareness of self in the play session

    o Play portion of videotape that parent has a question about or would particularly like to show

    o Ask what the parent thinks he/she does <u>well</u>

    o Ask what area the parent would like to work on in his/her next play session

____ III.   **Self-Esteem Building**

- Review handout: *Esteem-Building Responses* (refer parents to page 31 in the *Parent Notebook*)

☞ **Rule of Thumb: "Never do for a child that which he can do for himself."**

When you do, you rob your child of the joy of discovery and the opportunity to feel competent. You will never know what your child is capable of unless you allow him to try!

____ IV.   **Role-Play/Video Clip or Live Demonstration of Play Session Skills, Self-Esteem-Building Responses, and Responses that Return Responsibility to the Child**

- Always allow time for parents to see a demonstration of play session skills that you want them to emulate, focusing on those skills they report the most difficulty with

- After viewing demonstration, ask parents to role-play a few scenarios they believe are most difficult for them, including at least one self-esteem-building response in role-play

____ V.   **Arrange for One to Two Parents to Do Videotaping This Week**

Name/phone number _____ day/time (if taping at clinic)_____

Name/phone number _____ day/time (if taping at clinic)_____

Remind parent(s) who are videotaping this week to make note on their Parent Notes & Homework handout

____ **VI.**   **Homework Assignments** (refer parents to homework section in their notebook)

1) Read *Esteem-Building Responses*—practice giving at least one esteem-building response <u>during</u> your play session (note on *Play Session Skills Checklist*), also practice giving one esteem-building response <u>outside</u> of your play session.
   What happened outside of play session_____
   What you said _____
   How child responded (verbally or nonverbally)_____

2) Write a note to your child of focus, as well as other children in the family, pointing out a positive character quality you appreciate about the child (see *Positive Character Qualities handout*). Continue to write a note each week for three weeks (mail first note to child, if possible). Write down the following sentence:

   "Dear _____, I was just thinking about you, and what I was thinking is you are so _____ (thoughtful, responsible, considerate, loving, etc.). I love you, _____ (Mom, Dad)."

   Say to the child, in your own words, after the child reads the note (or you read it to the child), "That is such an important quality; we should put that note on the refrigerator (bulletin board, etc.)." <u>Reminder</u>: Don't expect a response from your child.

3) Conduct play session (same time & place)—review *Play Session Do's & Don'ts & Play Session Procedures Checklist*
   a.   Complete *Parent Play Session Notes*.
   b.   Use *Play Session Skills Checklist* to note what you thought you did well, and select one skill you want to work on in your next play session: note at least one self-esteem building response

____ *I will bring my videotape for next week (if videotaping at clinic: my appt. day/time _____).*

4) Additional Assignment:

____ **VII.**   **Close With Motivational Poem, Story, or Rule of Thumb (optional)**

Suggest reading: "The Struggle to Become a Butterfly: A True Story" (see parent handout: *Esteem-Building Responses* on page 31 in *Parent Notebook*)

Remember the butterfly: Without the struggle, there are no wings!

☝ RULE OF THUMB TO REMEMBER:

"Never do for a child that which he can do for himself."

When you do, you rob your child of the joy of discovery and the opportunity to feel competent. You will never know what your child is capable of unless you allow him to try!

👍 RULE OF THUMB TO REMEMBER:

"Never do for a child that which he can do for himself."
When you do, you rob your child of the joy of discovery and the opportunity to feel competent.
You will never know what your child is capable of unless you allow him to try!

Notes (use back for additional notes):

_____
_____
_____
_____
_____
_____
_____
_____
_____
_____
_____
_____
_____
_____
_____

Homework Assignments:

1. Read *Esteem-Building Responses*—practice giving at least one esteem-building response <u>during</u> your play session (note on *Play Session Skills Checklist*). Also practice giving one esteem-building response <u>outside</u> of your play session.
    What happened outside of play session_____
    What you said _____
    How child responded (verbally or nonverbally)_____

2. Write a note to your child of focus, as well as other children in the family, pointing out a positive character quality you appreciate about the child (see *Positive Character Qualities* handout). Continue to write a note each week for three weeks (mail first note to child, if possible). Write down the following sentence:

    "*Dear _____, I was just thinking about you, and what I was thinking is you are so _____ (thoughtful, responsible, considerate, loving, etc.). I love you, _____ (Mom, Dad).*"

    Say to the child, in your own words, after the child reads the note (or you read it to the child), "That is such an important quality; we should put that note on the refrigerator (bulletin board, etc.)." <u>Reminder</u>: Don't expect a response from your child.

3. Conduct play session (same time & place)—review *Play Session Do's & Don'ts & Play Session Procedure Checklist*

    a. Complete *Parent Play Session Notes*.

    b. Use *Play Session Skills Checklist* to note what you thought you did well, <u>specifically focus on esteem-building responses</u>, and select one skill you want to work on in your next play session.

    _____ *I will bring my videotape for next week (if videotaping at clinic: my appt. day/time _____).*

4. Additional assignment:

CHILD-PARENT-RELATIONSHIP (C-P-R) TRAINING
Esteem Building Responses:
Developing Your Child's Sense of Competence - Session 7

✎ **Rule of Thumb: "Never do for a child that which he can do for himself."**

When you do, you rob your child of the joy of discovery and the opportunity to feel competent.
You will never know what your child is capable of unless you allow him to try!

Parents help their child develop a positive view of "self," not only by providing their child with love and unconditional acceptance, but also by helping their child feel competent and capable. Parents help their child feel competent and capable by first allowing the child to **experience** what it is like to discover, figure out, and problem-solve. Parents show faith in their child and their child's capabilities by allowing him to struggle with a problem, all the while providing encouragement (encouragement vs. praise is covered in detail in Session 8). For most parents, allowing children to struggle is hard—but a necessary process for children to truly feel capable. The next step in helping children develop a positive view of self as competent and capable is learning to respond in ways that give children credit for ideas, effort, and accomplishments, without praising.

Esteem-Building Responses to Use in Play Sessions:

"You did it!"   "You decided that was the way that was supposed to fit together."
"You figured it out."   "You know just how you want that to look."
"You like the way that turned out." "You're not giving up—you're determined to figure that out."
"You decided…"   "You've got a plan for how…"

Example 1: Child works and works to get the lid off the playdough and finally gets it off.
Parent response: **"You did it."**

Example 2: Child works and works to get the lid off the playdough but can't get it off.
Parent response: **"You're determined to figure that out."**

Example 3: Child struggles to get the dart to fit into the gun and pushed in all the way and finally gets it in.
Parent response: **"You figured it out."**

Example 4: Child spends time drawing, cutting, and gluing a nondescript piece of "art" and shows you with a smile when he is finished.
Parent response: **"You really like the way that turned out."**

Example 5: Child is carefully setting up army soldiers and telling you all about a battle that is going to take place, what is going to happen, and how one side is going to sneak up, and so forth.
Parent response: **"You've got a plan for how that side is…"** or **"You've got that all planned out."**

Note: If your child tends to ask you to do things for him without trying first, ask the therapist to role-play how to return responsibility to your child to do things he is capable of figuring out for himself.

****

The Struggle to Become a Butterfly: A True Story (Author Unknown)

A family in my neighborhood once brought in two cocoons that were just about to hatch. They watched as the first one began to open and the butterfly inside squeezed very slowly and painfully through a tiny hole that it chewed in one end of the cocoon. After lying exhausted for about 10 minutes following its agonizing emergence, the butterfly finally flew out the open window on its beautiful wings.

The family decided to help the second butterfly so that it would not have to go through such an excruciating ordeal. So, as it began to emerge, they carefully sliced open the cocoon with a razor blade, doing the equivalent of a Caesarean section. The second butterfly never did sprout wings, and in about 10 minutes, instead of flying away, it quietly died.

The family asked a biologist friend to explain what had happened. The scientist said that the difficult struggle to emerge from the small hole actually pushes liquids from deep inside the butterfly's body cavity into the tiny capillaries in the wings where they harden to complete the healthy and beautiful adult butterfly.

Remember: WITHOUT THE STRUGGLE, THERE ARE NO WINGS!

CHILD-PARENT-RELATIONSHIP (C-P-R) TRAINING
Positive Character Qualities – Session 7

accountable	affectionate	appreciative	assertive
brave	careful	caring	clever
compassionate	confident	considerate	cooperative
courageous	courteous	creative	decisive
dependable	determined	direct	empathic
enjoyable	enthusiastic	energetic	feeling
forgiving	friendly	fun	generous
gentle	goal oriented	good sport	grateful
helpful	honest	humble	idealistic
insightful	intelligent	inventive	joyful
kind	loving	loyal	modest
neat	orderly	outgoing	patient
peaceful	persistent	polite	purposeful
punctual	quiet	reliable	resourceful
respectful	responsible	self-assured	self-controlled
self-disciplined	sensitive	sincere	smart
supportive	tactful	team player	tenacious
thoughtful	tolerant	trustworthy	truthful

CHILD-PARENT-RELATIONSHIP (C-P-R) TRAINING
In-Class Play Session Skills Checklist:
For Review of Videotaped (or Live) Play Session – Session 7

Directions: Indicate ✓ in blank when you observe a play session skill demonstrated in videotaped or live play session

1. ____ Set the Stage/Structured Play Session

2. ____ Conveyed "Be With" Attitudes
    Full attention/interested
    Toes followed nose

3. ____ Allowed Child to Lead
    Avoided giving suggestions
    Avoided asking questions
    Returned responsibility to child

4. ____ Followed Child's Lead
    Physically on child's level
    Moved closer when child was involved in play
    Joined in play when invited—took imaginary/pretend role when appropriate

5. ____ Reflective Responding Skills:

    ____ Reflected child's nonverbal play behavior (Tracking)

    ____ Reflected child's verbalizations (Content)

    ____ Reflected child's feelings/wants/wishes

    ____ Voice tone matched child's intensity/affect

    ____ Responses were brief and interactive

    ____ Facial expressions matched child's affect

6. ____ Used Encouragement/Self-Esteem-Building Responses

7. ____ Set Limits, As Needed, Using A-C-T

CHILD-PARENT-RELATIONSHIP (C-P-R) TRAINING
Parent Play Session Notes – Session 7

Play Session #_____ Date: _____

Significant Happenings:

What I Learned About My Child:

Feelings Expressed:

Play Themes:

What I Learned About Myself:

My feelings during the play session:

What I think I was best at:

What was hardest or most challenging for me:

Questions or Concerns:

Skill I Want to Focus on in the Next Play Session: _____

CHILD-PARENT-RELATIONSHIP (C-P-R) TRAINING
Play Session Skills Checklist - Session 7

Play Session #_____ Date: _____

(Note: Indicate ✓ in column if skill was used; — if skill was not used; and + if skill was a strength)

✓ — +	Skill	Notes/Comments
	Set the Stage/Structured Play Session	

	Conveyed "Be With" Attitudes
	   Full attention/interested
	   Toes followed nose	

	Allowed Child to Lead
	   Avoided giving suggestions
	   Avoided asking questions
	   Returned responsibility to child	

	Followed Child's Lead
	   Physically on child's level
	   Moved closer when child was involved in play
	   Joined in play when invited	

	Reflective Responding Skills:	
	Reflected child's nonverbal play (Tracking)	
	Reflected child's verbalizations (Content)	
	Reflected child's feelings/wants/wishes	
	Voice tone matched child's intensity/affect	
	Responses were brief and interactive	
	Facial expressions matched child's affect	
	Use of Encouragement/Self-Esteem-Building Responses	
	Set Limits, As Needed, Using A-C-T	

Child Parent Relationship Therapy (CPRT)

Session 8 – Treatment Outline

Note: Print material checklist for this session (CD-Rom, Appendix A – contains list of all materials and where to locate them)

_____ **I.** **Informal Sharing, followed by Review of Homework as Parents Report on Play Sessions and Generalizing Play Session Skills (Videotaped parents share test)**

- Parents report on the character quality note-writing activity

  Keep the sharing brief—caution parents not to expect an overt response from their children

- Parents report on practicing giving a self-esteem-building response <u>outside</u> the play session

  Parents report on practicing a self-esteem building response made <u>during</u> play sessions, as a lead into play session reports

- Continue debriefing play sessions, focusing on parents' perceived changes in their own behavior

  Focus on **Play Session Do's** (use poster for parents to refer to)

  Use examples from parents' comments to reinforce **Do's**

  Role-play with parents on how to respond to difficult situations.

- Remember the Donut Analogy: Encourage . . . Support . . . Connect!

_____ **II.** **Videotaped Play Session Review and Supervision**

- View one to two parent-child play sessions, following same procedure as last week

  Have parents report briefly on their home play sessions and their homework assignment to practice self-esteem-building responses during their play sessions

- Refer parents to handout, *In-Class Play Session Skills Checklist*, page 38 in the *Parent Notebook* and ask parents to check off skills they see being demonstrated

- Continue to refer to *Play Session Do's & Don'ts* poster/handout

_____ **III.** **Review Handout: *Encouragement vs. Praise*** (refer parents to page 37 in the *Parent Notebook*)

- Go over encouraging responses in handout to use in play sessions

    ✥ **Rule of Thumb: "Encourage the effort rather than praise the product."**

        Children need encouragement like a plant needs water.

_____ **IV.** **Role-Play/Video Clip or Live Demonstration of Play Session Skills and Prizing (Encouraging) Responses**

- Always allow time for parents to see a demonstration of play session skills that you want them to emulate, focusing on those skills they report the most difficulty with

- After viewing demonstration, ask parents to role-play a few scenarios they believe are most difficult for them, including at least one encouragement in role-play

_____ **V.** **Arrange for One to Two Parents to Do Videotaping This Week**

Name/phone number _____ day/time (if taping at clinic)_____

Name/phone number _____ day/time (if taping at clinic)_____

Remind parent(s) who are videotaping this week to make note on their Parent Notes & Homework handout

_____ **VI.** **Homework Assignments** (refer parents to homework section of their notebook)

1) Read *Encouragement vs. Praise*—practice giving at least one encouragement response <u>during</u> your play session (note on *Play Sessin Skill Checklist*). Also, practice giving atleast one encouragement <u>outside </u>of your play session.

    What happened or what child said (outside of play session) _____
    What you said _____
    How child responded (verbally ot nonverbally)_____

2) Write down one issue you are struggling with most <u>outside</u> of play session time.
_____

    It may be one they have brought up before, or they may have already solved that one on their own and have a new issue they want help with.

3) Conduct play session (same time & place)—review *Play Session Do's & Don'ts*
    a. Complete *Parent Play Session Notes.*
    b. Use *Play Session Skills Checklist* to note what you thought you did well, select one skill you want to work on in your next play session, and note at least one encouraging statement.

_____ *I will bring my videotape for next week (if videotaping at clinic: my appt. day/time___).*

4) Additional Assignment:
    Reminder: Write second note to your child of focus, as well as other children in the family, pointing out <u>another</u> positive character quality you appreciate about the child. (Vary how the note is

delivered, for example, placing in child's lunchbox, taped to mirror in bathroom, on the child's pillow, under the child's dinner plate, etc.)

_____ **VII.   Close With Motivational Poem, Story or Rule of Thumb (optional)**

☝ RULE OF THUMB TO REMEMBER:
"Encourage the effort rather than praise the product!"
Children need encouragement like a plant needs water.

_____

CHILD-PARENT-RELATIONSHIP (C-P-R) TRAINING
Parent Notes & Homework – Session 8

👍 RULE OF THUMB TO REMEMBER:

"Encourage the effort rather than praise the product!"
Children need encouragement like a plant needs water.

Notes (use back for additional notes):

_____
_____
_____
_____
_____
_____
_____
_____
_____
_____
_____
_____
_____
_____

Homework Assignments:

1. Read *Encouragement vs. Praise*—practice giving at least one encouragement response <u>during</u> your play session (note on *Play Session Skills Checklist*). Also practice giving at least one encouragement <u>outside</u> of your play session.

   What happend or what child said (outside of play session) _____
   What you said _____
   How child responded (verbally or nonverbally)_____

2. Write down one issue you are struggling with most <u>outside</u> of play session time.

   _____

3. Conduct play session (same time & place)—review *Play Session Do's & Don'ts & Play Session Procedure Checklist*

   a. Complete *Parent Play Session Notes*.

   b. Use *Play Session Skills Checklist* to note what you thought you did well, <u>specifically focus on encouragement responses</u>, and select one skill you want to work on in your next play session.

   _____ **I will bring my videotape for next week (if videotaping at clinic: my appt. day/time_____).**

4. Additional assignment:

Reminder: Write second note to your child of focus, as well as other children in the family, pointing out <u>another</u> positive character quality you appreciate about the child. (Vary how the note is delivered, for example, placing in child's lunchbox, taped to mirror in bathroom, on the child's pillow, under the child's dinner plate, etc.)

CHILD-PARENT-RELATIONSHIP (C-P-R) TRAINING
Encouragement vs Praise – Session 8

👍 **Rule of Thumb:** "Encourage the effort rather than praise the product"

Praise: Although praise and encouragement both focus on positive behaviors and appear to be the same process, praise actually fosters dependence in children by teaching them to rely on an external source of control and motivation rather than on self-control and self-motivation. Praise is an attempt to motivate children with external rewards. In effect, the parent who praises is saying, "If you do something I consider good, you will have the reward of being recognized and valued by me." Overreliance on praise can produce crippling effects. Children come to believe that their worth depends upon the opinions of others. Praise employs words that place value judgments on children and focuses on external evaluation.

<u>Examples</u>:   "You're such a good boy/girl." *The child may wonder, "Am I accepted only when I'm good?"*
"You got an A. That's great!" *Are children to infer that they are worthwhile only when they make As?*
"You did a good job." "I'm so proud of you." *The message sent is that the parent's evaluation is more important than the child's.*

Encouragement: Focuses on internal evaluation and the contributions children make—facilitates development of self-motivation and self-control. Encouraging parents teach their children to accept their own inadequacies, learn from mistakes (mistakes are wonderful opportunities for learning), have confidence in themselves, and feel useful through contribution. When commenting on children's efforts, be careful not to place value judgments on what they have done. Be alert to eliminate value-laden words (good, great, excellent, etc.) from your vocabulary at these times. Instead, substitute words of encouragement that help children believe in themselves. Encouragement focuses on effort and can always be given. Children who feel their efforts are encouraged, valued, and appreciated develop qualities of persistence and determination and tend to be good problem-solvers. *Note: Parent's voice should match child's level of affect; if child is excited about getting an "A" on a test, parent responds likewise with excitement in her voice, "You're really proud of that!" Use after-the-event celebrations (based on child's pride in achievement) instead of rewards (external motivators to get the child to achieve) to recognize achievement. In the above example, the parent could add "Sounds like something to celebrate; let's make a cake!" or "You choose the restaurant, my treat!"*

<u>Encouraging Phrases That Recognize Effort and Improvement</u>:
"You did it!" or "You got it!"
"You really worked hard on that."
"You didn't give up until you figured it out."
"Look at the progress you've made..." (Be specific)
"You've finished half of your worksheet and it's only 4 o'clock."

<u>Encouraging Phrases That Show Confidence</u>:
"I have confidence in you. You'll figure it out."
"That's a rough one, but I bet you'll figure it out."
"Sounds like you have a plan."
"Knowing you, I'm sure you will do fine."
"Sounds like you know a lot about_____."

<u>Encouraging Phrases That Focus on Contributions, Assets, and Appreciation</u>:
"Thanks, that was a big help."
"It was thoughtful of you to_____" or "I appreciate that you_____."
"You have a knack for _____. Can you give me a hand with that?"

<u>In summary, encouragement is:</u>
1. Valuing and accepting children as they are (not putting conditions on acceptance)
2. Pointing out the positive aspects of behavior
3. Showing faith in children, so that they can come to believe in themselves
4. Recognizing effort and improvement (rather than requiring achievement)
5. Showing appreciation for contributions

Adapted from Dinkmeyer, D., & McKay, G.D. <u>The Parent's Handbook</u>, (1982). Circle Pines, Minn: American Guidance Service.

CHILD-PARENT-RELATIONSHIP (C-P-R) TRAINING
In-Class Play Session Skills Checklist:
For Review of Videotaped (or Live) Play Session – Session 8

Directions: Indicate ✓ in blank when you observe a play session skill demonstrated in videotaped or live play session

1. ____ Set the Stage/Structured Play Session

2. ____ Conveyed "Be With" Attitudes
    Full attention/interested
    Toes followed nose

3. ____ Allowed Child to Lead
    Avoided giving suggestions
    Avoided asking questions
    Returned responsibility to child

4. ____ Followed Child's Lead
    Physically on child's level
    Moved closer when child was involved in play
    Joined in play when invited—took imaginary/pretend role when appropriate

5. ____ Reflective Responding Skills:

    ____ Reflected child's nonverbal play behavior (Tracking)

    ____ Reflected child's verbalizations (Content)

    ____ Reflected child's feelings/wants/wishes

    ____ Voice tone matched child's intensity/affect

    ____ Responses were brief and interactive

    ____ Facial expressions matched child's affect

6. ____ Used Encouragement/Self-Esteem-Building Responses

7. ____ Set Limits, As Needed, Using A-C-T

CHILD-PARENT-RELATIONSHIP (C-P-R) TRAINING
Parent Play Session Notes – Session 8

Play Session #_____   Date: _____

Significant Happenings:

What I Learned About My Child:

Feelings Expressed:

Play Themes:

What I Learned About Myself:

My feelings during the play session:

What I think I was best at:

What was hardest or most challenging for me:

Questions or Concerns:

Skill I Want to Focus on in the Next Play Session: _____

CHILD-PARENT-RELATIONSHIP (C-P-R) TRAINING
Play Session Skills Checklist - Session 8

Play Session #_____   Date: _____

(Note: Indicate ✓ in column if skill was used; — if skill was not used; and + if skill was a strength)

✓ — +	Skill	Notes/Comments
	Set the Stage/Structured Play Session	

	Conveyed "Be With" Attitudes
	    Full attention/interested
	    Toes followed nose	

	Allowed Child to Lead
	    Avoided giving suggestions
	    Avoided asking questions
	    Returned responsibility to child	

	Followed Child's Lead
	    Physically on child's level
	    Moved closer when child was involved in play
	    Joined in play when invited	

	Reflective Responding Skills:	
	Reflected child's nonverbal play (Tracking)	
	Reflected child's verbalizations (Content)	
	Reflected child's feelings/wants/wishes	
	Voice tone matched child's intensity/affect	
	Responses were brief and interactive	
	Facial expressions matched child's affect	
	Use of Encouragement/Self-Esteem-Building Responses	
	Set Limits, As Needed, Using A-C-T	

Child Parent Relationship Therapy (CPRT)

Session 9 – Treatment Outline

⊕ <u>Time</u>

<u>Marker</u>

Note: Print material checklist for this session (CD-Rom, Appendix A – contains list of all materials and where to locate them)

_____ **I.** **Informal Sharing, followed by Review of Homework as Parents Report on Play Sessions**

- Parents report on practicing giving an encouragement response <u>during</u> their play session

  If parents bring up homework responses <u>outside</u> play sessions, ask them to share those responses when skills outside play sessions are discussed in a few minutes

- Continue debriefing play sessions, focusing on parent's perceived changes in their own behavior

  Focus on **Play Session Do's** (use poster for parents to refer to)

  Use examples from parents' comments to reinforce **Do's**

  Role-play with parents on how to respond to difficult situations

- Remember the Donut Analogy: Encourage . . . Support . . . Connect!

_____ **II.** **Videotaped Play Session Review and Supervision**

- View one to two parent-child play sessions, following same procedure as last week

  Have parents report briefly on their home play sessions—model encouragement and facilitate peer feedback

  Ask particularly about the homework assignment of writing down one thing that didn't go well and one thing that went really well in the play session

- Refer parents to handout, *In-Class Play Session Skills Checklist,* page 48 in the *Parent Notebook* and ask parents to check off skills they see being demonstrated

- Continue to refer to *Play Session Do's & Don'ts* poster/handout

- Review limit setting and discuss advanced limit-setting strategies to use during play sessions when child does not comply with limit (refer parents to handout: *Advanced Limit Setting: Giving Choices as Consequences for Noncompliance*). page 42 & 43 in the *Parent Notebook.*

_____ **III.   Using Skills Outside the Play Session**

- Invite parents to comment on homework assignments from Session 8 about using skills <u>outside</u> the play session

  o Giving the child encouragement

  o Second note pointing out positive characteristic

  o Any other skills used outside the play session

- Review written list of parent's concerns from past eight weeks—ask which concerns remain troublesome. Briefly explore use of CPRT skills to address concerns (further discussion in Session 10)

☝ **Rule of Thumb: "Don't try to change everything at once!"**

Focus on 'big' issues that ultimately will mean the most to your child's development of positive self-esteem and feelings of competence and usefulness.

- Discuss how to use limit setting outside of play sessions (refer parents to handout: *Generalizing Limit Setting to Outside the Play Session*) page 44 & 45 in the *Parent Notebook*

☝ Rule of Thumb: "Where there are no limits, there is no security."

Consistent Limits = Secure Relationship

When you don't follow through, you lose credibility and harm your relationship with your child.

- If time allows Review handout as time allows: *Structured Doll Play for Parents* (refer parents to page 46 in the *Parent Notebook*)

_____ **IV.   Role-Play/Video Clip or Live Demonstration of Play Session Skills and Giving the Child Encouragement**

- Always allow time for parents to see a demonstration of play session skills that you want them to emulate, focusing on those skills they report the most difficulty with

- After viewing demonstration, ask parents to role-play a few scenarios they believe are most difficult for them, including at least one instance of giving encouragement in role-play

_____ **V.   Arrange for One to Two Parents to Do Videotaping This Week**

Name/phone number _____day/time (if taping at clinic)_____

Name/phone number _____ day/time (if taping at clinic)_____

Remind parent(s) who are videotaping this week to make note on their Parent Notes & Homework handout

_____ **VI.**   **Homework Assignments** (refer parents to homework section of their notebook)

1) Review Generalizing Limit Setting to Outside the Play Session—if applicable, report on a time you used A-C-T outside of the play session.

What happened _____
What you said _____
How child responded (verbally or nonverbally)_____

2) Notice the number of times you touch your child in interactions outside the play session (hugging, patting on the head, a touch on the arm, etc.) and keep count this week. # of physical contacts: _____

3) A related assignment is to play-wrestle with your children. (Example: In a two-parent family with small children, Mom and kids can sneak up on Dad and try to get him down on the floor, accompanied by lots of fun and laughter.)

4) Choose one issue you are struggling with outside of the play session to focus on and report back next week on how you can use your play session skills to respond to the issue. _____
_____

5) Conduct play session (same time & place)—review *Play Session Do's & Don'ts & Play Session Procedures Checklist*

a. Complete *Parent Play Session Notes.*
b. Use *Play Session Skills Checklist* to note what you thought you did well, and select one skill you want to work on in your next play session.

_____ *I will bring my videotape for next week (if videotaping at clinic: my appt. day/time _____).*

6) Additional assignment:

Reminder: Write third note to your child of focus, as well as other children in the family, pointing out <u>another</u> positive character quality you appreciate about the child. (Vary how the note is delivered.)

_____ **VII.**   **Close With Motivational Poem, Story, or Rule of Thumb (optional)**

☞ RULES OF THUMB TO REMEMBER:

1. **"Where there are no limits, there is no security."** Consistent Limits = Security in the Relationship. When you don't follow through, you lose credibility and harm your relationship with your child.

2. **"Don't try to change everything at once!"** Focus on 'big' issues that ultimately will mean the most to your child's development of positive self-esteem and feelings of competence and usefulness.

☝ RULES OF THUMB TO REMEMBER:

1. **"Where there are no limits, there is no security."** Consistent Limits = Security in the Relationship. When you don't follow through, you lose credibility and harm your relationship with your child.

2. **"Don't try to change everything at once!"** Focus on 'big' issues that ultimately will mean the most to your child's development of positive self-esteem and feelings of competence and usefulness.

Notes (use back for additional notes):

_____
_____
_____
_____
_____
_____
_____

Homework Assignments:

1. Review *Generalizing Limit Setting to Outside the Play Session*—if applicable, report on a time you used A-C-T outside of the play session.
   What happened _____
   What you said _____
   How child responded (verbally or nonverbally)_____

2. Notice the number of times you touch your child in interactions outside the play session (hugging, patting on the head, a touch on the arm, etc.) and keep count this week. # of physical contacts: _____

3. A related assignment is to play-wrestle with your children. (Example: In a two-parent family with small children, Mom and kids can sneak up on Dad and try to get him down on the floor, accompanied by lots of fun and laughter.)

4. Choose one issue you are struggling with outside of the play session to focus on and report back next week on how you can use your play session skills to respond to the issue. _____
   _____

5. Conduct play session (same time & place)—review *Play Session Do's & Don'ts & Play Session Procedure Cheklist*
   a. Complete *Parent Play Session Notes*.
   b. Use *Play Session Skills Checklist* to note what you thought you did well, and select one skill you want to work on in your next play session.
   _____ **I will bring my videotape for next week (if videotaping at clinic: my appt. day/time _____).**

6. Additional assignment:

Reminder: Write third note to your child of focus, as well as other children in the family, pointing out <u>another</u> positive character quality you appreciate about the child. (Vary how the note is delivered.)

CHILD-PARENT-RELATIONSHIP (C-P-R) TRAINING
Advanced Limit Setting: Giving Choices as Consequences for Non-Compliance - Session 9

Play Session Example: After parent has stated that the playdough is for playing with on the tray, 5-year-old Billy dumps it on the floor. Next, parent follows the A-C-T method of limit setting: "**Billy, I know that you want to play with the playdough over there, but the floor (carpet, etc.) is not for putting playdough on; (pointing to tray) the tray is for putting the playdough on.**" Billy continues to ignore parent and begins to smash the playdough on the floor. Parent may patiently restate limit up to three times before beginning the next step of stating "If-Then" choices (consequences) for following or not following limit. Note: This example assumes that parent has chosen a location for the play session where the floor surface can be cleaned by parent after the session. (if child *begins* to put playdoh on carpet, parent can reach out and guide the playdoh can to the tray as the A-C-T limit is set)

Next step: <u>Begin "If-Then" choice-giving method to provide consequence for unacceptable behavior</u>. *Note the number of times the words "choose" or "choice" are used! Remember that the intent is for the child to bring himself under control; therefore, patience is the order of the day. Children need time and practice to learn self-control.*

Example: "**Billy, <u>If you choose</u> to play with the playdough on the tray (pointing to tray), <u>then you choose</u> to play with the playdough today. <u>If you choose</u> to continue to play with the playdough on the floor, <u>then you choose</u> not to play with the playdough for the rest of today.**" (Pause.) Patiently restate if child does not make the choice to comply with the limit. (If no answer and Billy continues to play with playdough on floor, then he has made his choice.) "**Billy, looks like you've <u>chosen</u> to put the playdough up for today. You can <u>choose</u> to give me the playdough, or you can <u>choose</u> for me to put the playdough up for you; which do you <u>choose</u>?**" If child begins to cry and beg for the playdough, parent must be tough and follow through, acknowledging child's feelings and giving child hope that he will have a chance to make a different choice in the next play session. "**Billy, I understand that you're unhappy that you <u>chose</u> to have the playdough put up for today, but you can <u>choose</u> to play with it in our next play session.**"

In the above example, if at any point the child took the playdough and put it on the tray to play with, the parent must be careful to respond matter-of-factly, "**Looks like you decided you wanted to play with it some more today.**"

Practice:
1. Your child aims a loaded dart gun at you.

    A   *I know you'd like to shoot me,* _____.

    C   *But I'm not for shooting* _____.

    T   *You can shoot the Bop Bag or the doll (pointing at each)* _____.

Your child continues to aim the gun at you after you have set the limit using A-C-T three times.

If you choose to *aim the gun at me*
then you choose to *not to get to play with the gun.*

If you choose to *aim the gun somewhere else*
then you choose to *get to play with the gun.*

If your child aims and shoots the gun at you, you say:

I see you've chosen not to get to play with the gun.

If your child puts the gun down, you say:

Looks like you decided to shoot that.

2. Describe a situation in which you think you might need to set a limit during the play session and you anticipate the child might not comply.
Situation: _____

_____

_____

_____

A _____

C _____

T _____

If/Then _____

_____

_____

_____

_____

_____

CHILD-PARENT-RELATIONSHIP (C-P-R) TRAINING
Generalizing Limit Setting to Outside the Play Session – Session 9

Acknowledge the feeling
Communicate the limit
Target alternatives

Three-Step A-C-T Method of Limit Setting Followed by Choices (Consequences) for Non-compliance:

Scenario: *Child found your hidden stash of candy, has a piece in his hand, and is starting to unwrap it. (It is 3 minutes before dinner.)*

1. **A**cknowledge your child's feeling or desire (*your voice must convey empathy and understanding*).
   (Empathically) **"Billy, I know you'd really like to have the candy…"**
   Child learns that his feelings, desires, and wishes are valid and accepted by parent (but not all behavior).
   Just empathically reflecting your child's feeling often defuses the intensity of the feeling or need.

2. **C**ommunicate the limit. (Be specific and clear—and brief.)
   "…but candy is not for eating before dinner."

3. **T**arget acceptable alternatives. (Provide one or more choices, depending on age of child.)
   "You can choose to have a piece of fruit now (underline: pointing to bowl of fruit) **and choose to have the piece of candy after dinner."** (If you do not want your children to ever have candy, don't keep it around.)
   The goal is to provide your child with acceptable alternatives—ones that are acceptable to you, the parent, and ones that you believe will allow your child to get his need met (in this case, to have a piece of candy, but not until after dinner—and if he is hungry, to meet that need with an acceptable before-dinner snack).
   Note: Pointing helps redirect child's attention. *If child chooses fruit, stop here.*
   Patiently restate the limit up to three times, depending on the age of the child, to allow child to struggle with self-control before proceeding to the next step.

4. **Choice-Giving (consequences) as next step after noncompliance** (examples of possible responses):
   Billy continues to say that he doesn't want fruit; he wants the candy.
   — **"Billy, having candy now is not one of the _choices_. You can choose to give me the candy now and _choose_ to eat it after dinner, or you can _choose_ for me to put the candy up and _choose_ not to have the candy after dinner. Which do you _choose_?"** *(Pause—Billy says nothing.)* **"If you choose not to choose, you choose for me to choose for you."** *(Pause.)*
   a) (Billy gives you the candy.) **"I can tell that was a hard decision—I'll put it up here for you for after dinner."**
   b) (Billy continues to hold on to candy.) **"I see you've chosen for me to choose for you"** *(as you reach for the candy to put it up).* After dinner, if Billy comes to you and says "Now can I have the candy?" your response is, **"Remember when you chose not to give me the candy before dinner—at that very moment, you chose not to have candy after dinner."** *Child may continue to plead and cry (because it has worked in the past). Be FIRM—don't give in!*

Practice: It is a school night and 5-year-old Billy wants to watch just 30 more minutes of television before he goes to bed, because his favorite Charlie Brown special is coming on next.

A   *"I know you're disappointed that you can't watch Charlie Brown right now,_____.*

C   *but, it's time for bed_____.*

T   *We can borrow Charlie Brown from the library, and you can watch it tomorrow after school"_____.*
Patiently restate the limit up to three times; Billy doesn't comply. It's important to remain empathic & calm, but firm.
"Billy, I wish we had time to watch Charlie Brown, but it's time for bed now. You can choose to watch it tomorrow after school, but it's time for bed now."
(It may help to refocus child to bedtime by giving him a choice related to bedtime routine) Ex: "Do you want me or mom to read you a story tonight?"

What To Do Affect A-C-T

After you've followed the three-step A-C-T process with empathy and firmness:

1. If you are satisfied with your response to the child's question and the question or plea is repeated, DON'T DISCUSS.
2. If you think the child doesn't understand your response, say:
   — "I've already answered that question. You must have some question about my answer."
3. If you think the child understands, say:
   — "I can tell you'd like to discuss this some more, but I've already answered that question."
   OR
   — "I can tell you don't like my answer. If you are asking again because you want me to change my mind, I will not."
   OR
   — "Do you remember the answer I gave you a few minutes ago when you asked that same question?"
   If child answers, "No, I don't remember," say, "Go sit down in a quite place and think. I know you'll be able to remember."
4. If you are not satisfied with your response to the child's question:
   — If you are open to persuasion, say:
   "I don't know. Let's sit down and discuss it."
   — If you intend to answer the question later but are not prepared to answer now, say:
   "I can't answer that question now because (I want to talk it over with someone; I want to get more information; I want to think about it, etc.). I'll let you know (specific time)."
   — If child demands an answer now, say:
   "If you must have an answer now, the answer will have to be 'NO.'"

What To Do When Limit Setting Doesn't Work

You have been careful <u>several times</u> to calmly and empathically use **A-C-T and Choice-Giving**. Your child continues to deliberately disobey. What do you do?

1. <u>Look for natural causes for rebellion</u>: Fatigue, sickness, hunger, stress, and so forth. Take care of physical needs and crises before expecting cooperation.
2. <u>Remain in control, respecting yourself and the child</u>: You are not a failure if your child rebels, and your child is not bad. All kids need to "practice" rebelling. Remember: At this very moment, nothing is more important than your relationship with your child, so respond in a way that respects your child and yourself. *If you find yourself feeling angry at your child and losing control, walk outside or to another room.*
3. <u>Set reasonable consequences for disobedience</u>: *Let your child choose to obey or disobey*, but set a reasonable consequence for disobedience. Example: "If you choose to watch TV instead of going to bed, then you choose to give up TV all day tomorrow" (or whatever is a meaningful consequence for child).
4. <u>Never tolerate violence</u>: Physically restrain the child who becomes violent, without becoming aggressive yourself. Empathically and calmly **REFLECT** the child's anger and loneliness; provide compassionate control and alternatives as child begins to regain control.
5. <u>If the child refuses to choose, you choose for him</u>: The child's refusal to choose is also a choice. Set the consequences. Example: "If you choose not to (choice A or B), then you have chosen for me to choose for you."
6. <u>ENFORCE THE CONSEQUENCES</u>: Don't state consequences that you cannot enforce. If you crumble under your child's anger or tears, you have abdicated your role as parent and lost your power. **GET TOUGH!** When you <u>don't follow through</u>, you lose credibility and harm your relationship with your child.
7. <u>Recognize signs of more serious problems</u>: Depression, trauma (abuse/neglect/extreme grief/stress). The chronically angry or rebellious child is in emotional trouble and may need professional help. Share your concern with the child. Example: "John, I've noticed that you seem to be angry and unhappy most of the time. I love you, and I'm worried about you. We're going to get help so we can all be happier."

CHILD-PARENT-RELATIONSHIP (C-P-R) TRAINING
Structured Doll Play for Parents – Session 9

What is structured doll play?

Structured doll play is a lively way of storytelling for parents to help children who are feeling anxious or insecure. It provides a brief and specific experience for the children to prepare them for anxiety-provoking experiences, such as parents' divorce, going over to the babysitter, and so forth, or to help them regain a sense of normalcy and routine after a significant change in their life. It has a specific purpose and a clear message (e.g., Mom is going to come back at the end of the day to pick Lucy up).

Can my child benefit from structured doll play?

If your child is showing anxiety or fear, or has been through a traumatic experience, he/she can probably benefit from you using structured doll play with him/her. Structured doll play works best with children from ages 2–6. However, older or younger children can also benefit from it.

How do I do structured doll play?

1. Creating the story

    Structured doll play is basically creative storytelling about specific real life happenings. It is similar to reading a story from a storybook to your child; the major differences are:

    A. You create the story instead of reading out of a storybook.

    B. The story involves real life characters, such as Mom, Dad, Lucy (your child), babysitter Jane, Grandma, schoolteacher, dentist, and so forth.

    C. The story is about real life happenings, usually about future events that are coming up in the next day or two. It can also be a story of routine daily happenings.

    D. You have a specific purpose and a clear message. For example: Lucy is reluctant to go to the new day care. She would not let you leave when you dropped her off at day care. Your purpose is helping Lucy to feel more comfortable about going to day care. Your message may be, "Mom is going to return at the end of the day." (It's important that the message fit what the parent believes is of most concern to the child.)

    E. You use dolls to enhance the dramatic effect and help your child remember. You can also use sound effects to enrich the story and make it more powerful and fun. Remember, young children understand concrete things like dolls and scenes better than promises and reasons.

2. The making of a story (think about a beginning, middle, and an end)

Beginning	Don't start off by saying Lucy is going to the babysitter. Start off by giving some background for the story (e.g., a predictable routine, like waking up in the morning).
Middle	Give content to the story by putting in details (e.g., putting on shoes or buckling seat belt). Remember to exaggerate and use sound effects (you'll probably feel silly at first, but children love it!).
End	Remember to end the story. Don't leave your child hanging. End the story with a big kiss. *"Mom drives to the babysitter's (Jane) house and rings the bell (ding-dong). Jane opens the door and Lucy sees Mom. Lucy jumps into Mom's lap. Mom gives Lucy a big hug and a kiss (make kissing noise). Mom and Lucy drive home together. They talk about the day on the way home."*

    Steps to making a story:
    A) Start with a title sentence (e.g., "This is a story about Lucy going to the babysitter").
    B) Introduce the characters by using real names of people.
    C) Tell the story (don't use "you" to refer to the doll representing your child. Use your child's name to stay objective e.g., "Lucy is saying goodbye to Mom" rather than "You are saying goodbye to Mom").

3. Props and place

    Remember: This is a creative business. So you need to decide on a comfortable time and place to do structured doll play and prepare your props (dolls) ahead of time. A good time might be in your child's bedroom in the evening before bedtime (to avoid disruptions and create a routine). You don't need to buy any special dolls—use your child's dolls and stuffed animals or puppets. (Save your money to give yourself a treat after telling a good story—it's a lot of work to tell a really good story!) You can also involve your child in picking out the dolls/stuffed animals by saying "I've got a special story to tell you tonight. It's about a little girl name Lucy who goes to Jane's (the babysitter). To tell the story, we need a Lucy doll, a Mommy doll, a Daddy doll, and a Jane doll. Can you help me pick out a doll (stuffed animal) for each character? (Make sure you have a selection of your child's dolls/stuffed animals lined up to choose from.) *Note: You need to remember who is who, and the doll figures stay the same person thereafter (you can add new dolls as you use this method to tell different stories, like going to the dentist for the first time, etc.).*

4. How do I start?

    You can start this new play experience by using nonthreatening, general daily life activities as the content of the story (e.g., going to the grocery store). This will help you practice and gain skills before plunging into more challenging themes. Focus your story on one theme and don't go beyond five minutes. You can think the story out in your head, or you can jot down brief notes to use as the script.

Helpful hints:

1. It may seem awkward to tell stories and act them out. Be patient with yourself—YOUR CHILD WILL THINK IT'S FUN AND WON'T NOTICE IF YOU MESS UP!

2. Include only those elements in the story that you have control over. Don't say how much fun Lucy is going to have (she may not be having much fun, if she's anxious). If you say something is going to happen at the babysitter's (going to the park, etc.), make sure you ask that the babysitter follow through on that activity the next day. The entire point of the story is to help the child feel more secure by being able to predict what will happen.

3. Don't build on your own feelings when you are telling the story. For example, "Mom is working in the office while Lucy is playing in day care. Mom is thinking of Lucy <u>and she misses Lucy.</u>" (Take away the underlined phrase; including your own feelings in the story may make the child feel guilty for you missing her). Remember: The goal is to help Lucy go to day care without feeling anxious, so she can relax and have fun.

4. Make the story realistic and positive. You are the author of the story, so you can make it the way you want it to turn out in real life. Instead of focusing the story on how Lucy doesn't want to leave Mom, make the story go like this: "Lucy and Mom ring the doorbell together (ding-dong!). The door opens and Lucy smiles when she sees Jane. Lucy gives Mom a big hug, and she and Jane wave goodbye to Mom together...." (Remember to let Jane know about your story.)

5. Always end the story on a positive note THAT YOU CAN CONTROL. If the story involves the child not seeing you for several hours (especially if that is part of the concern), always include an "I'm so glad to see you!" reunion with kisses and hugs. The graphic representation of using dolls is more powerful than a verbal promise.

6. Your child may get distracted and interrupt the story. Briefly attend to the child, but be sure to finish the story. Telling the story after the child is already in bed helps with distractions. Parent can respond to requests to play with something else by saying, "You can play with your other dolls tomorrow; it's bedtime now." Or, if your child asks for a drink, "As soon as we've finished the story, I'll get you a drink."

CHILD-PARENT-RELATIONSHIP (C-P-R) TRAINING
In-Class Play Session Skills Checklist:
For Review of Videotaped (or Live) Play Session – Session 9

Directions: Indicate ✓ in blank when you observe a play session skill demonstrated in videotaped or live play session

1. ___ Set the Stage/Structured Play Session

2. ___ Conveyed "Be With" Attitudes
   Full attention/interested
   Toes followed nose

3. ___ Allowed Child to Lead
   Avoided giving suggestions
   Avoided asking questions
   Returned responsibility to child

4. ___ Followed Child's Lead
   Physically on child's level
   Moved closer when child was involved in play
   Joined in play when invited—took imaginary/pretend role when appropriate

5. ___ Reflective Responding Skills:

   ___ Reflected child's nonverbal play behavior (Tracking)

   ___ Reflected child's verbalizations (Content)

   ___ Reflected child's feelings/wants/wishes

   ___ Voice tone matched child's intensity/affect

   ___ Responses were brief and interactive

   ___ Facial expressions matched child's affect

6. ___ Used Encouragement/Self-Esteem-Building Responses

7. ___ Set Limits, As Needed, Using A-C-T

CHILD-PARENT-RELATIONSHIP (C-P-R) TRAINING
Parent Play Session Notes – Session 9

Play Session #_____ Date: _____

Significant Happenings:

What I Learned About My Child:

Feelings Expressed:

Play Themes:

What I Learned About Myself:

My feelings during the play session:

What I think I was best at:

What was hardest or most challenging for me:

Questions or Concerns:

Skill I Want to Focus on in the Next Play Session: _____

CHILD-PARENT-RELATIONSHIP (C-P-R) TRAINING
Play Session Skills Checklist - Session 9

Play Session #_____ Date: _____

(Note: Indicate ✓ in column if skill was used; — if skill was not used; and + if skill was a strength)

✓ — +	Skill	Notes/Comments
	Set the Stage/Structured Play Session	

	Conveyed "Be With" Attitudes
	    Full attention/interested
	    Toes followed nose	

	Allowed Child to Lead
	    Avoided giving suggestions
	    Avoided asking questions
	    Returned responsibility to child	

	Followed Child's Lead
	    Physically on child's level
	    Moved closer when child was involved in play
	    Joined in play when invited	

	Reflective Responding Skills:	
	Reflected child's nonverbal play (Tracking)	
	Reflected child's verbalizations (Content)	
	Reflected child's feelings/wants/wishes	
	Voice tone matched child's intensity/affect	
	Responses were brief and interactive	
	Facial expressions matched child's affect	
	Use of Encouragement/Self-Esteem-Building Responses	
	Set Limits, As Needed, Using A-C-T	

Child Parent Relationship Therapy (CPRT)

Session 10 – Treatment Outline

⊕ Time
Marker

Note: Print material checklist for this session (CD-ROM, Appendix A – contains list of all materials and where to locate them)

_____ **I.** **Informal Sharing, followed by Review of Homework**

- Parents report on number of times they physically touched their child

- Invite parents to discuss play-wrestling experience

_____ **II.** **Show Last Videotape(s) and Briefly Debrief Play Sessions**

Focus on observed growth and change in both parent and child

- What part of training was most helpful?

- What part is of greatest concern?

- Any other concerns or issues?

_____ **III.** **Review Handout: *Rules of Thumb & Other Things to Remember***
(refer parents to page 50 & 51 in the *Parent Notebook*) Share the Rule of Thumb that has been most meaningful for them.

_____ **IV.** **Closing Process**

- Review important things each parent learned

- Discuss how each perceives their child now as compared with 10 weeks ago

  Review notes from *Parent Information Form*

  ○ Encourage feedback within group on positive changes made

  ○ Has the child really changed that much or has the parent's perception changed, i.e., become more accepting?

_____ **V.** **Decide on a Date and Time for Follow-Up Meetings**

Ask for a volunteer to coordinate and suggest parents write the date, time, and volunteer name in blanks provided on their homework sheet:

- Date and time for follow-up meetings: _____

- Volunteer meeting coordinator: _____
  Make sure parents (with consent)—give phone numbers to the coordinator to make a phone list.

- Optional: Date & Time for follow-up with Therapist _____

_____ **VI.   Homework Assignments: Emphasize the Importance of Continuing Play Sessions** (refer parents to homework section in their notebook)

Make arrangements as needed for parents who want to continue play sessions with the child of focus and/or begin special playtime with a child other than their child of focus

Hand out additional appointment cards as needed

Schedule additional professional help for parents and/or children needing such help

1. <u>Continue play sessions</u>: If you stop now, the message is that you were playing with your child because you had to, not because you wanted to:

   I agree to continue my play sessions with my child of focus for _____ weeks and/or begin sessions with _____ and do for ___ weeks.

   ☝ **Rule of Thumb: "Good things come in small packages."**

   Don't wait for big events to enter into your child's world—the little ways are always with us. Hold onto precious moments!

_____ **VII.   Recommended Reading:**

1. *Relational Parenting* (2000) and *How to Really Love Your Child* (1992), Ross Campbell

2. *Between Parent and Child* (1956), Haim Ginott

3. *Liberated Parents, Liberated Children* (1990), Adele Faber and Elaine Mazlish

4. *How to Talk So Kids Will Listen and Listen So Kids Will Talk* (2002), Adele Faber and Elaine Mazlish

5. *"SAY WHAT YOU SEE" for Parents and Teachers* (2005), Sandra Blackard (Free online resource available at www.languageoflistening.com)

_____ **VIII.   Hand Out *Certificate of Completion* to Each Parent**

_____ **IX.   Close With Motivational Poem, Story, or Rule of Thumb (optional)**

CHILD-PARENT-RELATIONSHIP (C-P-R) TRAINING
Parent Notes & Homework – Session 10

👍 RULES OF THUMB TO REMEMBER:

"Good things come in small packages."
Don't wait for big events to enter into your child's world—
the little ways are always with us. Hold onto precious moments!

Notes (use back for additional notes):

_____
_____
_____
_____
_____
_____
_____
_____
_____
_____
_____
_____
_____

Homework Assignments:

Continue play sessions: If you stop now, the message is that you were playing with your child because you had to, not because you wanted to:

I agree to continue my play sessions with my child of focus for ____ weeks and/or begin sessions with _____ and do for ____ weeks.

Date and time for follow-up meetings: _____

Volunteer meeting coordinator: _____

Recommended Reading:

1. *Relational Parenting* (2000) and *How to Really Love Your Child* (1992), Ross Campbell

2. *Between Parent and Child* (1956), Haim Ginott

3. *Liberated Parents, Liberated Children* (1990), Adele Faber and Elaine Mazlish

4. *How to Talk So Kids Will Listen and Listen So Kids Will Talk* (2002), Adele Faber and Elaine Mazlish

5. *"SAY WHAT YOU SEE" for Parents and Teachers* (2005), Sandra Blackard (Free online resource available at www.languageoflistening.com)

> # CHILD-PARENT-RELATIONSHIP (C-P-R) TRAINING
> ## Rules of Thumb & Other Things to Remember – Session 10

☝ Rules of Thumb

1. **Focus on the donut, not the hole!**
   Focus on the relationship (your strengths and your child's strengths), NOT the problem.

2. **Be a thermostat, not a thermometer!**
   Learn to RESPOND (reflect) rather than REACT. The child's feelings <u>are not</u> your feelings and needn't escalate with him/her.

3. **What's most important may not be what you do, but what you do after what you did!**
   We are certain to make mistakes, but we can recover. It is how we handle our mistakes that makes the difference.

4. **The parent's toes should follow his/her nose.**
   Body language conveys interest.

5. **You can't give away what you do not possess.**
   (Analogy: oxygen mask on airplane) You can't extend patience and acceptance to your child if you can't first offer it to yourself.

6. **When a child is drowning, don't try to teach her to swim.**
   When a child is feeling upset or out of control, that is not the moment to impart a rule or teach a lesson.

7. **During play sessions, limits are not needed until they are needed!**

8. **If you can't say it in 10 words or less, don't say it.**
   As parents, we tend to overexplain, and our message gets lost in the words.

9. **Grant in fantasy what you can't grant in reality.**
   In a play session, it is okay to act out feelings and wishes that in reality may require limits.

10. **Big choices for big kids, little choices for little kids.**
    Choices given must be commensurate with child's developmental stage.

11. **Never do for a child that which he can do for himself.**
    You will never know what your child is capable of unless you allow him to try!

12. **Encourage the effort rather than praise the product.**
    Children need encouragement like a plant needs water.

13. **Don't try to change everything at once!**
    Focus on 'big' issues that ultimately will mean the most to your child's development of positive self-esteem and feelings of competence and usefulness.

14. **Where there are no limits, there is no security. (Consistent Limits = Secure Relationship)**
    When you don't follow through, you lose credibility and harm your relationship with your child.

15. **Good things come in small packages.**
    Don't wait for big events to enter into your child's world—the little ways are always with us. Hold onto precious moments!

CHILD-PARENT-RELATIONSHIP (C-P-R) TRAINING
Page 2—Rules of Thumb & Other Things to Remember – Session 10

Other Things to Remember:

1. Reflective responses help children to feel understood and can lessen anger.

2. In play, children express what their lives are like now, what their needs are, or how they wish things could be.

3. In the playtimes, the parent is not the source of answers (reflect questions back to child: "Hmm—I wonder").

4. Don't ask questions you already know the answer to.

5. Questions imply non-understanding. Questions put children in their minds. Children live in their hearts.

6. What's important is not what the child knows, but what the child believes.

7. When you focus on the problem, you lose sight of the child.

8. Support the child's feeling, intent, or need, even if you can't support the child's behavior.

9. Noticing the child is a powerful builder of self-esteem.

10. Empower children by giving them credit for making decisions: "You decided to_____."

11. One of the best things we can communicate to our children is that they are competent. Tell children they are capable, and they will think they are capable. If you tell children enough times they can't do something, sure enough, they can't.

12. Encourage creativity and freedom—with freedom comes responsibility.

13. "We're about to institute a new and significant policy immediately effective within the confines of this domicile."

14. When we are flexible in our stance, we can handle anger much more easily. When parents are rigid in their approach, both parent and child can end up hurt (remember the stiff arm!).

15. When unsure of what to say to child or what to do, ask yourself, "What action or words will most preserve the relationship or do least harm?" Sometimes walking away and saying nothing, or telling the child, "I need to take a time-out to cool off, and then we can talk," is best. Always remember: "Nothing at this moment is more important than my relationship with my child."
    (Also applies to spouses, significant others, etc.)

16. Live in the moment—today is enough. Don't push children toward the future.

CHILD PARENT RELATIONSHIP THERAPY(CPRT)

STUDY GUIDE

Using the CPRT Study Guide

The **Study Guide** is designed to be studied <u>prior to</u> each CPRT training session. It is not intended for use <u>during</u> the training sessions. The *Study Guide* is an expanded version of the *Therapist Notebook* and is designed to provide a more in-depth explanation of content for the novice CPRT/filial therapist. This section begins with an overview, *Helpful Hints for Conducting CPRT*. Embedded within each treatment outline are shaded text boxes with additional information and examples for each training concept or activity to aid you in preparing for each session. The material in the shaded text boxes is not meant to be presented in full or memorized. In several cases, the authors have shared personal parenting experiences to illustrate a point, but it is important to use your own stories and metaphors, making teaching points in a way that feels comfortable and congruent. If you are not a parent and have little personal experience with children, do not try to pretend that you do. You can draw on your professional experience as a play therapist, teacher, and so forth, or share stories of friends' or relatives' experiences with children. For the experienced CPRT/filial therapist, the *Study Guide* can serve as a brief review.

We suggest that therapists have the *Therapist Notebook* at hand when reviewing the *Study Guide* in preparation for each session, making any additional notes directly on the session treatment outline for that session (or electronically adapting the outline as needed). Never use the *Study-Guide* during treatment sessions; training should not be scripted. The CPRT curriculum is designed to be used by experienced play therapists with prior training and experience in both Child-Centered Play Therapy (CCPT) and group therapy, and who have a solid understanding of CPRT skills, concepts and procedures. This training and experience base is necessary in order to facilitate a lively, spontaneous, and interactive group training process. Reading from the *Study Guide* would interfere with this process and impede the development of a therapeutic connection between the parents and therapist. The therapist should become familiar enough with the material in the *Study Guide* to deliver the training in his or her own unique way of engaging parents in the treatment process. As noted earlier, it is expected that the therapist will exercise clinical judgement in using these materials in order to best meet the specific needs of a particular group of parents. Note: It is also necessary to refer to the *Materials Checklist* (See Appendix A on CD-ROM) as you prepare for each training session.

Helpful Hints for Conducting CPRT

Note: Print material checklist for this session (CD-Rom, Appendix A–contains list of all materials and where to locate them)

Excerpted from Chapter 4 of "Child-Parent Relationship Therapy (CPRT):
A 10-Session Filial Therapy Model" (Landreth & Bratton, 2006)

The CPRT/filial therapy process is characterized by **two key components: a didactic component and a group process component in the context of a safe, reassuring, supportive, and nonthreatening environment** that encourages parents to explore feelings, attitudes, and perceptions about themselves, their children, and about parenting.

The supportive format in a CPRT group often resembles group therapy as the therapist responds empathically to parents' issues and emotional reactions related to their family or their role as parents. Likening the emotional exploring and supportive component of CPRT to group therapy does not imply that the objective is to provide group therapy, only that some aspects of the group interaction and process take on the nature of group therapy for short periods of time as parents explore their feelings about themselves, their children, and their families. The transition from this empathic group therapy type element of exploring an emotional issue to the didactic element can be accomplished by limiting the group therapy exploration to a few minutes of interaction, making an empathic reflection that summarizes the parents' feelings, and then making a teaching point that is related to the content of the parents' sharing.

Processing parents' reactions and feelings about their children promotes the beginning of change in parents' perceptions about their children. The CPRT therapist must maintain a delicate balance between the didactic and process dimensions without being rigid in covering the scheduled training material or allowing the group to become bogged down in the group therapy dimensions of the process.

It is imperative that the therapist intersperse the teaching component of CPRT with building **group cohesiveness**, especially in the first two or three training sessions. This is accomplished when the therapist generalizes parent disclosures to help parents identify with each other by asking questions: "Does this sound familiar to anyone else?" or "Anyone else ever yell at your child?" and "What was that like for you?" when a parent responds affirmatively. When parents nod their heads understandingly as a parent describes a problem, the therapist can comment: "So the rest of you know what that is like." This **linking of parents** helps break down barriers of isolation and the feeling, "I'm the only one who feels this way" or "I'm the only one who ever yells at her child."

If a parent describes a point of difficulty in a play session, the therapist can ask, "Group, what Rule of Thumb applies here?" The therapist can also encourage group interaction by inviting parents to respond to each other's questions: "Linda, how would you suggest Erika respond when her son wants to paint her glasses?" This question not only facilitates interaction, but also decreases parents' dependence on the therapist for solutions by inviting parents to contribute their ideas. If a parent seems to be thoughtful about something, the therapist can invite sharing: "Angela, what are you thinking?" The guiding principle for the therapist is careful adherence to the **Rule of Thumb: The therapist is a facilitator of interaction, not just a trainer.** An objective is that, as the training progresses, the interaction among the parents will increase, and they will be more actively supportive and offer suggestions to one another.

The following teaching components should be observed in conducting the training sessions:

- Presenting the information to be learned in **simple, concise teaching points** is the key to parents learning and assimilating new information.

- **Simple homework assignments** and concise informational handouts are provided to reinforce teaching points made in the training sessions.

- **Active affirmation** of parents' efforts is considered to be a critical key to the effectiveness of CPRT.

- Employing a variety of teaching tools such as **stories, analogies, and metaphors to emphasize teaching points** helps to maintain a high level of parent interest and facilitates the learning process. Parents may have difficulty recalling a teaching point in isolation, but when the point is attached to a short interest-catching story, parents will remember the story and, in turn, the teaching point.

- Catchy **"Rules of Thumb"** also help make teaching points easier for parents to remember.

- The therapist's responses to parents should consistently **model basic child-centered play therapy principles and skills.**

- The therapist can **use self-disclosure** about his or her efforts and mistakes as a parent to illustrate teaching points and to model permission to make mistakes.

- Modeling is also utilized by **showing videotapes of the therapist's play sessions** or by the therapist conducting a live play session to demonstrate the kind of responses hoped for by parents in their play sessions.

- When viewing the video of a parent's play session, the video should be stopped frequently to validate and affirm the parent's efforts. **The focus is on what the parents are doing correctly** rather than focusing on mistakes.

Child Parent Relationship Therapy (CPRT)
Session 1 – Study Guide

Note: Print material checklist for this session (CD-Rom, Appendix A – contains list of all materials and where to locate them)

I. Give Name Tags and *Parent Notebooks* to All Parents as They Arrive
(Ask parents who need to complete intake information to stay afterward.)

Introduce self/welcome group—have parents briefly share about themselves and why they are here; help them feel supported and they are not alone in their struggles.

Tell parents in your own words: "I appreciate you making time in your busy schedules to be here. I know it's not easy to juggle everything you have to do to be here, and I know you are here because you care about your children. The purpose of this course is to add to the good things you are already doing as a parent."

Critical objectives of the first session are to enable parents to help their children by:

- Encouraging and empowering parents to make a difference in their children's lives

- Empathizing (seeing the world through the parents' eyes)

- Normalizing parents' relationships with their children

Remember to see the world through the parents' eyes. Many parents who attend the training are doing so because they have become discouraged about their ability to be good parents. They may be dealing with difficult feelings during the first session, such as inadequacy, guilt, or anger. The therapist needs to communicate encouragement and empowerment to the parents by acknowledging the parent's effort to come to the class and pointing out the abilities the parents already have. Some parents may be defensive, uncooperative, or judgmental of their children, of other parents, or of the therapist as a way to deal with their feelings. It's important for the therapist to empathize with the parents about how difficult and frustrating it can be to be a parent, so that parents feel safe enough to become aware of their feelings. It's also important to normalize any confessions a parent makes about yelling or losing his or her temper, so that everyone in the group gets the message that they will not be judged. When talking about behaviors that need to be changed, it's important to use examples from your own life about mistakes you've made with children, so that parents don't feel singled out or criticized.

Parenting styles can sometimes give therapists a clue about how to empathize with the parent. For example, an authoritative parent usually fears losing control or being embarrassed by his or her child, while a permissive parent may fear hurting or damaging his or her child, or may fear not being loved by the child. Both feel an enormous burden of responsibility, because they have a hard time having faith in their children's abilities. The authoritative parent's burden is that he or she must control the child's behavior, because he or she believes the child cannot control himself or herself. The permissive parent's burden is that he or she must make the child happy all the time, because the parent believes the child cannot cope with being upset.

II. Overview of CPRT Training Objectives and Essential Concepts

☞   **Rule of Thumb: "Focus on the donut, not the hole!"**

CPRT focuses on the relationship, your strengths and your child's strengths,
NOT the problem.

You might demonstrate this by holding up a donut if you've brought some for refreshments, pointing out that most people see what is missing (the hole), but the important part is the good stuff that's around it. For the therapist, this is a reminder to focus on the relationship and parent/child strengths, not the problem.

- Play is the child's language

  - Children sometimes don't have the ability to articulate what they are thinking or feeling; a child's thoughts and feelings are expressed through play.

  - In play, children express what their lives are like now, what their needs are, or how they wish things could be.

  - A child uses words <u>and</u> actions to communicate.

  - Acting out can be seen as an attempt to communicate a message—when a child feels understood, the need to act out a message ends.

- Helps prevent problems because parent becomes aware of child's needs

The training prevents problems by helping parents become aware of their children's needs in play sessions that require only 30 minutes of focused attention per week.

☝ Rule of Thumb: "Be a thermostat, not a thermometer!"

Learn to RESPOND (reflect) rather than REACT. The child's feelings <u>are not</u> your feelings and needn't escalate with him/her.

When your child's feelings and behavior escalate, you can learn to respond in a helpful way, rather than simply reacting and allowing your feelings and behavior to escalate, too. Remember: In-control parents are thermostats; out-of-control parents are thermometers.

Explain that a thermometer merely reacts to the temperature, whereas the thermostat controls the environment. As parents, we can create the kind of environment we want, rather than just reacting to our children's behavior. (*Show how to RESPOND [reflect] rather than REACT.*) When the children's feelings and behaviors escalate, the parents can learn to respond in a helpful way, rather than simply reacting and allowing their feelings and behaviors to escalate, too. Remind parents that in-control parents are thermostats; out-of-control parents are thermometers. Remember to put parents at ease, saying in your own words: "Everybody is a thermometer sometimes, myself included. We're all just human."

● You will learn the same basic play therapy skills that graduate students learn in a semester course

<u>These skills will</u>:

o Return control to you as parent—and help child develop self-control

Share your own experience and introduce demonstration. For example: "Sometimes I feel like my kids are the ones in control. Anybody else ever feel that way? That's stressful, because I still have all the responsibility, even if I don't have control; so then I overcompensate and become really, really strict. I don't let them get away with one little thing. I become controlling because I think if I'm not, then they will be in control. But that never works, does it? It just seems to make things more stressful; then I feel guilty, too, on top of all that."

<u>Note</u>: Throughout the *Study Guide*, when the suggestion is made that the therapist share a personal reaction to her child, therapists who are not parents can share similar experiences they have had with children of relatives or neighbors or experiences in play therapy.

    o   Provide closer, happier times with your child—more joy and laughter, warm memories

    Ask parents: *"What do you want your child to remember about you/your relationship 20 years from now?"* (What are parents' best memories from childhood?)

Share your own experience. For example: "Sometimes I get so wrapped up in trying to make sure my children are successful or polite or doing what they are supposed to do or becoming the person I think they should be, that I forget to just enjoy being with them. That's what I love about special playtime; I can just let all of that go and enjoy being with my kids. Without all of that pressure, I can appreciate how wonderful they really are, that they are much more wonderful than I could ever try to make them."

Note: Therapists who are not parents can share similar experiences they have had with children of relatives or neighbors or experiences in play therapy.

    o   Give key to your child's inner world—learn how to really understand your child and how to help your child feel that you understand

Tell parents in your own words: "Special playtime can give you the key to your child's inner world. You can learn how to really understand your child and how to help your child feel understood. The uppermost thought in your mind during the play sessions is, 'I want to know my child better.' You will be wondering, 'Does the love, the warmth I feel for my child show in my face? Does my tone of voice reveal kindness? Does my child know that I think he is important, the most important person in the world at this moment? Do my eyes show that? Is my caring about how my child feels inside being communicated? Do my words convey that caring?'"

•   Best of all—you only have to practice these new skills and do something different 30 minutes per week!

Tell parents in your own words: "This will be the most important 30 minutes per week you will ever spend with your child, and it will make a significant difference!"

•   Patience is important in learning a new language

Explain to parents that they are learning a language that allows them to see the world through their children's eyes, and just like any other language, it takes practice and patience. Also ask parents if they have ever tried to learn a new language. For the parents who have, ask in your own words, "Did you feel funny or awkward when you first started speaking the new language?" Explain that it is the same way with this language; it might feel funny or unnatural at first, but that's just a part of the learning process.

Teach parents to respond to their children's comments or questions about the new way they are talking by saying, for example, "I'm learning a new language that helps me see the world through your eyes."

Encourage parents by telling them:

"In 10 weeks, you are going to be different and your relationship with your child will be different."

III. Group Introductions

- Describe entire family–help pick child of focus if not identified during intake

Ask parents to introduce themselves, describe their families, and tell why they want to participate in the training. Ask parents in your own words: "Which child needs you the most right now?" If they have trouble answering that question, ask, "Which child is having the most difficulty or getting into trouble more?"

- Tell concerns about this child (take notes on *Parent Information Form*)
- Facilitate sharing

Sometimes parents will be hesitant to talk about their problems. It can be especially intimidating to be the first parent to share. Support the parent by being empathic and reflecting the good things he or she shares.

Ask questions that help the parent identify the problems he/she may be having at home, such as, "How is bedtime at your house?" or "Describe the most challenging times you have with your child," etc.

- Make generalizing, normalizing comments to other parents

  (Example: "Anyone else feel angry with their child this week?")

For example, if parents are able to share an annoying behavior or a behavioral problem their child is having, normalize their child's behavior by saying something like, "Anyone else here have a child who ____? (Say whatever the parent has shared about the child, for example: whines.) Then, after parents respond, say, "Sure, all kids whine sometimes."

Ask about the parent's response to his/her child's challenging behavior. Normalize the parent's responses by asking the rest of the group, by saying something like, "Anyone else ever ____ at their kids? (Insert whatever the parent has admitted doing, for example: yell.) If parent's example is not something all parents might confess to, simply say, "Anyone else here been so frustrated with your child that you felt like doing something you wouldn't normally do?" Finally, say something like, "Sure, all parents yell at their kids. There is no such thing as a perfect parent."

👍 **Rule of Thumb: "What's most important may not be what you do, but what you do after what you did!"**

We are certain to make mistakes, but we can recover. It is how we handle our mistakes that makes the difference.

Manage the introductions:

Limit amount of time each parent shares, by acknowledging concerns: Example: "Debbie, sounds like you've got a real problem, and we're going to work on that in your play sessions with Rachel." Make a note to be sure you do that.

Don't try to solve parents' problems—there is no quick fix!

Look for ways to highlight parents' love for their children. For example, if a mom confesses to being frustrated with her child for not "trying hard" at school, say, "It's upsetting to you because you want the best for her. You want her to know that she can be successful if she works hard."

End the responding parent's dialogue on a positive note asking him/her to identify the child's strengths or times he/she enjoys most with the child.

Close introductions with encouragement:

Thank the parents for being candid about their children and themselves.

Reassure parents that the course can help with the problems they are having.

If limit setting issues or questions arise during the first three sessions, respond by explaining that limits are very important and will be introduced in Session 4.

IV. Reflective Responding

Prepare parents to use reflective responding (reflecting feelings):

Remember to see the world through the parents' eyes. Reflecting feelings is hard for some parents because of the responsibility they feel to make everything right or okay. Both the authoritative and permissive parent are likely to be uncomfortable with their children's feelings and unknowingly give their children the message not to talk about their feelings. The authoritative parent might say something like, "That's nothing to be upset about" or "If you don't stop crying, we are not going anywhere." The permissive parent may say something like, "It's OK honey. I'll buy you a new one," attempting to fix the problem or rescue the child. When parents share these types of responses with the class, empathize with them by saying something like, "When your child is hurting, you hurt. You want to make everything better or make the pain go away." Some parents will say, "No, I just get angry when they cry." Reflect their feelings by saying, for example, "Right, it's a very powerless feeling when your child is upset. That's what anger is, a reaction to feeling powerless."

Share your own experience. For example: "Nothing hurts worse than when your child hurts. I remember when we moved to our new house and my son had to change schools. You know how cruel kids can be sometimes to the new kid at school. My son had had a really rough day and came home to tell me about it. He said, 'Mom, I don't have any friends. Nobody likes me.' My response was, 'Oh sure you do, you have me and Daddy (not at all what he was talking about); you have your sister and your friends in the old neighborhood. They still like you.' (still totally unrelated to what he was talking about). I thought I was trying to make my son feel better, but what I was really saying was, 'Please don't tell me when you're hurt. I can't handle it. It hurts too badly. Pretend like everything is okay. Think about how I need you to feel.' I would never want to give my son that message, but that was the message I was giving him. All I needed to say was, 'Sounds lonely. You had a rough day.' By letting him know that I understand how he feels and not trying to fix it or make it go away, I'm letting him know I can be there with him in his feeling, and he is free to share it with me. That's the point of the first skill I'm going to teach you—reflective responding."

<u>Note</u>: Therapists who are not parents can share similar experiences they have had with children of relatives or neighbors or experiences in play therapy.

- Way of following, rather than leading

<u>Share your experience</u>: For example: "When I understand how my child feels and let him know that I understand, without trying to make him feel the way I want him to feel, I make room for his feelings and allow him to go deeper into his feelings. He is able then, if he wants, to take the relationship to a deeper level. I give him the room to move where he needs to and follow him there."

<u>Note</u>: Therapists who are not parents can share similar experiences they have had with children of relatives or neighbors or experiences in play therapy. They can also take a teaching point approach, saying, for example: "When you understand how your child feels and let him know that you understand without trying to make him feel the way you want, you make room for his feelings."

- Reflect behaviors, thoughts, needs/wishes, and feelings (<u>without asking questions</u>)

<u>Tell parents in your own words</u>: "When I stop trying to make him feel the way I want him to, I can just say what I see in his face or in his words. I say, 'I noticed you...' or 'You think that...' or 'You need...' or 'You really wish...' or 'You feel....' It's important, too, not to ask him questions, because then I'm leading the relationship."

Continue by asking parents something like: "What do children usually do when you ask a question?" Most parents will say that their children either shut down or try to say what they think they are supposed to say. Respond by saying, "Right, that's exactly right!" Tell them also, "Sometimes a child will answer a question directly, but regardless, questions place the parent in a leading position. Generally, **if you have enough information to ask a question, you have enough information to make a statement.** Often, questions imply non-understanding. 'Did that make you angry?' communicates a lack of understanding, even though you do understand. Instead say, 'You feel angry about that.' Empathic statements go into the child's heart and soul; questions go to the mind to be processed and evaluated."

●   Helps parent understand child <u>and</u> helps child feel understood

<u>Tell parents in your own words</u>: "Reflecting feelings communicates understanding and acceptance of children's feelings and needs. It also shows children that you are interested and that you want to understand them. This process helps children understand, accept, label, and communicate. If a feeling, desire, or need is expressed and goes unrecognized, children may think that the feeling or expression is not acceptable."

"Be With" Attitudes convey:	Not:
I am here; I <u>hear</u> you	I always agree
I understand	I must make you happy
I care	I will solve your problems

I am here: Nothing will distract me. I will be fully present physically, mentally, and emotionally. I want to be so fully present that there will be no distance between myself and my child. I want to enter fully into my child's world, to move about freely in my child's world, to sense what my child senses, to feel what my child feels. Once I have achieved this kind of knowing contact, it is easy to know when I am not in touch with my child. Can I enter so fully into my child's world that I have no need to evaluate or judge my child?

I hear you: I will listen fully with my ears and eyes to everything about my child—what is expressed and what is not expressed. I want to hear my child completely. Can I experience and hear my child as she is? To accomplish this kind of hearing, I must be secure enough within myself to allow my child to be separate from me.

I understand: I want my child to know I understand what she is communicating, feeling, experiencing, and playing, so I will work hard to communicate that understanding to my child. I want to understand the inner depth and meaning of my child's experiences and feelings. The crucial dimension in special playtimes is the communication to the child of this kind of understanding and acceptance.

I care: I really do care about my child and want my child to know that. If I am successful in communicating fully the first three messages, I will not be perceived as a threat, and the child will allow me into his world; then the child will know I care. This kind of caring releases the dynamic potential that already exists in children.

Explain to parents that the purpose of these attitudes is to strive to understand their child's world, so that the child is free to explore, to test boundaries, to share frightening parts of their lives, or to change until they experience a relationship in which the world as they see it is understood and accepted.

V.   Optional – Show Video Clips: *Life's First Feelings*

(See *CPRT Training Resources*)

Video clip #1 – Discuss

Video clip #2 – Discuss reactions (especially difference in mad/sad) as lead-in to *Feelings Response: In-Class Practice Worksheet* (refer parents to page 3 in the *Parent Notebook*)

VI.   Complete *Feelings Response: In-Class Practice Worksheet*

Complete worksheet together with parents, asking them, <u>as a group,</u> to decide on the feeling word that best describes how the child is feeling, and next, <u>as a group</u>, decide on a short response.

See *Therapist Notebook* for worksheet with example responses.

VII. Role-Play

Demonstrate with co-leader or ask a parent to tell you about his or her day and simply reflect as the parent talks about it: then pair-up parents & have them take turns being the "listener".

Most parents will hesitate at first, trying to think about what they are supposed to say. Reassure them by telling them, "There is no wrong way to do this. Just think back to this morning and tell what happened." As they begin to tell you, empathize with what their morning felt like and respond, saying, "Sounds like a hectic morning" or "You had a relaxing morning for a change" or "You had a lot to think about this morning." Remember to reflect the feeling, also saying, "Sounds stressful" (or blissful, exciting, etc.).

Ask parents: "Did you notice what I was doing? I was just trying to understand how she felt and saying it back to her—just what we've been working on in class. Now you try. Everybody find a partner and practice."

After parents have reflected for a while, ask them to share what it was like.

VIII. Video Demonstration (optional, if time permits)

Show demonstration of play session skills of reflection of feeling and allowing the child to lead

IX. Homework Assignments (refer parents to homework section in their notebook)

(See *Therapist Notebook*)

1) Notice one physical characteristic about your child you haven't seen before:
    _____

2) Practice reflective responding—complete *Feelings Response: Homework Worksheet* and bring next week.

3) Bring your favorite, heart-tugging picture of your child of focus.

4) Practice giving a 30-second Burst of Attention. If you are on the telephone, say, "Can you hold for 30 seconds? I'll be right back." Put the phone aside, bend down, and give your child undivided, focused attention for 30 seconds; then say, "I have to finish talking to ___." Stand back up and continue talking with your friend.

Explain to parents that they can say this to the person they are talking with on the phone when their child wants their attention.

X. Close With Motivational Poem, Story, or Rule of Thumb (optional)

In the *Therapist Notebook,* at the end of the treatment outline for each session, you will find a list called "Rules of Thumb To Remember." A corresponding list is found at the beginning of each *Parent Notes & Homework* handout. The list will not be repeated in this *Study Guide.* The purpose of the list is to facilitate a quick review of the Rules of Thumb introduced in each session to reinforce their importance.

Child Parent Relationship Therapy (CPRT)
Session 2 – Study Guide

Note: Print material checklist for this session (CD-Rom, Appendix A – contains list of all materials and where to locate them)

I. Informal Sharing and Review of Homework

Ask about each parent's week and reflect briefly

Review homework from Session 1:

1. 30-second burst of attention

2. *Feelings Response: Homework Worksheet*—refer parents to worksheet for reflecting feelings review and practice

   Remember to reflect

Parent's experiences/model encouragement as parents share

Encourage participation: Typically, a few parents will not have completed this assignment or forgot to bring their worksheet, but encourage them to participate by asking for an example of a time during the week when they remember their child feeling ____, and help them formulate a response. **The message is that homework and practice are important—and you will hold them accountable!**

No matter what parents report, remember to reflect! Most parents will report positive results from the homework. When they do, emphasize their effort and the impact they had on their child. Example: "You put your feelings aside for your daughter to be happy and were right there with her. It sounds like you made a huge impact on her." Occasionally, parents will report that the reflection or the 30-second Burst of Attention "doesn't work on my child." Simply reflect, "Sounds like you're disappointed in the way your child responded. Tell me what happened." The parent may say something like, "My son got mad and started screaming and throwing a fit, and I said 'You're mad,' but he didn't change." Encourage the parent by saying something like, "It's really hard to use this skill in the heat of the moment; it's even hard to remember to use it at a time like that, but you did it. The most important thing is that you communicated to your son that you understood how he felt. He hasn't learned how to behave appropriately when he feels angry yet. It takes time to learn that. In fact, I think I'm still working on that one! We will talk more about that in Session 4 when we practice setting limits. Keep doing exactly what you did last time, just reflect the feeling and set limits however you usually would for now." If the parent continues to be skeptical about the training helping her, saying, "You just don't understand, this is not going to work on my son," reflect again, saying something like, "It sounds like you're discouraged, like you've tried everything you know how to do and nothing has worked." Make room for however the parent is feeling. Let her know that you understand and tell her that if she still needs help with her son after the training, you will help her or refer her to someone.

It's important to emphasize to parents that when they are using these new skills, **they should not expect something back from their child.** Explain to parents in your own words that, "Your child probably won't say, 'Yeah, you're right.' But your child hears you and takes it in. Sometimes you may get a smile or a nod that lets you know your child heard you, but sometimes your child may just take it in and continue what she was doing." Of course, all parents would like to see quick and dramatic results for their efforts, but for some parents, this is more of a need than for others. The therapist must caution parents to be patient and point out that **these new ways of responding therapeutically to their children are working, even when they seem not to be working.**

In essence, the therapist is asking parents to **trust the process** when, for most parents, they've had no similar experience on which to base their trust. The therapist may find it helpful to use an analogy that parents can relate to, such as asking parents what they do when they cut their finger badly. Parents know from experience that although you respond immediately by putting some medicine and a bandage on the wound, it doesn't work (heal) immediately. But they would not remove the bandage and wash off the medicine after a few hours, just because the wound had not healed yet; they would trust that over time, by continuing to apply the medicine, the wound would heal. Their experience has taught them that they have to be patient and trust the process of healing—and the deeper the wound, the longer the process of healing.

3. Physical Characteristic/Favorite Picture

   Ask questions and reflect answers: Ask parents to report a physical characteristic of their child that they hadn't noticed before.

Ask them, "What was that like for you to do that exercise?" Reflect their answers. Also ask, "Did your child react to you looking at him/her?" Some parents will report that their child liked the attention. When they do, explain to them that the point of the exercise was to remember what it was like when their child was a baby. For example, "Remember how, when your child was a baby, she didn't have to do anything special to get your approval? A baby can just put her toe in her mouth and we just 'ooo' and 'ah' over it. You just love your baby because she exists on the planet. As parents, we feel so much pressure to make sure our kids turn out right that sometimes we forget that feeling. That's the point of the exercise, to give you some time to pay attention to your child and treasure who the child is without any pressure on you or your child."

Explain to parents that, just by using their eyes, they can begin to know and understand their child better. This discussion can be coupled with having parents show their favorite picture of their child as they report on something new they noticed in their child. Parents typically bring pictures of their children as babies or toddlers, which can lead to a brief but lively discussion of why that stage in their child's development holds more special memories than the child's current developmental phase. (Hint: Less discipline problems and power struggles!) Sharing pictures is another way of enhancing parent connectedness in the group and developing rapport among group members. In addition, this activity focuses parents on their child's strengths—what they love or enjoy most about their child.

Prize the child: As parents share the picture of their child, reflect their love and pride in their child. Prize the child in the picture saying, "Look at that smile. It's like she's smiling with her whole body."

4. (Optional) Supplemental worksheet: *Feelings Response Practice Worksheet* can be assigned for additional homework this week, if needed—go over a couple of examples together before sending it home as homework (see Appendix C on CD-ROM for supplemental worksheet and answer sheet for therapist).

II. Handout: *Basic Principles of Play Sessions* (refer parents to page 9 in the *Parent Notebook*)

(See *Therapist Notebook* for handout)

1. Parent allows child to lead and parent follows, without asking questions or making suggestions

   ● Show keen interest and closely observe

It is important for parents to be comfortable, not detached, during their play sessions with their children. When the parent's whole body turns toward the child, and the parent conveys genuine interest and full attention, the child feels the parent's presence.

✥ Rule of Thumb: "The parent's toes should follow his/her nose."

Body language conveys interest and full attention.

Explain the importance of body language in conveying interest:

   ● Get down to child's eye level.

   ● Face the child.

   ● Parents are to keep their eyes focused on the child.

- Listen with their eyes and ears.

- Point out that parental boredom can be overcome by maintaining focus on the child.

- Parents should move closer to their child when the child is intent and focused on his/her play, and join in when invited.

- The parent can be quite active in conveying interest and involvement by shifting body posture or by leaning forward to be closer to the child's activity.

- Actively join in when invited

When invited to play, the parent should think of himself or herself as an actor without a script or any knowledge of the character he or she is playing and the child as the director/writer of the play.

For example, if the child says, "Hey Mom, you be the bad guy," the parent says, "OK, show me what to do." If the child says, "You rob the bank and try to get away," then follow along in a way you think is appropriate, careful not to add any of your own ideas into the play. If the child has a sense that he is in charge of the play, he will begin to correct any details of the play, for example, saying, "No, you don't have a getaway car; you have to run away from the police."

- Parent is "dumb" for 30 minutes

In this case, "dumb" means "knows nothing"; it does not mean "silent." Parents are usually in the position of being "the expert." Children look to parents for direction, permission, and answers. During the play session, the parent is not the teacher or a person who corrects children's responses. The child can add five plus one and get an answer of seven. In addition, the child can choose to spell any way the child decides.

When children ask questions or seek assistance, the parent will make a response that returns the responsibility to the child. These responses encourage children to make their own decisions and to take responsibility for a current concern. For example:

Child: "What should I play with first?"
Parent: "In here, you can decide what you want to play with first."

At the beginning of the first playtime, a child often wants the parent to identify what to do, what things are used for, and how to "undo" difficult things. The child may hold up a toy that the child obviously knows the name for and ask, "What's this?" This is a moment when the parent does not know for sure the motivation behind the question. To name the item may inhibit the child's creativity, structure the child's expression, or keep responsibility in the hands of the parent. Responsibility could be returned to the child by responding, "That can be whatever you want it to be." Similar responses, depending on the child's request, might be, "You can decide" or "That's something you can do." If the child needs help to complete a task he/she is not capable of completing without assistance, the parent can respond, "Show me what you want done." These responses allow a child to assume responsibility and make a decision. Typically, by the end of the session, the child is stating what things are without asking for the parent's decision.

2. The parent's major task is to empathize with the child

    ●   See and experience the child's play through the child's eyes

> Tell parents in your own words to imagine in every way they can what it is like to be the child. For example: "Imagine what it feels like to play out what the child is playing. What does it feel like to hold the toy the child is holding? Is it cold, soft, textured? What does the carpet or tile feel like on his knees? What does everything look like from the child's perspective?"

    ●   To understand child's needs, feelings, and thoughts expressed through play

> <u>Tell parents in your own words</u>: "Ask yourself (but not your child), 'What is the mood of this play? What feelings and thoughts would promote that type of play?'"

3. Parent is then to communicate this understanding to the child

    ●   Describing what the child is doing/playing

> <u>Example</u>: "You've decided to paint." "You're hitting it right in the face."

    ●   Reflecting what the child is saying

> <u>Example</u>: Child says, "We have one of these at school." Parent says, "You've seen one of those before."

    ●   Reflecting what the child is feeling

> <u>Example</u>: Child says, "Wow! Look at all these toys!" Parent says, "You're excited!"

4. The parent is to be clear and firm about the few "limits" that are placed on the child's behavior

    ●   Gives child responsibility for behavior

Example: Child asks, "What should I play with?" Parent says, "In here, you get to decide."

- Limits set on time, for safety, and to prevent breaking toys or damaging play area

Example: Child says, "I'm not through playing yet." Parent says, "You want to keep playing, but special playtime is up for the day. Let's go get some milk and cookies, and then you can play with the toys in your room."

- Stated only when needed, but consistently

Tell parents in your own words: "In special playtime, you only set a limit at the time it is needed, not before. If you state all of the limits before they are needed, it implies you are in control of the session and in control of the child's behavior. Your child needs to be responsible for his or her behavior and learn self-control and self-responsibility."

5. Note: If time allows, briefly review goals of play sessions on handout

a. To allow the child—through the medium of play—to communicate thoughts, needs, and feelings to his/her parent, and then for the parent to communicate that understanding back to the child.

b. Through feeling accepted, understood and valued—for the child to experience more positive feelings of self-respect, self-worth, confidence, and competence—and ultimately develop self-control and responsibility for actions and learn to get needs met in appropriate ways.

c. To strengthen the parent-child relationship and foster a sense of trust, security, and closeness for both parent and child.

d. To increase the level of playfulness and enjoyment between parent and child.

III. Demonstration of Toys for Play Session Toy Kit

- Briefly review Toy Categories on *Toy Checklist for Play Sessions* (refer parents to page 10 in the *Parent Notebook*)

See *Therapist Notebook* for *Toy Checklist for Play Sessions* handout

- Demonstrate/show toys and briefly explain rationale—especially for toys that may concern parents (dart gun and baby bottle)

- As toys are shown, briefly provide examples of how you might respond to child playing with that toy (co-leader can role-play with you)

Be Playful: The more fun and uninhibited you are with the toys, the less parents will worry about looking childish or silly when they play with the toys.

Give a brief discussion of the overall rationale and importance of inclusion of specific toys and materials within three broad categories:

Real life/nurturing toys include the following: (examples of responses to a child playing with the toy are in parentheses)

    small baby doll: (child wraps baby in blanket) "You're making sure she's warm"
    nursing bottle: (child takes a drink) "You decided to take a sip out of the bottle."
    doctor kit (with stethoscope and three Band-Aids)
        Tell parents to take all but three Band-Aids out of the Band-Aid box and put the rest in a ziplock bag for later play sessions, so that the child won't use all of the Band-Aids in one session: (child puts a Band-Aid on the baby) "You're helping her get well."
    two toy phones
    doll family
    domestic animal family
    wild animals
    play money: (child organizing the money) "You're getting it just the way you want it."
    car/truck
    plastic kitchen dishes
    optional toys in this category include: puppets, doll furniture, small dress-up items

Acting out/aggressive release toys include:

    dart gun: (child aims gun at you) "You'd like to shoot me, but I'm not for shooting; you can shoot the wall and pretend it's me."
    rubber knife
    piece of rope
    aggressive animal or two
    small toy soldiers (12–15 of two different colors to specify two teams, good guys and bad guys)
    inflatable bop bag
    mask (Lone Ranger type)
    optional toys in this category include: toy handcuffs with a key

Creative/expressive toys include:

   playdough
   crayons
   plain paper
   child scissors
   transparent tape
   egg carton
   ring toss game
   deck of playing cards
   soft foam ball
   two balloons (not inflated)
   optional toys in this category include:
      a selection of arts and crafts materials in a ziplock bag,
      Tinkertoys® or small assortment of building blocks,
      binoculars, tambourine (drum or other small musical instrument),
      magic wand

Explain briefly that the toys included in the filial kit were carefully selected, because they provide opportunities for a wide range of expression, mastery, imagination, fantasy play, creativity, and activity. Caution against including mechanical toys that limit children's creativity. Remind parents that the toys collected for the filial kit should be selected with safety in mind, to keep limit setting to a minimum.

●   Discuss finding used, free, and inexpensive toys

Toys don't have to be expensive. They can come from garage sales or the dollar store.

Toys can be homemade:

●   Make the dollhouse furniture out of small cardboard boxes.

●   Make dollhouse dolls out of magazine cutouts glued onto a cardboard stand or pipe cleaners.

●   Make a sock puppet aggressive by adding pointy teeth made out of felt and angry eyebrows made with a permanent marker. You can make happy and sad sock puppets, too.

●   Use old Tupperware®, pots, pans, and wooden spoons for play dishes.

●   Make a punching bag out of a pillowcase stuffed with old clothes tied with a rope and hung from a door frame.

The child's own toys can only be used with permission of the child, because special playtime toys can't be played with any other time than special playtime.

- Emphasize the importance of the toys—get commitment that each parent will have over half of the toys by next week—preferably all

  If they don't, they likely won't be ready for their first play session

- Discuss pros and cons of involving child in collecting toys for play session kit

If your child doesn't like the toys or complains about not getting the toys he or she wants, just reflect, "You really don't like these toys. You were hoping for different ones. You're disappointed."

IV. Choosing a Place and Time for Play Sessions

- Suggest a room that parent believes will offer the fewest distractions to the child and the greatest freedom from worry about breaking things or making a mess

  Kitchen area is ideal if no one else at home—otherwise, you need to be able to close a door

The child's room is not a good choice because there are too many other toys and distractions.

Let parents know that most families don't have an ideal playroom. If there is no other private room, the parents may choose their bedroom.

The room should be somewhat orderly for special playtime.

- Set aside a regular time in advance
  - ○ This time is to be undisturbed—no phone calls or interruptions by other children
  - ○ Most importantly, a time when the parent feels most relaxed, rested, and emotionally available to child

If the phone rings during special playtime and the child asks, "Aren't you going to answer the phone?" tell the child, "No, nothing is more important than our time together." You may also take the child with you and unplug the phone, explaining that you don't want anything to disturb your time with your child.

☝ **Rule of Thumb: "You can't give away that which you don't possess."**

(Analogy: oxygen mask on airplane take care of yourself first, then your child)

You can't extend patience and acceptance to your child if you can't first offer it to yourself.

As your child's most significant caregiver, you are asked to give so much of yourself, often when you simply don't have the resources within you to meet the demands of parenting. As parents, you may be deeply aware of your own failures, yet you can't extend patience and acceptance to your child while being impatient and un-accepting of yourself.

Analogy: "If you've ever been on an airplane, you've seen the flight attendant demonstrate how to use an oxygen mask. Does anyone remember though, the proper procedure if the oxygen mask drops and you are sitting next to a baby or child who needs your help to use the oxygen mask? Do you put the mask on yourself or the baby first? (Most parents will answer that they should put the mask on the baby first.) You put it on yourself first, because if you pass out, no one is there to help the baby. You have to take care of yourself first, then your child."

Sense of humor: Tell a specific parent, "Ask me for a million dollars." When the parent says, "Give me a million dollars," reply saying, "I can't. I don't have a million dollars." Explain, "I can't give away what I don't possess. It's impossible. It's important to remember to be accepting of yourself and forgiving of your mistakes so that you can be accepting and forgiving toward your child. Remember, you're just human. There is no such thing as a perfect parent. If you expect yourself to be perfect, it's likely you will expect your child to be perfect too."

    o   Note: Let parents know that you will be asking each of them to report next week on the place and time they have chosen

V.   Role-Play and Demonstration of Basic Play Session Skills (video clip or live)

Make sure to allow at least 15–20 minutes of demonstration, stopping to answer questions and get reactions, and another minimum of 5–10 minutes for paired parent role-plays, followed by at least 5–10 minutes for therapist to role-play "scenarios" parents had difficulty with in their role-play with parent partners

1. Show video clip that clearly demonstrates the concept of setting the stage, allowing the child to lead (without asking questions), tracking, and conveying the "Be With" Attitudes (or conduct live demo focusing on same attitudes and skills)

    ○   Review the "BE WITH" ATTITUDES: I'm here, I hear you,
            I understand, and I care!

(Optional—see Appendix B on CD-ROM for *Play Session Do's & Don'ts* poster with "Be With" Attitudes)

<u>Tell parents in your own words</u>: "All right, I want to show you a videotape of one of my play sessions. You will see me doing what I would like for you all to do. Let's watch the video, and then we'll talk about it."

Show a section of a video that clearly illustrates one of the concepts discussed earlier in the class, such as "let the child lead" or "set the stage" (or demonstrate the concepts with a volunteer parent for a minute or two).

Stop video or demonstration and say something like: "Now, let's talk about what you saw me do."

Use parents' responses to teach them how to let the child lead. Emphasize the child's choices and your willingness to watch and listen to see what the child does, rather than suggest or tell the child what to do.

Below is a sample exchange during a training session between the therapist and the parents:

Dr. L.:   *What did you all see me do?*

Sonya: *You got down to his level.*

Dr. L.:   *Yes, I got down to his level. Don't stand. You will say to your child, "It's time for our special playtime." Walk your child back to your bedroom, close the door, and say, "This is our special playtime, and this is a time when you can play with these toys in a lot of the ways you would like to." Sit down, sit on the floor. If you'd rather sit in a chair, sit in a chair. But then when your child settles in, show interest in what he or she is doing by moving to be close to your child. Lie on the floor and prop your chin on your hand, and fiddle with the things that your child is fiddling with, but don't take over. Your child is to be in the lead. Now, I'd like for you to listen to who leads the conversation.*

Ask parents "What else did you see me do?" until all of the key concepts that were demonstrated in the video are discussed.

Follow the same procedure to demonstrate "Returning Responsibility." Your demonstration should include phrases such as, "Hmm, I wonder what that is?" and "In here it can be whatever you want it to be," when the child asks what something is.

Follow the same procedure to demonstrate the concept of "Actively join in when invited." Your demonstration should include phrases such as, "Show me what to do," when invited to play.

Below is a sample exchange during a training session between the therapist and a parent:

Dr. L.:   *"Tell me what I am to do next." If you just start building, then you've taken over. The child may say, "You play with the toy soldiers," and I would say, "Show me what you want done with them." "Well, you take these, and I'll take these, and you line them up." "Okay, show me where you want them lined up, and I'll line mine up." "Well, you line yours up right there. I'll line mine up right here." Now you know exactly what he wants done. So you start lining the soldiers up, and he starts lining his up. But you keep getting your direction from the child.*

Play more of the video or demonstrate the concept of the parent's "Be With" Attitudes. Play more of the video or demonstrate the concept of the parent "tracking." Tell parents in your own words, "Tracking means just saying what you see, reflecting the behavior of your child. For example, if your child picks up a toy truck and flies it over the dollhouse, you say, "That flew right over the top of that." Don't use labels such as car or house, because in the child's imagination, the car and house can be anything—a rocket ship and a castle."

    2. Use filial toy kit or toys in playroom for parents to take turns role-playing child and parent in play session, practicing the skills just demonstrated

VI. Homework Assignments (refer parents to homework section in their notebook)

(See *Therapist Notebook*)

    1) Priority—Collect toys on *Toy Checklist for Play Sessions.*

        Brainstorm ideas and sources and suggest parents sharing resources

    2) Select a consistent time and an uninterrupted place in the home suitable for the play sessions and report back next week. Whatever room you feel offers the fewest distractions to the child and the greatest freedom from worry about breaking things or making a mess. Set aside a regular time in advance. This time is to be undisturbed—no phone calls or interruptions by other children.
        Time _____ Place _____

3) Additional Assignment:

(Optional additional assignment) Complete supplemental *Feelings Response Practice Worksheet* begun in class. Worksheet can be handed out and assigned to provide parents with play session scenarios for additional practice. Ask parents to write in reminder on homework sheet.

VII. Close With Motivational Poem, Story, or Rule of Thumb (optional)

End session with a motivational book, poem, or story, such as "I'll Love You Forever"

(See *CPRT Training Resources*)

Child Parent Relationship Therapy (CPRT)
Session 3 – Study Guide

Note: Print material checklist for this session (CD-Rom, Appendix A – contains list of all materials and where to locate them)

I. Informal Sharing, and Review of Homework

Ask about each parent's week and reflect briefly.

Review homework from Session 2:

1. Toys collected

Ask parents about collecting toys for the kits, their children's reactions, and toys they had trouble finding. Ask parents about suggestions for difficult-to-find toys.

2. Time and place for play sessions

Very important to ask very specific questions about when and where

Write down the time and place for the play sessions in your notes.

Hand out appointment cards—one for parent and one for child to keep

(See Appendix A on CD-ROM for *Appointment Cards.*) Explain that this appointment is as important as a doctor's appointment and should be kept.

3. Any questions

4. (Optional) Review parent responses on *Feelings Response Practice Worksheet* if assigned in Session 2 homework

II. Handout: *Play Session Do's & Don'ts* (refer parents to page 13 in the *Parent Notebook*)

(See *Therapist Notebook* for handout.)

● Ask parents to refer to *Play Session Do's & Don'ts* handout as you refer to poster and provide examples

The *Play Session Do's & Don'ts* handout will be referred to many times during the following weeks. To make the list easy for parents to find, print it out on colored paper (yellow is suggested), then you can simply ask parents to refer to the "yellow" handout. You may also want to laminate this list for parents.

<u>Note</u>: There is a poster of the *Play Session Do's & Don'ts* handout included in Appendix B on CD-ROM for therapists to use. Remember to bring it to this session and all of the following sessions.

- Demonstrate: **Play Session Do's** physically with toys as you go over each one (or role-play with co-leader)

If you are running short on time, go over #1, #2, #3, and #6 on the following Do's List (highlighted in bold).

<u>Do:</u>

1. Do set the stage (structuring).

Prepare play area ahead of time:

- An old blanket or vinyl tablecloth can be used to establish a visual boundary of the play area, as well as provide protection for flooring.

- A cookie sheet under the arts/crafts materials provides a hard surface for playdough, drawing, and gluing, and provides ease of clean up.

- Display the toys in a consistent manner around the perimeter of the play area; Ziplock® bags and Tupperware® containers can be used to help organize the toys

Convey freedom of the special playtime through your introductory words: "During our special playtime, **you** can play with the toys in lots of the ways you'd like to."

Demonstrate all of the following Do's (#2–#8) using the toys in ways that the child might play with them:

2. Do let the child lead.

Allow your child to lead by <u>returning responsibility.</u>

Do this by responding, "That's up to **you**," "**You** can decide," or "That can be whatever **you** want it to be."

Allowing the child to lead during the playtime helps you to better understand your child's world and what your child needs from you. Convey your willingness to follow your child's lead through your responses: "Show me what **you** want me to do," "**You** want me to put that on," "Hmmm...," or "I wonder...." Use whisper technique (coconspirators) when child wants you to play a role: "What should I say?" or "What happens next?" (modify responses for older kids: use conspiratorial tone, "What happens now?" "What kind of teacher am I?" etc.).

3. Do join in the child's play actively, as a follower.

Convey your willingness to follow your child's lead through your responses and your actions, by actively joining in the play (child is the director, parent is the actor): "So I'm supposed to be the teacher," "**You** want me to be the robber, and I'm supposed to wear the black mask," "Now I'm supposed to pretend I'm locked up in jail, until **you** say I can get out," or "**You** want me to stack these just as high as yours." Use whisper technique in role-play: "What should I say?" or "What happens next?"

4. Do verbally track child's play (describe what you see).

Verbally tracking your child's play is a way of letting your child know that you are paying close attention and that you are interested and involved: "**You're** filling that all the way to the top ...," "**You've** decided you want to paint next ...," or "**You've** got 'em all lined up just how you want them."

5. Do reflect the child's feelings.

Verbally reflecting children's feelings helps them feel understood and communicates your acceptance of their feelings and needs: "**You're** proud of your picture," "That kinda surprised you," "**You** really like how that feels on your hands," "**You** really wish that we could play longer," "**You** don't like the way that turned out," or "**You** sound disappointed." (Hint: Look closely at your child's face to better identify how your child is feeling.)

6. Do set firm and consistent limits.

Consistent limits create a structure for a safe and predictable environment for children. Children should never be permitted to hurt themselves or you. Limit setting provides an opportunity for your child to develop self-control and self-responsibility. Using a calm, patient, yet firm voice, say, *"The floor's not for putting playdough on; you can play with it on the tray"* or *"I know you'd like to shoot the gun at me, but I'm not for shooting. You can choose to shoot at that"* (point to something acceptable).

7. Do salute the child's power and encourage effort.

Verbally recognizing and encouraging your child's effort builds self-esteem and confidence and promotes self-motivation: "**You** worked hard on that!" "**You** did it!" "**You** figured it out!" "**You've** got a plan for how you're gonna set those up," "**You** know just how you want that to be," or "Sounds like **you** know lots about how to take care of babies."

8. Do be verbally active.

Note: Emphasize the bolded **Do's** for parents to focus on in first play session:

Being verbally active communicates to your child that you are interested and involved in her play. If you are silent, your child will feel watched. <u>Note</u>: Empathic grunts—"Hmm..." and so forth—also convey interest and involvement when you are unsure of how to respond.

Explain to parents that the **Do's** list provides a remedy for the following **Don'ts** list. Ask them which **Don't** will be the most difficult and what remedy would be the most helpful.

Don't:
1. Don't criticize any behavior.
2. Don't praise the child.
3. Don't ask leading questions.
4. Don't allow interruptions of the session.
5. Don't give information or teach.
6. Don't preach.
7. Don't initiate new activities.
8. Don't be passive or quiet.
(Don'ts 1–7 are taken from Guerney, 1972)

<u>Sense of humor</u>: "I've just told you don't criticize, don't praise, don't ask questions, don't teach, don't preach, and don't make suggestions; and then I tell you not to be quiet! That doesn't seem fair does it? So don't worry about that last one so much during your first session."

III. View Demonstration Video Clip or Do a Live Demonstration Illustrating the Do's

Video clip should primarily focus on demonstrating the "Be With" Attitudes and the skill of "allowing the child to lead"

It is best for you to show a video clip of yourself doing a play session with a child you know. After showing the clip, ask, "Did you see me do anything really difficult? Does this look hard to do?" Emphasize how anyone can do this.

Try to show a section of the tape where you do something you've told parents not to do, such as ask a question. Stop the tape right after the mistake and ask, "What did I just do?" Emphasize that you have never had a perfect special playtime and that you don't expect them to either.

IV. **Handout: *Play Session Procedures Checklist*** (refer parents to page 14 in the *Parent Notebook*)

(See *Therapist Notebook* for handout and photograph of toys set up for a play session.)

Briefly go over handout—especially what to do before the session to structure for success; ask parents to read over carefully at least two days before their play session

The *Play Session Procedures Checklist* is referred to frequently while teaching, so it is recommended that this handout be printed on colored paper [blue] to make it easy for parents to find

Refer parents to photograph in their handouts of toys set up for play session

Discuss placing toys in groups according to categories and repeating general placement of groups each time for predictability, to help the child find the toy needed for the desired expression.

V. **Parent Partners Role-Play—focusing on skills they saw you demonstrate, as well as practice beginning and ending the session**

VI. **Discuss with Parents How to Explain the "Special Playtime" to Their Child**

Example explanation: "You may wish to explain to your child that you are having these special playtimes with her because, 'I am going to this special play class to learn some special ways to play with you!'"

VII. Arrange for One to Two Parent(s) to Do Videotaping This Week

Ask a parent who appears to have the best grasp of the skills, and who is confident and most likely to follow through, to videotape. If parents express anxiety about videotaping the session or showing it in class, empathize with them. Share a story of showing your first tape in supervision. Reassure them that you have never had a perfect play session and that you don't expect them to either.

Name/phone number _____ day/time (if taping at clinic) _____

Name/phone number _____ day/time (if taping at clinic) _____

Remind parent(s) who are videotapping this week to make note on their Parent Notes & Homework handout

☞ Rule of Thumb: "Be a thermostat, not a thermometer."

Learn to RESPOND (reflect) rather than REACT. The child's feelings <u>are not</u> your feelings and needn't escalate with him/her.

Reflecting/responding to child's thoughts, feelings, and needs creates a comfortable atmosphere of understanding and acceptance for child.

During the 30-minute play session, parents are asked to be a thermostat for their child.

VIII. Homework Assignments (refer parents to homework section in their notebook)

(See *Therapist Notebook*)

1) Complete play session toy kit—get blanket/tablecloth and other materials (see *Photograph of Toys Set Up for Play Session* in handouts) and confirm that the <u>time and place you chose will work.</u>— make arrangements for other children.

2) Give child appointment card and make "Special Playtime—Do Not Disturb" sign with child one to three days ahead (depending on child's age). See *Template for Do Not Disturb Sign* in handouts.

   The younger the child, the closer to time of play session

Explain that keeping this appointment is very important and that having the appointment at the same time, in the same place, and with the same toys, allows the child to learn to "trust" at a deeper level during special playtime, because everything is predictable.

3) Read handouts prior to play session:
   Play Session Do's & Don'ts
   Play Session Procedures Checklist

4) Play sessions begin at home this week—arrange to videotape your session and make notes about problems or questions you have about your sessions.

_____ I will bring my videotape for next week (if videotaping at clinic: my appt. day/time _____).

Encourage parents to tape all of their sessions. Explain that this will allow them to see their progress and show clips of their sessions when they have a question about specific happenings in their sessions.

VII. Close With Motivational Poem, Story, or Rule of Thumb (optional)

Child Parent Relationship Therapy (CPRT)
Session 4 – Study Guide

Note: Print material checklist for this session (CD-Rom, Appendix A – contains list of all materials and where to locate them)

Note: Prior to this session, either meet the parent(s) to be videotaped at the clinic or follow-up with a phone call to help prepare them for home play session—and ask them to let you know if videotaping worked out OK.

The World Through the Parent's Eyes:

Most parents will come to class excited to share their experience in special playtime, but also at least a little anxious about whether or not they did the playtime the way they were "supposed to." The parent who videotaped her session may be especially anxious. Other parents may have experienced frustration at not being able to control the session or at not seeing the changes or having the experience they had expected or hoped for. Regardless of what the parent is feeling, it is important that each parent's feelings are validated through reflective responding. Encourage parents by focusing on the **Do's** they practiced in the play session. Reassure parents who are disappointed that changes take time.

Resistant parents often share the behavioral problems they are having with their children, often citing examples of how they tried to use a skill and it didn't work: "Nothing works with my child." Remind parents of the Band-Aid: that it's working even when they don't see it working. Ask them to trust the process, and don't take the Band-Aid off yet! The therapist can also use resistant parents' reports of frustration with their children's behavior as an opportunity to reflect that what they are doing doesn't seem to be getting them the results they want. Ask them to consider that their child may have special needs that require a different response, and that the 30-minute special playtime will teach them a new way to respond to their child's needs. This is a good time to introduce the **Rule of Thumb: "When a child is drowning, don't try to teach her to swim."** (See below.) Ask parents what they would do if their child were drowning. Do you look into the pool and try and tell your child what to do or give him/her a crash course in how to swim? Of course not! You jump in and save your child. You would then wait until the next week to teach your child how to swim. Liken the 30-minute special playtime to a time the parent is jumping in to save the child (hence, the name of the course, CPR Therapy). The special playtime is a time for a parent to respond to her/his child's need, without trying to teach a lesson, change behavior, and so forth. Reflective responding is the tool that parents use to respond to their children's needs. When a child is feeling upset or out of control, that is not the moment to teach, preach, or impart a rule.

☞ **Rule of Thumb: When a child is drowning, don't try to teach her to swim.**

When a child is feeling upset or out of control, that is not the moment to impart a rule or teach a lesson.

The facilitator must be sensitive to the difficulty parents have with the concept of focusing only on the special playtimes, especially when they are having significant behavior problems that they want solved NOW! Continue to affirm their frustrations and struggles, writing down their concerns and assuring them that you will come back to those issues in a few weeks.

I. Informal Sharing, followed by Parent Highlights of Preparing for and Conducting Home Play Sessions (parents with video go last)

Be aware of time—keep group process moving!

- Look for something positive to reflect for each parent

- Model encouragement by prizing parents' efforts

- Use parents' sharing to emphasize examples of **Play Session Do's**

  (Refer to poster or handout and encourage parents' efforts to recognize the **Play Session Do's**)

- Seize opportunities to forge connections between parents with similar struggles

If you see a parent indicating she identifies with what another parent is sharing in her story, say what you see; for example, "Sarah, I saw you nodding your head. Looks like you've had a similar experience."

A general rule of thumb in critiquing a parent play session is to make only one suggestion about something they could do differently. Work hard to find something you can be positive about in the parent's session.

II. Videotaped Play Session Review and Supervision

- Comment primarily on the positive, taking a few words the parent said or nonverbal behavior and turning that into a **Play Session Do** or another teaching point

  Focus on parent's strengths (remember the Donut Analogy applies to parents, too)

  o Encourage the parent who videotaped the session to share what it was like to be videotaped knowing that she would have to share it with the class

○   Play videotape until a strength is evident

Stop the tape and model reflective responses, prizing the parent's effort.

Focus discussion on positive points: Look for something the parent did that he/she thought would be hard to do. Model reflective responses, prizing the parent's effort. Hold up the **Do's** list and ask the other members of the group, "What is being demonstrated here?"

Example: "The way you're leaning in shows that you're really focused on your child. Just imagine how it feels to your child to have you pay such close attention…"

Example (for very quiet parent): "I can tell you're really interested in Sarah's play, and that you're thinking about how you should respond." (That is a positive because most parents first have to stop themselves from saying what they would typically say and then figure out what they are supposed to say—a lot to learn in one week!)

○   Focus on importance of parent's awareness of self in the play session

Example: "Just now, as you watched your child playing, what were you aware of?"

○   Ask if the parent has a question about some part of the session or if there is some part he/she would particularly like to show—play that portion of the videotape

○   Identify only one thing the parent might do differently

Note: In case of absences or technical problems, have backup play session videotapes available and/or extend the previous discussion of other parents' home play sessions to fill the time.

● Continue to refer to *Play Session Do's & Don'ts* poster or handout, asking parents to try and identify the **Do's** they see demonstrated in videotaped play session.

An issue that is usually brought up following the parents' first play session is that a child is enjoying the play session and doesn't want to stop when the time is up. Parents are reminded that it is their responsibility to end the sessions, even though children may want to continue playing, and that this happening provides a perfect opportunity to demonstrate an example of limit setting. "Rachel, I know you would like to play with the doctor kit longer, but our special playtime is over for today. You can choose to play with the doctor kit next week." For the younger child who may need a more immediate alternative: "Rachel, I know you want to play longer, but our special playtime is over for today. We can go to the kitchen and have a snack." This example of how to end a play session with a reluctant child leads into instruction of the skill of limit setting.

III. Handout: *Limit Setting: A-C-T Before It's Too Late* (refer parents to page 19 in the *Parent Notebook*)

See *Therapist Notebook* for handout.

(Optional) Show video clip on limit setting

- Briefly review the A-C-T model—go over importance of consistency

- Parent is in charge of the structure for the play session: selecting the time and place, establishing necessary limits, and enforcing the limits

- Child is responsible for choices and decisions, within the limits set by parent during playtimes

- Briefly give a few examples of possible limits to set during play sessions

Examples:

- You want to shoot me, but I'm not for shooting. You can shoot the wall.

- You're so frustrated with that ring toss that you want to break it, but it is not for breaking. You can tear up the phone book or hit the bobo doll.

- Throw in a funny one, like: You're so excited you want to hang from the chandelier, but the chandelier is not for hanging on. You may ___ (ask the parents what the alternative is, then add one if needed) draw a picture of yourself hanging from the chandelier or jump up and down and say "Hooray!"

👌   **Rule of Thumb: "During play sessions, limits are not needed until they are needed!"**

- Review *Limit Setting: A-C-T Practice Worksheet* (refer parents to page 20 in the *Parent Notebook*)

See *Therapist Notebook* for worksheet with example responses.

Read over and do at least two or three examples together—discuss the rest next week as completed homework; point out question #7, where parents are asked to write down a limit they think they will need to set for their child

- Be prepared for discussion regarding parent concerns about guns (used in limit-setting example)

Emphasize that the dart gun is an outlet for aggression during special playtimes; parent limits how gun is used—for shooting targets, toys, and so forth, not people. Through pretend play, parent has opportunity to reinforce that people aren't for shooting.

The World Through the Parents Eyes:

Some parents may have very strong feelings about their children playing with guns. Tell parents that the rules outside the play session can be the same as always, but that in special playtime, the gun is important in expressing anger and aggression. Explain that taking away the gun in special playtime is like taking away some of the child's vocabulary. It is analogous to asking a therapist to help you with anger issues and then having her say to you, "OK, I'll help, but don't talk about your anger at all." If a parent is opposed to having the gun in the playtime because the child has experienced some kind of trauma involving the gun, explain that having the gun in special playtime is even more important because the child needs to be able to work on those feelings in the play session.

IV. Role-Play/Video Clip or Live Demonstration of Play Session Skills and Limit Setting

- Always allow time for parents to see a demonstration of play session skills that you want them to emulate, focusing on those skills they report the most difficulty with

- After viewing demonstration, ask parents to role-play a few scenarios they believe are most difficult for them, including at least one limit-setting role-play

Ask parents in your own words: "What was it like to be the child and test the limits?" Most will say it was fun. Reflect by saying something like, "It's nice to let your playful side come out. When you're playful, you're not worried about what you're supposed to do."

V. Arrange for One to Two Parents to Do Videotaping This Week

Name/phone number _____ day/time (if taping at clinic) _____

Name/phone number _____ day/time (if taping at clinic) _____

Remind parent(s) who are videotaping this week to make note on their Parent Notes & Homework handout

VI. Homework Assignments (refer parents to homework section in their notebook)

(See *Therapist Notebook*)

1) Complete *Limit Setting: A-C-T Practice Worksheet*.

2) Read over handouts prior to play session:

   Limit Setting: A-C-T Before It's Too Late!

   Play Session Do's & Don'ts (from Session 3)

   Play Session Procedures Checklist (from Session 3)

3) Conduct play session and complete *Parent Play Session Notes.*

   Notice one intense feeling in yourself during your play session this week.

   _____ *I will bring my videotape for next week (if videotaping at clinic: my appt. day/time _____).*

VII. Close With Motivational Poem, Story, or Rule of Thumb (optional)

Child Parent Relationship Therapy (CPRT)
Session 5 – Study Guide

Note: Print material checklist for this session (CD-Rom, Appendix A – contains list of all materials and where to locate them)

The major focus of this session is supporting and encouraging parents as they learn and practice their new play session skills. No new material is introduced, to avoid overwhelming parents. As in each of the remaining training sessions, the majority of the session is spent on parents' reports of home play sessions, with the most time allocated to reviewing the video(s) of the one or two parents who volunteered to be videotaped for this week's focused supervision. A specific focus during group supervision is on increasing parents' self-awareness of their own feelings, particularly in relation to their children. The therapist also uses supervision and feedback to review and reinforce previously taught CPRT principles and skills, with an emphasis on the play session "Do's."

I.   **Informal Sharing, followed by Review of Homework as Parents Report on Play Sessions**
     (Videotaped parents share last)

- Parents share an intense feeling they were aware of during their play sessions

     Focus on importance of self-awareness of parents' feelings in the play session; model by reflecting parents' feelings

     Model the importance of parents' awareness of themselves by being sensitive to feelings expressed by parents and reflecting them.

     The World Through the Parent's Eyes:

     Authoritarian parents may be resistant to this exercise because they tend to cut themselves off from their emotions as a way to cope with them, while permissive parents may be resistant because they are easily overwhelmed by their emotions.

- Parents share limit-setting attempts <u>during</u> play sessions

     Remember to focus only on play session happenings—redirect limit-setting questions about outside of play sessions to end of session

     Let parents know you will be reviewing limit-setting homework later in the session after videotape review

     Example Dialogue:

     Parent: "I don't have any problems with Robert during the play session because he gets to be in control there. What I need help with is how to handle him when he's screaming at me in the grocery store."

Therapist: "Oh boy! That is so stressful, isn't it? Anyone else here ever had your child embarrass you at the grocery store or out in public? Looks like that is something everyone can relate to; probably something everyone would like help with. We're going to talk about limit setting at the end of this session. I'll make a note so I remember to address that. You said something else important, though. You indicated that your relationship with Robert is different during special playtime. Tell us more about that."

● Focus on **Play Session Do's** (use poster for parents to refer to)

Use examples from parents' comments to reinforce **Do's**—point out difficult situations and spontaneously role-play with parent on how to respond

Example Dialogue:

Therapist: When your child asked you to open the playdough, you told her you didn't know how. You were demonstrating: "Do let the child lead." That's not an easy thing to do. What was that like for you?

Parent: It was really hard; and I think it was confusing to Sarah, because she knows that I do know how.

Therapist: You are demonstrating one the most important things you can do during a play session; you are seeing the world through your child's eyes. You know that acting as though you can't do something that you can do is confusing to Sarah. Let's role-play how you can handle that situation if it comes up again. You be Sarah, and ask me to open the play dough.

Parent: (Handing the play dough to therapist) Mommy, open this for me.

Therapist: (Now pretending to be the parent) I saw you tugging on the lid right there. You tug there, and I'll tug on this side. (Lid pops open). There, you did it. [Pointing out what the child does "right" helps her remain engaged.]

● Remember the Donut Analogy: Focus on strengths & Positive Examples

Find something in each parent's sharing that can be encouraged and supported—facilitate "connecting" among group members; help them see they are not alone in their parenting difficulties

II. Videotaped Play Session Review and Supervision

● View one to two parent-child play sessions, following same procedure as last week

- Model encouragement and facilitate peer feedback

- Refer parents to handout, *In-Class Play Session Skills Checklist,* page 26 in the *Parent Notebook* and ask parents to check off skills they see being demonstrated as therapist or other parents point them out

(See *Therapist Notebook*)

- Continue to refer to *Play Session Do's & Don'ts* poster/handout (from Session 3)

  o Encourage the parent who videotaped to share a bit about the play session before starting video.

Comment <u>only</u> on the positive; taking a few words the parent said or non-verbal behavior and turning them into a **Do** or another teaching point. **Encouragement is the Order of the Day!** Focus on parent's strengths [remember that the Donut Analogy applies to parents, too].

  o Play videotape until a <u>strength</u> is evident

  o Focus on importance of parent's awareness of self in the play session

  o Play portion of videotape that parent has a question about or would particularly like to show

  o Ask what the parent thinks he/she does <u>well</u>

  o Ask what area the parent would like to work on in his/her next play session

(Refer to Session 4 in the *Study Guide* for further discussion and examples.)

III. Limit-Setting Review

(Optional) Show video clip on limit setting

<u>The World Through the Parent's Eyes</u>:

Often parents tend toward extremes when setting limits. Authoritarian parents have high expectations for how their children should behave and feel responsible for making them behave properly. Some parents become controlling when they fear being embarrassed or humiliated by their children's behavior. Permissive parents may be afraid of hurting or damaging their children. Many of these parents view themselves as damaged by the way they were treated as children; they fear their child will not love them if they make a mistake, so they often feel as though they are walking on eggshells.

Authoritarian parents may have difficulty tuning in to their children's emotions for fear they will lose control of their children if they empathize with them. Permissive parents may have difficulty because they feel overly responsible for their children's emotions. Permissive parents may also be prone to extreme swings from permissive to authoritarian parenting styles, because they feel taken advantage of and because of the chaos that the lack of structure creates. The permissive parent, though, likely feels guilty for being "mean and controlling" and shifts fairly quickly back to a permissive style. A-C-T limit setting provides a balance of empathy and faith in the child and helps both types of parents focus on the child's needs, rather than on the parents need to control or rescue. A-C-T also helps permissive parents avoid emotionally charged swings from one extreme to the other.

Keeping these ideas in mind may help the therapist empathize with parents and understand what is most important to them. Authoritarian parents may respond best to the idea that their child is learning self-control, while permissive parents may respond best to the idea that their child is learning coping skills.

- Review A-C-T Method

    Limit Setting: A-C-T Before It's Too Late! (refer parents to page 19 in the *Parent Notebook*)

    Emphasize importance of using all three steps

    Ask for questions

<u>Use a simple example to review A-C-T limit setting</u>:

<u>Example</u>: "Remember, limits in the play session are not punitive, they are therapeutic. When we take responsibility for stopping our children from doing something, then we deprive them of the experience of learning how to stop themselves. So when we set a limit by saying, "I'm not for shooting; that's for shooting," the child is responsible because he is in a position to choose. The way to set limits can be remembered with the letters A-C-T, which stand for the three steps in limit setting. The first step is A, acknowledge the feeling. For example, "Jessie, I know you want to color on the wall...." The second step is C, for communicate the limit. For example, "...but the wall is not for coloring on." The third step is T, for target the alternatives. For example, "You can color on the paper.""

<u>Tell parents in your own words</u>: "This way of setting limits follows the rule: 'It's OK to feel any way you want to feel; it's just not OK to act any way you want to act.' Usually, we are trying to change the way the child feels, for example, by saying, 'That's nothing to be upset about' or 'You don't hate your sister; you love your sister.' With A-C-T, there is no attempt to change the feeling. In fact, you communicate to the child that you understand the feeling. You empathize with the child. That first step is important because in order to target a satisfying alternative, you have to really understand how the child feels."

<u>Share your experience</u>: "I remember when I learned how to use A-C-T; my daughter was about 3 years old. Every morning, she would argue with everything I said. There was a power struggle every 30 seconds. I would be brushing her hair or trying to help her get ready or saying, 'Good morning,' and she would yell, 'No! Stop it! I don't want to! No!' I tried using A-C-T, saying, 'Deva, I know you're mad, but I'm not for yelling at. You can tell me you're mad without yelling at me.' It didn't work; my daughter kept yelling. The next morning, though, I realized I hadn't empathized. I hadn't understood how she was feeling. I used A-C-T again, only this time I said, 'Deva, I know you want to be in charge. You want to tell me what to do. You're tired of everyone telling you what to do, but I'm not for bossing around. You can line up your stuffed animals and tell them what to do—you can boss them around.' It worked like a charm! It worked because I understood what she was feeling and gave her a way to express it in a satisfying but appropriate way. For years, wherever we went, she would line up stuffed animals or chairs with imaginary people in them and tell them what to do. She's now 12 and wants to be the first female president. I think there is a definite connection."

<u>Note</u>: Therapists who are not parents can share similar experiences they have had with children of relatives or neighbors or share experiences in play therapy.

Emphasize the importance of stating clear and concise limits:

- Review principles of limit setting on *Limit Setting:A-C-T Before It's Too Late!* (refer parents to page 19 in the *Parent Notebook*)

(See *Therapist Notebook* for handout)

- Review homework worksheet: *Limit Setting: A-C-T Practice Worksheet* (refer parents to page 20 in the *Parent Notebook*)

(See *Therapist Notebook* for worksheet with example answers)

Go over any scenarios not covered in Session 4

Discuss limits parents might need to set and help with one they generated

Ask for questions

- Review handout: *Limit Setting: Why Use the Three-Step A-C-T Method?* (refer parents to page 25 in the *Parent Notebook*)

(See *Therapist Notebook* for worksheet with example answers)

If not enough time, ask parents to read over at home

IV. Role-Play/Video Clip or Live Demonstration of Play Session Skills and Limit Setting

- Always allow time for parents to see a demonstration of play session skills that you want them to emulate, focusing on those skills they report the most difficulty with

- After viewing demonstration, ask parents to role-play a few scenarios they believe are most difficult for them, including at least one limit-setting role-play

Be Playful! Test the limits with the parents by pretending to be the child.

Example: Aim the dart gun at the parents and ask them to set a limit. When they say, "I know you want to shoot me, but I'm not for shooting. You can shoot the doll and pretend it's me," aim the gun a millimeter away from their head and say, "I'm not going to shoot you. I'm just going to shoot the wall behind you. I won't hit you." The parent then must be more specific and say, "I know you want to shoot me, but I am not for shooting, and this whole wall behind me is not for shooting. You may shoot that wall or that one."

Example: Test the limit by pretending that you are going to draw on a parent's shoe. Resist the limit like a child would, saying, "It won't hurt your shoe. It will just make it look better." The limit would be, "I know you would like to decorate my shoe, but my shoe is not for drawing on. You can draw on the paper and tape it to my shoe." It's usually hard for parents to acknowledge the feeling, because they believe you are really going to draw on their shoe. Point out to parents how difficult this is to use in the heat of the moment unless it is practiced often.

Example: Test the limit suggesting that you play beauty shop; pretend you are going to pour water on a parent's head. Explain to parents that to get the child's attention right away, to stop the child, say the child's name. For example, "Daniel, I know you want to play beauty shop, but my head is not for getting wet during playtime. You can pour the water on the doll's head as you hold her over the sink, or you can use an empty bottle and pretend you're pouring water on my head."

Point out to parents that in all of these examples, it seemed as though they were really worried that you were going to cross the line. For example, say, "You really thought I was going to draw on your shoe" or "You really thought I was going to pour water on you." Ask them about the physical feeling they experienced. Explain that the physical sensation is important to tune in to, in order to know when they need to set a limit.

Tell parents in your own words: "Now, turn to the person next to you. One of you can be the child first. Use the toys, and do something children might do to break a limit. Pretend you're going to break the toys, or pretend you're going to splash paint, and let your parent practice setting limits."

V. Arrange for One to Two Parents to Do Videotaping This Week

Name/phone number _____ day/time (if taping at clinic) _____

Name/phone number _____ day/time (if taping at clinic) _____

Remind parent(s) who are videotaping this week to make note on their Parent Notes & Homework handout

VI. Homework Assignments (refer parents to homework section in their notebook)

(See *Therapist Notebook*)

1)   Give each of your children a Sandwich Hug and Sandwich Kiss.

Tell parents in your own words: "I have one more really important homework assignment for all of you to do with your child and another family member. You do this sometime other than your play session—and you do this with each of your children. It's called a **Sandwich Hug.** It looks like this (stand up to demonstrate): you and your husband get on either side of your child (pick your child up if she is little), and you say (playfully), 'We're going to make a sandwich hug; you're going to be the peanut butter (or whatever sandwich child likes best) and we're going to be the bread.' Then you give your child a big physical, noisy hug, 'ummm—ummm!' (the noise is very important—children love that!). Be sure to give each of your children one. Older children may be a little resistant; adapt how you present it to fit their age. Then, another time in the week, let your child know that you learned another funny assignment in this class that you are taking; it is called a **Sandwich Kiss.** Demonstrate a sandwich kiss by taking your fists (each representing one parent) and putting them up to your own cheeks and pushing in while making a big kissing noise, "ummm—smack!" Remind the parents again that making a really loud kissing noise is very important, and that parents are to do this with each child in the family.

2)   Read over handouts prior to play session:

   Limit Setting: A-C-T Before It's Too Late! (from Session 4)

   Play Session Do's & Don'ts (from Session 3)

   Play Session Procedures Checklist (from Session 3)

3)   Conduct play session (same time & place):

   a. Complete *Parent Play Session Notes.*

   b. Use *Play Session Skills Checklist* to note what you thought you did well, and select one skill you want to work on in your next play session.

   c. If you needed to set a limit during your playtime, describe on the checklist what happened and what you said or did.

   ____ *I will bring my videotape for next week (if videotaping at clinic: my appt. day/ time ____).*

4)   Additional Assignment:

Have parents write down additional assignments as needed.

VII. Close With Rule of Thumb

✋ Rule of Thumb: "If you can't say it in 10 words or less, don't say it"

As parents, we have a tendency to overexplain to our children, and our message gets lost in the words.

Child Parent Relationship Therapy (CPRT)
Session 6 – Study Guide

Note: Print material checklist for this session (CD-Rom, Appendix A – contains list of all materials and where to locate them)

<u>Overview of Sessions 6–9</u>: Enhancing feelings of parental efficacy, along with building self-esteem and self-confidence, is a primary aim for the therapist, just as a primary aim for parents in Sessions 6 through 9 is to actively respond to their child in ways that encourage and build their child's self-esteem.

Sessions 6 through 9 follow a similar format. First, each parent reports on their home play session, followed by the videotaped play session critique/supervision of one to two parents. The therapist provides suggestions and points out CPRT skills demonstrated as parents describe play session happenings, attending carefully to feelings expressed by parents. Greater attention is placed on common problems parents are experiencing. Taking the time to process parents' feelings as they arise is especially important and models for parents what you are asking them to do with their children...focus on feelings. The therapist helps parents see that they are not alone in their child rearing struggles by linking experiences shared by several parents. Parents are generally feeling more confident in their ability to give feedback to one another. Use group facilitation skills to help each member have a chance to give feedback. When parents can begin to notice skills in themselves and others, integration of skill and knowledge is occurring. Allow time to discuss common problems parents are experiencing and role-play solutions.

Continue to emphasize the **Do's and Don'ts** as parents report on play sessions. Reviewing and role-playing of play session principles and skills are continued each session. Limit setting is generally a "Hot Topic." In Sessions 6 through 8, the therapist continues to acknowledge parental concerns about long-term and crisis-related child problems not related to the special playtimes by listening and writing down concerns as they are expressed; typically, these issues aren't addressed until Session 9. As is true in all sessions, the inevitable sidetracking on discussions of minor child-related problems is carefully avoided by the therapist acknowledging the parent briefly with a word and refocusing the discussion to the point at hand. In limited cases of some minor child-related problems, a very brief suggestion might be offered but not explained in a prolonged discussion. By Sessions 8 and 9, many parents are beginning to integrate play session skills and spontaneously use skills successfully outside of session. As parents spontaneously begin to share happenings outside the play session that in any small way indicate generalization of CPRT skills, the therapist quickly acknowledges the newly developed coping strategy, with the aim of encouraging, empowering, and enhancing parental confidence. Session 9 focuses specifically on the use of these skills in everyday happenings.

I. Informal Sharing, followed by Review of Homework as Parents Report on Play Sessions

- Parents share experience giving each of their children a Sandwich Hug and Sandwich Kiss

- Parents share limit-setting attempts during play sessions. Review A-C-T Limit Setting as needed (refer to handout from Session 4 page 19 in the *Parent Notebook*)

Remember to focus only on play session happenings—redirect other questions about limit setting by letting parents know you will be focusing on limit setting more later in the session

- Continue debriefing play sessions, focusing on parents' perceived changes in their own behavior (videotaped parents go last)

  Focus on **Play Session Do's** (use poster for parents to refer to)

  Use examples from parents' comments to reinforce **Do's**

  Point out difficult situations and spontaneously role-play with parent on how to respond

- Remember the Donut Analogy: Focus on the Positive! Find something in <u>each</u> parent's sharing that can be encouraged and supported—facilitate "connecting" among group members.

II. Videotaped Play Session Review and Supervision

- View one to two parent–child play sessions, following same procedure as last week
- Model encouragement and facilitate peer feedback
- Refer parents to handout, *In-Class Play Session Skills Checklist,* page 35 in the *Parent Notebook* and ask parents to check off skills they see being demonstrated

(See *Therapist Notebook*)

- Continue to refer to *Play Session Do's & Don'ts* poster/handout

Emphasize importance of consistency over and over: consistency in holding play sessions, consistency in limit setting, consistency in daily routines, and so forth. Importance of consistency in conducting home play sessions **at the same time and place each week** is emphasized throughout, even if the child asks for changes and/or it would be more convenient for the parent to change the time. Parents often have great difficulty grasping the importance of consistency and predictability in children's lives.

Remind parents that, for children,

parental consistency > predictability > security > child feeling safe and loved!

👍 **Rule of Thumb: "Grant in fantasy what you cannot grant in reality."**

In a play session, it is okay to act out feelings and wishes that in reality may require limits.

Example: Three-year-old Margaret has a new baby sister and is naturally feeling a little jealous. During her play session, she takes the baby doll and throws it out of the play area. A helpful parent response would be, "You just didn't want the baby to be in here" or "You decided to just throw the baby over there." However, parents are generally disturbed by this kind of behavior, believing that if they accept this behavior during the session, their child will think it is permissible outside of the session. The same is true of any aggressive or regressive play behaviors; therefore, the filial therapist must be careful to explain this concept in a way that parents can understand.

III. Choice-Giving

- Review handout: *Choice-Giving 101: Teaching Responsibility & Decision-Making* (refer parents to page 31 in the *Parent Notebook*)

(See *Therapist Notebook*) As you discuss first paragraph, "Providing children with age-appropriate choices empowers children by allowing them a measure of control over their circumstances…," introduce the following Rule of Thumb:

👍 **Rule of Thumb: "Big choices for big kids, little choices for little kids."**

Choices given must be commensurate with child's developmental stage.

The concept of giving children choices is introduced to build on the principles of limit setting focused on in Sessions 4 and 5, and as a strategy for empowering children to make decisions and avoid power struggles outside of play sessions.

Tell parents that choice-giving requires a shift in attitude, creative thinking, and spontaneous reaction. The shift in attitude is a change from making decisions for the child to allowing the child to decide. For example, if a child doesn't want to take her medicine, taking the medicine is not a choice, that is a given; so the parent can say, "You may choose to have orange juice with your medicine, or you may choose to have apple juice with your medicine. Which do you choose?" The question calls for a commitment on the part of the child, and once the child has made a choice, the child is more willing to follow through. Allowing the child to be a part of the decision-making process usually results in cooperation or willingness to compromise. Tell parents to keep in mind that they must be willing to live with either choice the child makes.

Choice-giving is also a new approach to discipline (not punishment, but discipline) that helps a child learn how to engage in making appropriate choices and learn self-responsibility. For example, "If you choose to finish your homework by 4:00, you choose to get to play your computer game. If you choose not to finish you homework by 4:00, you choose not to play your computer game."

This method of choice-giving can be used in the special playtime to help children learn self-discipline and self-control as the fourth step in the A-C-T model. Engage the parents by discussing a choice-giving scenario such as: "You set the limit that walls are not for marking on, but your child keeps trying to mark on the wall. Now, what do you do? You've gone through the three steps, three or four times, and your child is still trying to mark on the wall." Have parents brainstorm ideas of possible choices.

- (Optional) Show video: *Choices, Cookies, and Kids* (suggest showing 15–20 minutes and finish video in Session 7)

Show optional video, if at all possible (the video *Choices, Cookies, and Kids* by Garry Landreth can be obtained from Center for Play Therapy, University of North Texas, PO Box 310829, Denton, TX, 76203, or see: www.centerforplaytherapy.com). The skill of choice-giving is most easily grasped by parents through demonstration and providing opportunities for practice. The *Choices, Cookies, and Kids* video is shown to clearly illustrate both the concept and the skill of choice-giving. The video is approximately 30 minutes in length and should be previewed prior to use. Because of time constraints, the therapist may want to show part of the video during Session 6 and the remainder during Session 7. The Oreo® Cookie Theory of choice-giving is covered approximately six minutes into the video and should be presented during Session 6, even if time restricts viewing the full tape.

- As time allows, review second choice-giving handout: *Advanced Choice-Giving: Providing Choices as Consequences* (refer parents to page 32 in the *Parent Notebook*). *Note: this handout can be deferred to Session 7 or partially covered in this session and completed in Session 7.*

(See *Therapist Notebook*)

Go over handout at least through "Oreo Cookie Method of Choice-Giving" and finish in Session 7, if more time is needed. <u>Share your experience</u>: "I didn't realize how much I was taking responsibility for things that were my son's responsibility, until I started doing this. I used to spend so much time in the morning trying to get Dylan to brush his teeth. I would get so frustrated. I'd ask him four or five times, and he still wouldn't do it. We'd be running late many mornings, because he just wouldn't do it until I stood there and made him do it. I was taking responsibility for something he needed to be responsible for. With choice-giving, I didn't need to lose my temper or get stressed out anymore. I just calmly stated, 'Dylan, if you choose to brush your teeth in the morning before it is time to go, you choose to get to eat what you want for lunch; if you choose not to brush your teeth before it's time to go, you choose to eat raw vegetables for lunch because that's the only thing that won't hurt your teeth.' It's the most powerful choice I ever gave him. He only chose veggies once!"

<u>Note</u>: Therapists who are not parents can share similar experiences they have had with children of relatives or neighbors or experiences in play therapy.

● (Optional) Supplemental worksheet: *Choice-Giving Practice Worksheet* can be assigned for additional homework, if needed—go over a couple of examples together before sending it home as homework (See Appendix C on CD-ROM for worksheet and answer sheet for therapist)

The skill of limit setting is an ongoing challenge for most parents and typically continues to be a major focus in Session 6. The therapist uses parents' spontaneous sharing of limit-setting struggles to review and practice the skill. The majority of parents struggle with following through once they have set a limit, especially when faced with their child's pleading, whining, and other behaviors that the child has learned to use to manipulate and wear down the parent. Remind parents about the importance of follow-through: **when they don't follow through on limits set or promises made, they lose credibility** and, ultimately, damage their relationship with their child. **Trust is the foundation of a healthy relationship.** When parents fail to follow through and provide consistency, the message to the child is, "You really can't count on me to do what I say." Humor can be used to get this very serious point across, for example, by having parents repeat after you three times, "**When Setting Limits, I WILL Follow Through—I Am Tough As Nails!**"

IV.   Role-Play/Video Clip or Live Demonstration of Play Session Skills and Choice-Giving

- Always allow time for parents to see a demonstration of play session skills that you want them to emulate, focusing on those skills they report the most difficulty with

- After viewing demonstration, ask parents to role-play a few scenarios they believe are most difficult for them, including at least one choice-giving role-play

<u>Say to parents in your own words</u>: "Let's practice generating some choices. You three are in a group and you three are in a group. Your assignment is to think of at least three things your children have done or might do and develop a choice for each of those situations. Then you can share your situations and choices with the rest of us."

V.   Arrange for One to Two Parents To Do Videotaping This Week

Name/phone number _____ day/time (if taping at clinic) _____

Name/phone number _____ day/time (if taping at clinic) _____

Remind parent(s) who are videotaping this week to make note on their Parent Notes & Homework handout

VI.   Homework Assignments (refer parents to homework section in their notebook)

(See Therapist Notebook)

1)   Read *Choice-Giving 101: Teaching Responsibility & Decision-Making* and *Advanced Choice-Giving: Providing Choices as Consequences.*

2)   Read *Common Problems in Play Sessions* and mark the top two to three issues you have questions about, or write in an issue you are challenged by that is not on the worksheet.

3)   Practice giving at least one kind of choice ("A" or "B") outside of the play session.

        A.   Provide choices for the sole purpose of <u>empowering your child</u>
           (two positive choices for child, where either choice is acceptable to you and
           either choice is desirable to child).
           What happened   _____
           What you said _____
           How child responded _____

        B.   Practice giving choices as a <u>method of discipline</u> (where choice-giving is used to
           provide a consequence for noncompliance of limit, family rule, or policy).
           What happened _____
           What you said _____
           How child responded _____

4)   Conduct play session (same time & place)—review *Play Session Do's & Don'ts &*
    Play Session Procedure Checklist

        a.   Complete *Parent Play Session Notes.*

        b.   Use *Play Session Skills Checklist* to note what you thought you did well, and
           select one skill you want to work on in your next play session.

        ____ ***I will bring my videotape for next week (if videotaping at clinic: my appt.***
    day/time ___).

5)   Additional assignment:

> (Optional additional assignment) Complete supplemental *Choice-Giving Practice*
> *Worksheet* begun in class. Worksheet can be handed out and assigned to provide parents
> with scenarios for additional practice. Ask parents to write in reminder on homework
> sheet.

VII. Close With Motivational Poem, Story, or Rule of Thumb (optional)

Child Parent Relationship Therapy (CPRT)
Session 7 – Study Guide

Note: Print material checklist for this session (CD-Rom, Appendix A – contains list of all materials and where to locate them)

The major focus of this session is supporting and encouraging parents' skill development and confidence through group supervision and feedback; thus, the majority of allotted time is devoted to this activity. The only new skill introduced in Session 7 is esteem-building responses.

I. Informal Sharing, followed by Review of Homework as Parents Report on Play Sessions

- Review *Choice-Giving 101* (refer parents to page 31 in the *Parent Notebook*)—reinforce basic concepts as parents report on homework assignment to practice giving a choice to their child outside the play session

Review optional homework worksheet and complete as needed: *Choice-Giving Practice Worksheet*

- (Optional) Complete video, *Choices, Cookies, and Kids,* from Session 6 as needed

- Review and complete as needed: *Advanced Choice-Giving: Providing Choices as Consequences* (refer parents to page 32 in the *Parent Notebook*)

   If parents raise questions about how choices can be used when the child doesn't comply with a limit, briefly discuss the use of choices as consequences. Inform parents that this more advanced skill will be covered in-depth in a later session (refer to handout in Session 9: *Advanced Limit Setting: Giving Choices as Consequences for Noncompliance* page 55 in the *Parent Notebook*)

Explain to parents in your own words: "If you go through the three A-C-T steps several times, and your child continues to test the limit (for example trying to shoot you with the dart gun), Step 4 is: 'If you choose to keep trying to shoot me, you choose not to play with the gun for the rest of our playtime. If you choose not to shoot me, you choose to get to play with the gun.' Or, 'If you choose to keep trying to mark on the table, then you choose not to play with the crayons for the rest of our playtime. If you choose not to mark on the table, you choose to get to play with the crayons.' We'll continue to work on giving choices next week."

- Briefly Review handout: *Common Problems in Play Sessions* (refer parents to page 33 & 34 in the *Parent Notebook*)

   Use as a chance to review reflective listening, setting limits, giving choices, and so forth.

- Continue debriefing play sessions, focusing on parents' perceived changes in their own behavior

  Focus on **Play Session Do's** (use poster for parents to refer to)

  Use examples from parents' comments to reinforce **Do's**

  Role-play with parent on how to respond to difficult situations

- Remember the Donut Analogy: Encourage–Support–Connect!

  Find something in <u>each</u> parent's sharing that can be encouraged and supported— facilitate "connecting" among group members

II. Videotaped Play Session Review and Supervision

- View one to two parent-child play sessions, following same procedure as last week

- Model encouragement and facilitate peer feedback

- Refer parents to handout, *In-Class Play Session Skills Checklist,* page 43 in the *Parent Notebook* and ask parents to check off skills they see being demonstrated

(See *Therapist Notebook*)

- Continue to refer to ***Play Session Do's & Don'ts*** poster/handout

  o   Play videotape until a <u>strength</u> is evident

  o   Focus on importance of parent's awareness of self in the play session

  o   Play portion of videotape that parent has a question about or would particularly like to show

  o   Ask what the parent thinks he/she does <u>well</u>

  o   Ask what area the parent would like to work on in his/her next play session

(Refer to Session 4 in the *Study Guide* for further discussion and examples.)

III. Self-Esteem Building

- Review handout: *Esteem-Building Responses* (refer parents to page 41 in the *Parent Notebook*)

(See *Therapist Notebook*) Suggestion to therapist: Save butterfly story at bottom of handout to read at close of session

In your own words, explain importance of self-esteem building responses. Parents help their child develop a positive view of "self," not only by providing their child with love and unconditional acceptance, but also by helping their child feel competent and capable. Parents help their child feel competent and capable by first allowing the child to *experience* what it is like to discover, figure out, and problem-solve. Parents show faith in their child and their child's capabilities by allowing him to struggle with a problem, all the while providing encouragement (encouragement vs. praise is covered in detail in Session 8). For most parents, allowing children to struggle is hard, but it is a necessary process for children to truly feel capable. The next step in helping children develop a positive view of self as competent and capable is learning to respond in ways that give children credit for ideas, effort, and accomplishments—<u>without praising</u>.

👆 **Rule of Thumb: "Never do for a child that which he can do for himself."**

When you do, you rob your child of the joy of discovery and the opportunity to feel competent. You will never know what your child is capable of, unless you allow him to try!

Many parents and children have difficulty with this concept. Most parents do too much for their children; in response, their children have learned to depend on their parents to solve their problems, believing they cannot do it by themselves. The therapist needs to take time to role-play how parents respond when the child says, "Here, Mommy (handing the playdough to Mom), take the lid off for me" or "Daddy, help me set the soldiers up." Parents need lots of practice in how to return responsibility to their child to do things he is capable of figuring out for himself. Parents benefit from seeing a video clip or live demonstration illustrating the use of esteem-building responses, in which that skill is the focus.

- (Optional) Supplemental worksheet: *Esteem-Building Responses Worksheet* can be assigned for additional homework, if needed—go over a couple of examples together before sending it home as homework (See Appendix C on CD-ROM for worksheet and answer sheet for therapist)

IV. Role-Play/Video Clip or Live Demonstration of Play Session Skills, Self-Esteem-Building Responses, and Responses That Return Responsibility to the Child

- Always allow time for parents to see a demonstration of play session skills that you want them to emulate, focusing on those skills they report the most difficulty with

- After viewing demonstration, ask parents to role-play a few scenarios they believe are most difficult for them, including at least one self-esteem-building response in role-play

V. Arrange for One to Two Parents To Do Videotaping This Week

Name/phone number _____ day/time (if taping at clinic)_____

Name/phone number _____ day/time (if taping at clinic)_____

Remind parent(s) who are videotaping this week to make note on their Parent Notes & Homework handout

VI. Homework Assignments (refer parents to homework section in their notebook)

(See *Therapist Notebook*)

1) Read *Esteem-Building Responses*—practice giving at least one esteem-building response <u>during</u> your play session (note on *Play Session Skills Checklist*). Also practice giving one esteem-building response <u>outside</u> of your play session.

What happened outside of play session_____

What you said _____

How child responded (verbally or nonverbally) _____

2) Write a note to your child of focus, as well as other children in the family, pointing out a positive character quality you appreciate about the child (see Positive Character Qualities handout). Continue to write a note each week for three weeks (mail first note to child, if possible). Write down the following sentence:

"Dear ____, I was just thinking about you, and what I was thinking is you are so ___ (thoughtful, responsible, considerate, loving, etc.). I love you, _____ (Mom, Dad)."

Say to the child, in your own words, after the child reads the note (or you read it to the child), "That is such an important quality; we should put that note on the refrigerator (bulletin board, etc.)." Reminder: Don't expect a response from your child.

Encourage parents to mail their notes; children seldom get mail, so this makes the note an extra special treat. If the child cannot read, arrange for someone else in the home to read the note to the child when it arrives in the mail, if possible; if not, the parent can read the note. Parents are to continue this assignment each week, identifying a different character quality for the remainder of the CPRT training and varying how the note is delivered, for example: placing in child's lunchbox, taped to mirror in bathroom, on the child's pillow, under the child's dinner plate, and so forth.

3) Conduct play session (same time & place)—review *Play Session Do's & Don'ts & Play Session Procedures Checklist*

    a. Complete *Parent Play Session Notes.*
    b. Use *Play Session Skills Checklist* to note what you thought you did well, and select one skill you want to work on in your next play session; note at least one self-esteem building response.
    ____ *I will bring my videotape for next week (if videotaping at clinic: my appt. day/ time_____).*

4) Additional Assignment:

    (Optional additional assignments) Complete supplemental *Esteem-Building Responses Worksheet* begun in class. Worksheets can be handed out and assigned, to provide parents with scenarios for additional practice. Ask parents to write in reminder on homework sheet.

VII. Close With Motivational Poem, Story, or Rule of Thumb (optional)

Suggest reading: "The Struggle to Become a Butterfly: A True Story" (see parent handout: *Esteem-Building Responses* on page 41 in the *Parent Notebook*).

Remember the butterfly: Without the struggle, there are no wings!

Child Parent Relationship Therapy (CPRT)
Session 8 – Study Guide

Note: Print material checklist for this session (CD-Rom, Appendix A – contains list of all materials and where to locate them)

As in Sessions 6 and 7, the major focus of this session is supporting and encouraging parents' skill development and confidence through group supervision and feedback; thus, the majority of allotted time is devoted to this activity. Encouragement is the only new skill introduced this week and builds on the training on esteem-building responses covered last week in Session 7.

I.   **Informal Sharing, followed by Review of Homework as Parents Report on Play Sessions and Generalizing Play Session Skills**

- Parents report on the character quality note-writing activity

   Keep the sharing brief—caution parents not to expect an overt response from their children

- Review optional homework worksheet(s) and complete as needed:
   Esteem Building Responses Worksheet (Appendix C – CD-Rom)

- Parents report on practicing giving a self-esteem-building response <u>outside</u> the play session

   Parents report on practicing a self-esteem building response made <u>during</u> play sessions, as a lead into play session reports

- Continue debriefing play sessions, focusing on parents' perceived changes in their own behavior

   Focus on **Play Session Do's** (use poster for parents to refer to)

   Use examples from parents' comments to reinforce **Do's**

   Role-play with parent on how to respond to difficult situations.

- Remember the Donut Analogy: Encourage . . . Support . . . Connect!

II. **Videotaped Play Session Review and Supervision**

- View one to two parent-child play sessions, following same procedure as last week

   Have parents report briefly on their home play sessions and their homework assignment to practice self-esteem-building responses during their play sessions

   Review of self-esteem-building responses continues to be a focus during focused supervision of videotaped parent. Model encouragement and facilitate peer feedback.

- Refer parents to handout, *In-Class Play Session Skills Checklist,* page 50 in the *Parent Notebook* and ask parents to check off skills they see being demonstrated

(See *Therapist Notebook*)

- Continue to refer to *Play Session Do's & Don'ts* poster/handout

Listen for opportunities in the parents' sharing of play session happenings to reinforce their skills; provide additional strategies as needed.

Monitor feedback: As the videotaped parent's session is reviewed, stop the video after an obvious CPRT skill has been demonstrated and ask parents if they have any feedback for that parent. This strategy encourages parents' sharing of feedback and keeps the focus on parent strengths.

Parents' growing confidence in themselves and their ability to use their newly acquired skills becomes evident in the interactions during the group supervision and feedback time in each session. Generally, by this session, parents begin to volunteer comments on changes they see in themselves, in their child, and in other parents in the group. Take this cue as an opportunity to facilitate parents' growth and learning to a higher level by asking them to give one another feedback as they watch and listen to one another's play sessions. Essentially, you are moving parents into the role of peer supervisor and helping them become more self-aware, with a goal of moving toward the skill of self-monitoring by Session 10.

Caution parents that the newness of the special playtime and the toys may begin to wear off, and their child may seem uninterested or bored. The playtime is still important. Continue to insist on having the playtime.

III. Review Handout: *Encouragement vs. Praise* (refer parents to page 49 in the *Parent Notebook*)

(See *Therapist Notebook*)

- Go over encouraging responses in handout to use in play sessions

Encouraging Phrases that Recognize Effort and Improvement:

"You did it!" or "You got it!"

"You really worked hard on that."

"You didn't give up until you figured it out."

"Look at the progress you've made…." (Be specific)

"You've finished half of your worksheet and it's only 4 o'clock."

Encouraging Phrases that Show Confidence:

"I have confidence in you. You'll figure it out."

"That's a rough one, but I bet you'll figure it out."

"Sounds like you have a plan."

"Knowing you, I'm sure you will do fine."

"Sounds like you know a lot about_____."

Encouraging Phrases that Focus on Contributions and Assets:

"Thanks, that was a big help."

"It was thoughtful of you to_____" or "I appreciate that you_____."

"You have a knack for _____. Can you give me a hand with that?"

In summary, encouragement is:

1. Valuing and accepting children as they are (not putting conditions on acceptance)

2. Pointing out the positive aspects of behavior

3. Showing faith in children, so that they can come to believe in themselves

4. Recognizing effort and improvement (rather than requiring achievement)

5. Showing appreciation for contributions

Introduce Rule of Thumb and discuss:

👆 **Rule of Thumb: "Encourage the effort rather than praise the product."**

Children need encouragement like a plant needs water.

● (Optional) Supplemental worksheet: *Encouragement vs. Praise Worksheet* can be assigned for additional homework, if needed—go over a couple of examples together before sending it home as homework (See Appendix C on CD-ROM for worksheet and answer sheet for therapist)

IV. Role-Play/Video Clip or Live Demonstration of Play Session Skills and Prizing (Encouraging) Responses

● Always allow time for parents to see a demonstration of play session skills that you want them to emulate, focusing on those skills they report the most difficulty with

- After viewing demonstration, ask parents to role-play a few scenarios they believe are most difficult for them, including at least one encouragement in role-play

V. Arrange for One to Two Parents to Do Videotaping This Week

Name/phone number _____ day/time (if taping at clinic)_____

Name/phone number _____ day/time (if taping at clinic)_____

Remind parent(s) who are videotaping this week to make note on their Parent Notes & Homework handout

VI. Homework Assignments (refer parents to homework section of their notebook)

(See *Therapist Notebook*)

As successful use of play session skills outside the play sessions naturally occurs (around Session 8 to 9), the therapist can begin to add homework assignments that encourage generalization of skills. As is true for all homework assignments, be specific in what you want parents to <u>write down</u> and report on the next week; then make sure to take a few minutes at the beginning of the next session for parents to share homework results.

1) Read *Encouragement vs. Praise*—practice giving at least one encouragement response <u>during</u> your play session (note on *Play Session Skills Checklist*). Also, practice giving atleast one encouragement <u>outside</u> of your play session.

What happend or what child said (outside of play session) _____
What you said _____
How child responded (verbally or nonverbally) _____

2) Write down one issue you are struggling with most <u>outside</u> of play session time. ___
_____
It may be one they have brought up before, or they may have already solved that one on their own and have a new issue they want help with

3) Conduct play session (same time & place)—review *Play Session Do's & Don'ts*
a. Complete *Parent Play Session Notes*.
b. Use *Play Session Skills Checklist to* note what you thought you did well, select one skill you want to work on in your next play session, and note at least one encouraging statement.

____ *I will bring my videotape for next week (if videotaping at clinic: my appt. day/time ___).*

4) Additional Assignment:

(Optional additional assignment) Complete supplemental *Encouragement vs. Praise Worksheet* begun in class. Worksheet can be handed out and assigned to provide parents with play session scenarios for additional practice. Ask parents to write in reminder on homework sheet.

Reminder: Write second note to your child of focus, as well as other children in the family, pointing out <u>another</u> positive character quality you appreciate about the child. (Vary how the note is delivered, for example: placing in child's lunchbox, taped to mirror in bathroom, on the child's pillow, under the child's dinner plate, etc.)

VII. Close With Motivational Poem, Story, or Rule of Thumb (optional)

Child Parent Relationship Therapy (CPRT)
Session 9 – Study Guide

Note: Print material checklist for this session (CD-Rom, Appendix A – contains list of all materials and where to locate them)

Although Session 9 follows a similar format to Sessions 6 through 8 (sharing how the week went, reporting on home play sessions, and focused supervision of the videotaped parent[s]), this session differs in the amount of time spent in group processing of the parents' week. Since the majority of homework assignments from last week focused on the use of skills outside of the play sessions, focusing more time and energy on the sharing of happenings outside of playtimes is warranted. The amount of time spent will vary depending on the needs of the group. The more advanced the group, the more they will usually generalize skills outside the play sessions; therefore, more time is spent on applying skills to everyday activities.

Typically, by Session 9, parents are demonstrating greater awareness of their own feelings and reporting greater sensitivity to their children's feelings; consequently, the therapist uses the parents' discussion of happenings outside of play sessions to facilitate parents' sharing of their feelings, as well as their recognition of their child's feelings. This informal sharing provides many opportunities for parents to continue to practice how to more effectively respond to their child's feelings, wants, and needs, without accepting all behaviors.

I. **Informal Sharing, followed by Review of Homework as Parents Report on Play Sessions**

- Review optional homework worksheet and complete as needed: *Encouragement vs. Praise Worksheet* (Appendix C – CD-Rom)

- Parents report on practicing giving an encouragement response <u>during</u> their play session

  If parents bring up homework responses <u>outside</u> play sessions, ask them to share those responses when skills outside play sessions are discussed in a few minutes

- Continue debriefing play sessions, focusing on parents' perceived changes in their own behavior

  Focus on **Play Session Do's** (use poster for parents to refer to)

  Use examples from parents' comments to reinforce **Do's**

  Role-play with parent on how to respond to difficult situations

- Remember the Donut Analogy: Encourage . . . Support . . . Connect!

- (Optional) Supplemental worksheet: *Advanced Limit Setting: Giving Choices as Consequences Worksheet* can be assigned for additional homework, if needed—go over a couple of examples together before sending it home as homework (see Appendix C on CD-ROM for worksheet and answer sheet for therapist)

II. Videotaped Play Session Review and Supervision

- View one to two parent-child play sessions following same procedure as last week

    Have parents report briefly on their home play sessions—model encouragement and facilitate peer feedback

    Ask particularly about the homework assignment of writing down one thing that didn't go well and one thing that went really well in the play session

- Refer parents to handout, *In-Class Play Session Skills Checklist,* page 61 in the *Parent Notebook* and ask parents to check off skills they see being demonstrated

(See *Therapist Notebook*)

- Continue to refer to *Play Session Do's & Don'ts* poster/handout

Monitor feedback: As the videotaped parent's session is reviewed, stop the video after an obvious CPRT skill has been demonstrated and ask parents if they have any feedback for that parent. The goal is to have parents become self-monitoring by Session 10.

The issue of pleasing their children may come up for parents, since they often believe they are responsible for their children's happiness—and unhappiness. This is addressed in a sample interaction between a therapist and a parent during Session 9:

Dr. L.:   *Kim, I heard you say something I want to check on. I think I heard you say that you have a hard time keeping Toby interested.*

Kim: *Yes, he has a short attention span; when we first started, the toys were new.*

Dr. L.:   *For 30 minutes, it is not your responsibility to keep Toby interested.*

Kim: *But, I wait all week for the playtime, and then he doesn't have fun.*

Dr. L.:   *So you're disappointed.*

The therapist uses this kind of sharing to generalize play session skills to outside the playtime—in this case, to emphasize that the parents are not responsible for their children's happiness. It is not their job to make sure their children are always occupied, interested, busy, or happy.

Remind parents that if they take responsibility for their child's happiness, how will the child ever learn to do that for himself? Although no new play session skills are introduced, the therapist may introduce strategies that will help parents with specific problems. Tell parents that when pressure begins to build, or things begin to fall apart in the relationship, or a stressful event occurs, they may add an extra playtime that week.

- Review limit setting and discuss advanced limit-setting strategies to use during play sessions when child does not comply with limit (refer parents to handout: *Advanced Limit Setting: Giving Choices as Consequences for Noncompliance* on pages 55 & 56 in the *Parent Notebook*)

(See *Therapist Notebook* for handouts with example responses.)

III. Using Skills Outside the Play Session

The therapist can use the homework assignments to lead into a discussion of generalizing skills.

- Invite parents to comment on homework assignments from Session 8 about using skills <u>outside</u> the play session
  - ❍ Giving the child encouragement
  - ❍ Second note pointing out positive characteristic
  - ❍ Any other skills used outside the play session

- Review written list of parents' concerns from past eight weeks—ask which concerns remain troublesome. Briefly explore use of CPRT skills to address concerns (further discussion in Session 10).

Although by this point in this session, the therapist has already addressed some parent concerns and discussed how the play session skills can be used to respond more effectively, be sure to allow time to review your written list of parents' concerns from the past eight weeks. It is our experience that many of the "problems" on the list are not "problems" anymore! Prioritize concerns by those shared by the most parents. When discussing the generalization of play session skills to problem areas, tell parents:

☞ **Rule of Thumb: "Don't try to change everything at once!"**

Focus on 'big' issues that ultimately will mean the most to your child's development of positive self-esteem and feelings of competence and usefulness.

- Discuss how to use limit setting outside of play sessions (refer parents to handout: *Generalizing Limit Setting to Outside the Play Session* on pages 57 & 58 in the *Parent Notebook*)

(See *Therapist Notebook* for handouts with example responses.)

Begin by reviewing the three-step A-C-T model: 1) **A**cknowledge the feeling, 2) **C**ommunicate the limit, and 3) **T**arget alternatives.

☞ **Rule of Thumb: "Where there are no limits, there is no security."**

Consistent Limits = Secure Relationship

When you don't follow through, you lose credibility and harm your relationship with your child.

<u>Share your own experience</u>: One of the great things about using A-C-T is that your kids will learn how to set limits for themselves in a respectful way. They don't even know they're using A-C-T. It becomes just a natural way of communicating. One of my favorite examples of this happened one day when I picked my daughter up from school. She was only 9 years old at the time. When she got in the car, she said, "Mom, I am so mad. Mr. (Vice Principal) told us all to shut up today in the lunchroom. That is not right! I want to do something about it!" Frankly, I was shocked more by my daughter saying she wanted to do something about it than by what the vice principal said. When I was a kid,

I never would have even considered talking with the principal or vice principal of the school. I was too intimidated.

"Well, what would you like to do?" I asked hesitantly. "I want to talk to him and tell him that's not right." "OK, honey, I'll talk to him," I responded. "No, Mom, I want to go in there myself and talk to him without you." "What are you going to say?" I asked in shock. "I'm just going to tell him, 'Mr. (Vice Principal), I know it's frustrating when the kids are too loud in the lunch room, but kids are not for saying shut up to. If you're angry, you can take away our recess or tell our teacher.'" "That sounds like a very respectful way to talk with him. You're considering his feelings and giving him a solution to the problem," I responded, hoping to reinforce her plan. She walked in the office determined that she could do this without me but decided to take her older brother with her, just in case. Mr. (Vice Principal) wasn't there, so she wrote him a note. He never said "shut up" to the kids again, that we know of.

<u>Note</u>: Therapists who are not parents can share similar experiences they have had with children of relatives or neighbors or experiences in play therapy.

- If time allows review handout as time allows: *Structured Doll Play for Parents* (refer parents to pages 59 & 60 in the *Parent Notebook*)

(See *Therapist Notebook*)

The therapist should introduce the handout, at least briefly, to let parents know about doll play. It is a lively way of storytelling for parents to help children who are feeling anxious or insecure about new or stressful situations. Following is a sample exchange concerning doll play during a training session between the therapist and a parent of a child in therapy:

Dr. L.: *For some reason, he's anxious about going into the playroom with the therapist, or he's anxious about you leaving him. Let's try something.*

Laura: *OK. Tell me what. We're supposed to go back Wednesday at 6:00.*

Dr. L.: *Today is Monday. Before he goes to bed tonight and again tomorrow, I would like for you to try a procedure I call structured doll play. (To the group) This is a procedure all of you can use when your child is anxious about something or your child is worried about something like being left with a babysitter, going to the dentist, going to school, or going to a birthday party for the first time. Laura, sit down with David and say to him, "I want to tell you a special story. For this story, we need a toy or stuffed animal that can be you and one that can be me." Let David choose the items. "We also need a car." David chooses, and the story begins. "You're playing in your room, and I say, 'Dinner is ready.'" You use the chosen characters to act out the story as you tell it. "You sit down at the table, and we eat. Then I wash the dishes. OK, it's time to get in the car and go to the university. Here I go, and here you go," as you show the characters going to the car. "You buckle your seat belt, click, and I buckle mine, click." Be sure to use lots of noise props in telling the story. Make motor noises, brrrmmm brrrmmm, as you drive. "Here we are at the university. Click, I lock the car and we walk across the parking lot to the special*

Child Parent Relationship Therapy (CPRT)
Session 10 – Study Guide

Note: Print material checklist for this session (CD-Rom, Appendix A – contains list of all materials and where to locate them)

Supervision, evaluation, and follow-up are the primary concerns of this session. Parents need to debrief the experience and prepare to disengage from the group. Parents evaluate the experience and share their perceptions of how they and their children have changed.

One of the most important things the therapist can do to prepare for this session is to let go of their expectations of what it will be. It is not unusual for the last session to be a profound experience for the therapist and the members of the group, but it doesn't happen all the time, and it never happens the same way. Often, parents are very emotional about the transformation they have made, the changes they have seen in their children, and their relationships with them. The extent to which this is shared and explored during the last session depends on several variables, most importantly, the quality of the relationships that have been formed within the group.

I.   Informal Sharing, followed by Review of Homework

- Parents report on number of times they physically touched their child

- Invite parents to discuss play-wrestling experience

II. Show Last Videotape(s) and Briefly Debrief Play Sessions

Focus on observed growth and change in both parent and child

- What part of training was most helpful?

- What part is of greatest concern?

- Any other concerns or issues?

Parents briefly report on their play sessions and the last one to two parent play session videotapes are viewed. Basic CPRT principles are reviewed; parents are asked to share what part of the training has been the most helpful and what parts they continue to have the most concerns about. Parents are asked if they have any lingering concerns about the special playtimes or other issues they would like to share. These questions project an attitude of continuing concern on the part of the therapist for parents in the group.

Depending on the size of the group, the discussion time on these topics will need to be limited. Avoid getting bogged down in new concerns of major significance that may not be of interest to the rest of the group. Keep the interaction moving and focused.

III. Review Handout: *Rules of Thumb & Other Things to Remember* (refer parents to pages 67 & 68 in the *Parent Notebook*)

Ask parents to share the Rule of Thumb that has been most meaningful for them.

(See *Therapist Notebook*)

IV. Closing Process

- Review important things each parent learned

- Discuss how each perceives their child now as compared with 10 weeks ago

   Review notes from *Parent Information Form*

   o   Encourage feedback within group on positive changes made

   o   Has the child really changed that much or has the parent's perception changed, i.e., become more accepting?

How Child Behaviors Have Changed

The therapist shares her notes of parents' original descriptions of their children as points of reference for parents to evaluate progress. This sharing usually facilitates accounts of dramatic changes and tremendous insight on the part of the parents.

Below is a sample exchange during a training session between the therapist and the parents, followed by a summary of behavior changes reported in other group members' children:

Dr. L.:   *Ten weeks ago, as you were talking about your child of focus, I wrote down your descriptions. I'd like to read these descriptions, and then you give us an update on what your child is like now. Jan, in our first session, you said Jennifer does a lot of attention seeking, especially at bedtime. She has severe headaches and gets attention because of her medication and medical problem. She doesn't get along very well with other children. She's been like a little adult. She argues a lot. She has several seizures a day and the medication doesn't help. You said, "I think she has learned to cause her own seizures to get attention." Has any of that changed?*

Jan: *Yes. She had only one seizure in the past four weeks and has complained of a headache only three or four times in the past four or five weeks.*

(Group applauds)

Dr. L.:   *What a dramatic change! That is a super report.*

Jan: *She was having as many as 10 seizures a day on some days.*

Dr. L.: *What has made the difference, Jan?*

Jan: *Well, I think a lot of it, ah…well, I've probably made some difference by the way I respond to her. I know the playtimes have really helped her.*

Dr. L.: *Yes, you have made a difference in your child's life.*

Jan: *She seems happier now. And there's a lot less stress at home.*

This is a remarkable description of behavior change, especially when considering the short time span of only 10 weeks. However, this description is not atypical of descriptions given by parents when they report behavioral changes in the 10th session. In the first CPRT training session, Erin described her 2-year-old daughter as a strong-willed child. She reported that they often engaged in power struggles, and that from the moment that her daughter was born, she found it difficult to connect with her. In the 10th session, Erin stated, with tears in her eyes, that she finally loved her daughter. She had stopped punishing her and was able to spend more quality time with her.

In Session 1, Michal reported that she rocked her 4-year-old daughter to sleep in her stroller every night in order to avoid bedtime arguments. In the 10th session, Michal reported that her daughter was going to sleep on her own, and that their relationship was much more calm and loving. She also stated her relationship with her two teenagers had improved and was now based on attitudes of understanding and respect.

In Session 1, Jeanie expressed fear of her 7-year-old son's anger and aggression. She wept as she described his behavior problems in school, her inability to control his behavior at home, and her shame. After two play sessions, she reported progress in her son's behavior and how excited he was that she was taking a class to learn how to play with him. In the 10th session, Jeanie beamed with excitement as she said her son was no longer angry or out of control, there were no behavioral problems at school, and she was no longer afraid of her son. She particularly benefited from the homework assignment in which she wrote her son a note saying she appreciated his honesty and mailed it to him. He was excited about the note and asked her hopefully, "Is it true?" The note had such an impact on her son that she decided to e-mail the exercise to all of her friends, as well as the school counselor.

How Parents Have Changed

Asking parents how they are different now, how they have changed, or how their feelings about their children have changed facilitates opportunities for insight and can result in parents feeling more empowered. Parents need an opportunity to formulate new descriptions of themselves. Succinctly summarizing parents' descriptions of themselves helps them to recognize their changes and their accomplishments.

Below is another sample exchange during Session 10 between the therapist and the parents:

Dr. L.: *Group, how are you different now?*

Kim: *I believed that parents had to be in charge of every single thing that kids did. I expected my children to make decisions and to behave kind of like adults. Now I see my children as so much more. They're not an extension of me. They are different. They are unique. Now my son knows I'm going to love him for who he is, and that I still love him and trust him even if he doesn't make the right choices.*

Sonya: *I was a sergeant-of-arms with my daughter, and we usually got into power struggles. Our interactions were like open-heart surgery crisis-type; I mean screaming and crying and slamming doors. My anger was abrupt and quick, and we yelled and hollered at each other at least four or five times a day. Now, I know a lot of her behavior is kinda normal, and I'm more accepting of her. CPRT has taught me how to set limits without getting angry to make my point.*

Debbie: *I used to yell at my daughter all the time. I don't do that anymore, so there's less stress. I spend more time with her now. I feel more in control. Even when I make a mistake, and things go wrong, I know I can do it differently next time.*

Laura: *I had a lot of my self-worth tied up in trying to make my children happy. I tried real hard not to do things that would make them mad at me. I felt completely responsible for their happiness. My children had to obey me so other people wouldn't think I was a bad mother. I learned in the play sessions that I don't have to fix things for my child. This one principle has changed my thinking and attitude about parenting. I have learned to acknowledge my children's feelings without having to fix them or do things for them. I can be there and offer what I have to offer, and I don't have to fix it.*

Kim: *I've discovered I don't have to be the perfect mom. I've been trying to be the perfect mom and provide everything for my child, meet all his needs, and I don't have to do that.*

Dr. L.: *And that feels good to you.*

Kim: *Yes, it does! It's a relief.*

Dr. L.: *Debbie, you're shaking your head.*

Debbie: *Yeah, I feel less stressed and a lot better about myself and the way I am responding to my daughter. I know I can handle the problems now. Before, I didn't think I could, so I wouldn't even try.*

Kathy: *I feel closer to my son. I don't love him any more, but I feel closer. I listen to him better now. I don't turn him off.*

Emily: *I'm more ready to be a parent now. I haven't had special playtimes with my other children, but I respond differently to them. I have realized that these situations with my children don't have to be resolved immediately, that it often takes time to work through the process.*

Sonya: *I would do this training forever even if I was perfect doing the techniques, because of the support of everyone in this group. And not just that, but also because we have Dr. Landreth sitting here, who is supposed to know everything. And he takes the pressure off when he doesn't know the answer by just saying, "I don't know." I need to know if I'm going to screw my kid up. I'll really miss that.*

Laura: *It's just nice having an outlet, somebody you can talk to that knows what you're talking about; a person who knows and understands and touches on your feelings; somebody who cares about you.*

Debbie: *The special playtimes started out being for my daughter, but now they are for me, too. I came from a really bad family background, and I don't have a good parenting role model; so you (Dr. L) have become my parent role model figure. I need more of this.*

Kim: *I wish this could be a once-a-week session until the kids are all grown! The supporting atmosphere with positive suggestions, comments, and stories in a safe, caring, nonjudgmental atmosphere is so wonderful. We didn't analyze what we were doing wrong, so there was no guilt trip.*

Emily: *Recently, my family experienced some problems, and I was truly grateful for the skills I learned here, because I think they helped keep some difficult times from going into disastrous times. When things got out of hand, I was aware of how automatically some of the new skills came to mind.*

It can also be helpful to ask parents to compare and contrast what is currently occurring in their family to what was happening 10 weeks ago, and what is currently happening in the play sessions to what happened in the first special playtime. The objective is to send parents away feeling empowered.

Parents Evaluate the Experience:

Parents are asked to share their reactions to the CPRT training and what part of the training has been most helpful to them. Sharing on this topic provides opportunities for review of basic skills that can serve as a reminder to parents of skills they will need to continue to focus on and utilize with their children. Parents can also be asked to share how what they have learned has been transferred or generalized to other children in the family. One mom shared about her increased confidence in a note, "I never dreamed parenting could be so easy and so very rewarding!!!"

Another parent from an earlier CPRT group with Dr. L had this to say:

"What I have learned from this experience has affected all areas of my life. In the group, I saw firsthand how feelings I reject in myself build a wall of shame internally and a wall of judgment and arrogance externally. I have learned to trust my feelings of rejection toward others as a guide to reclaiming that lost part of myself that they have brought to my attention.

I know that my son will still struggle and sometimes fail. I will still make mistakes that will deeply hurt him, and we will both experience painful feelings, but I no longer believe that to be healed means to never feel insecure or ashamed. Instead, I will strive to honor these feelings as an important part of us.

Through this experience, I have learned to value wholeness more than healing, allowing myself to embrace that part of me that will always be wounded. I have also come to know that finding my place in the world does not require me to be better or the best. In fact, those strivings have gotten in the way of belonging. As I learned to allow Dylan (my son) and myself to express our true feelings, I learned to appreciate that our emotional experience is what guides us, not just to a connection with each other, but to the depths of our being and to all that has been created."

V.   Decide on a Date and Time for Follow-Up Meetings

Ask for a volunteer to coordinate and suggest parents write the date, time, and volunteer name in blanks provided on their homework sheet:

Date and time for follow-up meetings: _____

Volunteer meeting coordinator: _____

Make sure parents (with consent) give phone numbers to the coordinator to make a phone list

Optional: Date & Time for follow-up with Therapist _____

Parents may be scared about their ability to continue what they have learned without the safety and support of the group! Discuss whether or not you, the therapist, should attend meetings.

If meetings are not scheduled, consider encouraging the group to exchange names and contact information for future support.

VI.   Homework Assignments: Emphasize the Importance of Continuing Play Sessions
(refer parents to homework section in their notebook)

(See *Therapist Notebook*)

Make arrangements as needed for parents who want to continue play sessions with the child of focus and/or begin special playtime with a child other than their child of focus

Hand out additional appointment cards as needed

(See Appendix A on CD-ROM for *Appointment Cards*)

Discuss with parents the need to start play sessions with other children in the family. Assess parents' need for support. If older children are to be involved, appropriate toys and materials will need to be discussed.

Schedule additional professional help for parents and/or children needing such help

Have parents turn to the contract in the homework section and determine the number of sessions they will have before the follow-up meeting. Ask them to sign contract:

1) Continue play sessions: If you stop now, the message is that you were playing with your child because you had to, not because you wanted to:

   I agree to continue my play sessions with my child of focus for ___ weeks and/or begin sessions with _____ and do for ___ weeks.

After parents complete their 10 sessions of training, about half of them tend to stop having special playtimes. The reasons vary—parents become involved in other projects that they placed on hold while they were in CPRT training; they no longer have the group or the therapist to answer to; or their children's behavior has improved, so they no longer feel a sense of urgency to get something done. The importance of encouraging parents to continue having their special playtimes cannot be overly emphasized.

The 10 sessions of CPRT training are considered to be minimal, and parents with children who have more severe problems certainly need more extensive training to equip them with the skills required. However, in all cases, parents should be encouraged to continue having their special playtimes.

One parent reported that the most important thing Dr. L. said to her group at the very end was that if they had trouble with something in the future and wanted to call him for support, they could, but because most situations that come up can be resolved by parents returning to play sessions, the first thing he would say would be, "Are you doing play sessions?" Many times in the next few years, when the parent had doubts about her parenting abilities and thought of calling him, she said she remembered what he said, skipped the call, and just started play sessions again. She reported that the play sessions worked every time for both of her children. She and her children did play sessions off and on until they were teenagers, then they just talked. She said it did wonders for her confidence as a parent to know she already had the answer—do play sessions!

Introduce this Rule of Thumb to emphasize the importance of continuing play sessions:

☞ **Rule of Thumb: "Good things come in small packages."**

   Don't wait for big events to enter into your child's world—the little ways are always with us. Hold onto precious moments!

VII. Recommended Reading:

(Refer parents to reading list on parent handout below homework assignment)

1.   *Relational Parenting* (2000) and *How to Really Love Your* Child (1992), Ross Campbell

2.   *Between Parent and Child* (1956), Haim Ginott

3.   *Liberated Parents, Liberated Children* (1990), Adele Faber and Elaine Mazlish

4.   *How to Talk So Kids Will Listen and Listen So Kids Will Talk* (2002), Adele Faber and Elaine Mazlish

5.   *"SAY WHAT YOU SEE" for Parents and Teachers* (2005), Sandra Blackard (Free online resource available at www.languageoflistening.com)

VIII. Hand Out *Certificate of Completion* to each parent

Prepare certificates ahead of time to hand out at end of session. (See Appendix A on CD-ROM)

IX. Close With Motivational Poem, Story, or Rule of Thumb (optional)

CHILD PARENT RELATIONSHIP (C-P-R) TRAINING

PARENT NOTEBOOK

Parent Handouts, Notes, and Homework Sessions 1-10

Using Parent Notebook

The **Parent Notebook** includes all of the printed materials that parents will need to complete CPRT training. It is strongly recommended that the entire *Parent Notebook* be printed from the CD-ROM (rather than copied from this manual). The CD-ROM version of the *Parent Notebook* provides for correct pagination (to correspond with the page numbers in the *Parent Notebook* that are referred to in the Treatment Outlines in the *Therapist Notebook)*. We suggest organizing the notebook into a three-ring binder to be given to each parent on the first day of training. However, some therapists may prefer to hand out the materials one section at a time at the beginning of each session. Providing tabs to identify each session enhances usability of the *Parent Notebook*. Other useful strategies for the organization of training materials include printing the two most used handouts, *Dos and Don'ts* and *Play Session Procedures Checklist,* on two different colors of paper or using tabs or similar tools to provide an easy method for parents to locate them in their notebooks (both handouts are introduced in Session 3, but referred to in every session thereafter).

Handouts are organized by the CPRT training session they are typically used in. Some flexibility in presenting materials is allowed, depending on the needs of a particular group of parents. Supplemental skill practice worksheets for parents are also included in Appendix C on the accompanying CD-ROM. Although these supplemental worksheets are provided as additional practice for CPRT skills that a particular group of parents may be having difficulty with, the therapist is cautioned to avoid over-whelming parents with too much information or homework. Again, it is expected that the therapist will exercise clinical judgment in determining when and if to use supplemental materials.

Please note that permission to copy the materials is granted to the therapist in conjunction with the purchase of this training. The copyright statement on the cover page of the *Parent Notebook* should be printed out and included in the notebook handed out to parents.

CHILD-PARENT-RELATIONSHIP (C-P-R) TRAINING
Parent Notes & Homework – Session 1

👍 RULES OF THUMB TO REMEMBER:

1. **"Focus on the donut, not the hole!"** Focus on the Relationship, NOT the Problem.
2. **"Be a thermostat, not a thermometer."** Learn to RESPOND (reflect) rather than REACT.
3. **"What's most important may not be what you do, but what you do after what you did!"**
   We all make mistakes, but we can recover. It is how we handle our mistakes that makes the difference.

Reflective Responding:

A way of following, rather than leading

Reflect behaviors, thoughts, needs/wishes, and feelings (<u>without asking questions</u>)

Helps parent understand child <u>and</u> helps child feel understood

"Be With" Attitudes Convey:	Not:
I am here; I <u>hear</u> you	I always agree
I understand	I must make you happy
I care	I will solve your problems

Notes (use back for additional notes):

_____

_____

_____

_____

_____

_____

_____

_____

Homework Assignments:

1. Notice one physical characteristic about your child you haven't seen before.

---

2. Practice reflective responding (complete ***Feeling Response: Homework Worksheet*** and bring next week).
3. Bring your favorite, heart-tugging picture of your child of focus.
4. Practice giving a 30-second Burst of Attention. If you are on the telephone, say, "Can you hold for 30 seconds? I'll be right back." Put the phone aside, bend down, and give your child undivided, focused attention for 30 seconds; then say, "I have to finish talking to ____." Stand back up and continue talking with your friend.

184

CHILD-PARENT-RELATIONSHIP (C-P-R) TRAINING
Feelings Response: In-Class Practice Worksheet – Session 1

Directions: 1) Look into child's eyes for clue to feeling. 2) After you've decided what child is feeling, put the feeling word into a short response, generally beginning with <u>you</u>, "you seem sad," or "you're really mad at me right now." 3) Your facial expression & tone of voice should match your child's (empathy is conveyed more through nonverbals than verbals).

HAPPY

Child: Adam is telling you all the things he's going to show Grandma and Grandpa when they get to your house.

Child Felt: _____

Parent Response: _____

SAD

Child: Sally gets in the car after school and tells you that Bert, the class pet hamster, died—and then tells you about how she was in charge of feeding Bert last week and how he would look at her and then get on his wheel and run.

Child Felt: _____

Parent Response: _____
_____

MAD

Child: Andy was playing with his friend, Harry, when Harry grabbed Andy's fire truck and wouldn't give it back. Andy tried to get it back and the ladder broke off. Andy comes to you crying and tells you what happened and that it's all Harry's fault.

Child Felt: _____

Parent Response: _____

SCARED

Child: Sarah was playing in the garage while you were cleaning it out, when a big box of books falls off the shelf and hits the floor behind her. She jumps up and runs over to you.

Child Felt: _____

Parent Response: _____

CHILD-PARENT-RELATIONSHIP (C-P-R) TRAINING
Feelings Response: Homework Worksheet – Session 1

Directions: 1) Look into child's eyes for clue to feeling. 2) After you've decided what child is feeling, put the feeling word into a short response, generally beginning with <u>you</u>, "you seem sad," or "you're really mad at me right now." 3) Remember the importance of your facial expression & tone of voice matching child's (empathy is conveyed more through nonverbals than verbals).

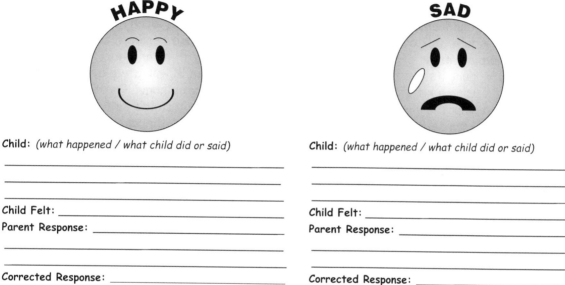

HAPPY

Child: *(what happened / what child did or said)*

_____
_____
_____

Child Felt: _____
Parent Response: _____
_____
_____

Corrected Response: _____
_____
_____

SAD

Child: *(what happened / what child did or said)*

_____
_____
_____

Child Felt: _____
Parent Response: _____
_____
_____

Corrected Response: _____
_____
_____

MAD

Child: *(what happened / what child did or said)*

_____
_____
_____

Child Felt: _____
Parent Response: _____
_____
_____

Corrected Response: _____
_____
_____

SCARED

Child: *(what happened / what child did or said)*

_____
_____
_____

Child Felt: _____
Parent Response: _____
_____
_____

Corrected Response: _____
_____
_____

CHILD-PARENT-RELATIONSHIP (C-P-R) TRAINING
What Is It and How Can It Help?

What Is It?

Child-Parent-Relationship (C-P-R) Training is a special 10-session parent training program to help strengthen the relationship between a parent and a child by using 30-minute playtimes once a week. Play is important to children because it is the most natural way children communicate. Toys are like words for children and play is their language. Adults talk about their experiences, thoughts, and feelings. Children use toys to explore their experiences and express what they think and how they feel. Therefore, parents are taught to have special structured 30-minute playtimes with their child using a kit of carefully selected toys in their own home. Parents learn how to respond empathically to their child's feelings, build their child's self-esteem, help their child learn self-control and self-responsibility, and set therapeutic limits during these special playtimes.

For 30 minutes each week, the child is the center of the parent's universe. In this special playtime, the parent creates an accepting relationship in which a child feels completely safe to express himself through his play—fears, likes, dislikes, wishes, anger, loneliness, joy, or feelings of failure. This is not a typical playtime. It is a special playtime in which the child leads and the parent follows. In this special relationship, there are no:

+ Reprimands
+ Put-downs
+ Evaluations
+ Requirements (to draw pictures a certain way, etc.)
+ Judgments (about the child or his play as being good or bad, right or wrong)

How Can It Help My Child?

In the special playtimes, you will build a different kind of relationship with your child, and your child will discover that she is capable, important, understood, and accepted as she is. When children experience a play relationship in which they feel accepted, understood, and cared for, they play out many of their problems and, in the process, release tensions, feelings, and burdens. Your child will then feel better about herself and will be able to discover her own strengths and assume greater self-responsibility as she takes charge of play situations.

How your child feels about herself will make a significant difference in her behavior. In the special playtimes where you learn to focus on your child rather than your child's problem, your child will begin to react differently because how your child behaves, how she thinks, and how she performs in school are directly related to how she feels about herself. When your child feels better about herself, she will behave in more self-enhancing ways rather than self-defeating ways.

CHILD-PARENT-RELATIONSHIP (C-P-R) TRAINING
Parent Notes & Homework – Session 2

☙ RULES OF THUMB TO REMEMBER:

1. **"The parent's toes should follow his/her nose."**

2. **"You can't give away that which you don't possess."** You can't extend patience and acceptance to your child if you can't first offer it to yourself. As your child's most significant caregiver, you are asked to give so much of yourself, often when you simply don't have the resources within you to meet the demands of parenting. As parents, you may be deeply aware of your own failures, yet you can't extend patience and acceptance to your child while being impatient and un-accepting of yourself.

Remember the analogy of the oxygen mask on an airplane!

Remember the "BE WITH" ATTITUDES: I'm here, I hear you, I understand, and I care!

Notes (use back for additional notes):

_____
_____
_____
_____
_____
_____
_____
_____
_____
_____
_____
_____
_____
_____
_____
_____
_____

Homework Assignments:

1. Priority—Collect toys on *Toy Checklist for Play Sessions*.

2. Select a consistent time and an uninterrupted place in the home suitable for the play sessions and report back next week—whatever room you feel offers the fewest distractions to the child and the greatest freedom from worry about breaking things or making a mess. Set aside a regular time in advance. This time is to be undisturbed—no phone calls or interruptions by other children.

Time _____ Place _____

3. Additional assignment:

CHILD-PARENT-RELATIONSHIP (C-P-R) TRAINING
Basic Principles of Play Sessions – Session 2

Basic Principles for Play Sessions:

1. The parent sets the stage by structuring an atmosphere in which the **child feels free** to determine how he will use the time during the 30-minute play session. The **child leads** the play and the **parent follows**. The parent follows the child's lead by showing keen interest and carefully observing the child's play, **without making suggestions or asking questions**, and by actively joining in the play when invited by the child. *For 30 minutes, you (parent) are "dumb" and don't have the answers; it is up to your child to make his own decisions and find his own solutions.*

2. The parent's major task is to empathize with the child: to understand the child's thoughts, feelings, and intent expressed in play by working hard to **see and experience the child's play through the child's eyes.** *This task is operationalized by conveying the "Be With" Attitudes below.*

3. The parent is then to **communicate this understanding to the child** by: a) verbally describing what the child is doing/playing, b) verbally reflecting what the child is saying, and c) most importantly, by verbally reflecting the feelings that the child is actively experiencing through his play.

4. The parent is to be clear and firm about the few "limits" that are placed on the child's behavior. Limits are stated in a way that give the child responsibility for his actions and behaviors—helping to foster self-control. Limits to be set are: time limits, not breaking toys or damaging items in the play area, and not physically hurting self or parent. **Limits are to be stated only when needed,** but applied consistently across sessions. *(Specific examples of when and how to set limits will be taught over the next several weeks; you will also have lots of opportunities to practice this very important skill.)*

"Be With" Attitudes:
Your <u>intent</u> in your actions, presence, and responses is what is most important and should convey to your child:
"I am here—I hear/see you—I understand—I care."

Goals of the Play Sessions:

1. To allow the child—through the medium of play—to communicate thoughts, needs, and feelings to his parent, and for the parent to communicate that understanding back to the child.

2. Through feeling accepted, understood, and valued—for the child to experience more positive feelings of self-respect, self-worth, confidence, and competence—and ultimately develop self-control, responsibility for actions, and learn to get needs met in appropriate ways.

3. To strengthen the parent-child relationship and foster a sense of trust, security, and closeness for both parent and child.

4. To increase the level of playfulness and enjoyment between parent and child.

CHILD-PARENT-RELATIONSHIP (C-P-R) TRAINING
Toy Checklist for Play Sessions – Session 2

Note: Obtain sturdy cardboard box with sturdy lid to store toys in (box that copier paper comes in is ideal–the deep lid becomes a dollhouse). Use an old quilt or blanket to spread toys out on and to serve as a boundary for the play area.

Real-Life Toys (also promote imaginative play)
- ☐ Small baby doll: *should not be anything "special"; can be extra one that child does not play with anymore*
- ☐ Nursing bottle: *real one so it can be used by the child to put a drink in during the session*
- ☐ Doctor kit (with stethoscope): *add three Band-Aids for each session (add disposable gloves/Ace bandage, if you have)*
- ☐ Toy phones: *recommend getting two in order to communicate: one cell, one regular*
- ☐ Small dollhouse: *use deep lid of box the toys are stored in–draw room divisions, windows, doors, and so forth inside of lid*
- ☐ Doll family: *bendable mother, father, brother, sister, baby, and so forth (ethnically representative)*
- ☐ Play money: *bills and coins; credit card is optional*
- ☐ Couple of domestic and wild animals: *if you don't have doll family, can substitute an animal family (e.g., horse, cow family)*
- ☐ Car/Truck: *one to two small ones (could make specific to child's needs, e.g., an ambulance)*
- ☐ Kitchen dishes: *couple of plastic dishes, cups, and eating utensils*

Optional
- ☐ Puppets: *one aggressive, one gentle; can be homemade or purchased (animal shaped cooking mittens, etc.)*
- ☐ Doll furniture: *for a bedroom, bathroom, and kitchen*
- ☐ Dress up: *hand mirror, bandana, scarf; small items you already have around the house*

Acting-Out Aggressive Toys (also promote imaginative play)
- ☐ Dart guns with a couple of darts and a target: *parent needs to know how to operate*
- ☐ Rubber knife: *small, bendable, army type*
- ☐ Rope: *prefer soft rope (can cut the ends off jump rope)*
- ☐ Aggressive animal: *(e.g., snake, shark, lion, dinosaurs—strongly suggest hollow shark!)*
- ☐ Small toy soldiers (12–15): *two different colors to specify two teams or good guys/bad guys*
- ☐ Inflatable bop bag (Bobo *clown style preferable*)
- ☐ Mask: *Lone Ranger type*

Optional
- ☐ Toy handcuffs with a key

Toys for Creative/Emotional Expression
- ☐ Playdough: *suggest a cookie sheet to put playdough on to contain mess—also serves as a flat surface for drawing*
- ☐ Crayons: *eight colors, break some and peel paper off (markers are optional for older children but messier)*
- ☐ Plain paper: *provide a few pieces of new paper for each session*
- ☐ Scissors: *not pointed, but cut well (e.g., child Fiskars®)*
- ☐ Transparent tape: *remember, child can use up all of this, so buy several of smaller size*
- ☐ Egg carton, styrofoam cup/bowl: *for destroying, breaking, or coloring*
- ☐ Ring toss game
- ☐ Deck of playing cards
- ☐ Soft foam ball
- ☐ Two balloons per play session

Optional
- ☐ Selection of arts/crafts materials in a ziplock bag *(e.g., colored construction paper, glue, yarn, buttons, beads, scraps of fabrics, raw noodles, etc —much of this depends on age of child)*
- ☐ Tinkertoys®/small assortment of building blocks
- ☐ Binoculars
- ☐ Tambourine, drum, or other small musical instrument
- ☐ Magic wand

Reminder: *Toys need not be new or expensive. Avoid selecting more toys than will fit in a box—toys should be small. In some cases, additional toys can be added based on child's need and with therapist approval. If unable to get every toy before first play session, obtain several from each category—ask therapist for help in prioritizing.*

Note: Unwrap any new toys or take out of box before play session. Toys should look inviting.

Good Toy Hunting Places: garage sales, attic, friends/relatives, "dollar" stores, toy aisles of grocery and drug stores

CHILD-PARENT-RELATIONSHIP (C-P-R) TRAINING
Parent Notes & Homework – Session 3

👍 RULE OF THUMB TO REMEMBER:

"Be a thermostat, not a thermometer."
Reflecting/responding to your child's thoughts, feelings, and needs
creates a comfortable atmosphere of understanding and acceptance for your child.

Basic Limit Setting:

"Sarah, "I know you'd like to shoot the gun at me, but I'm not for shooting. You can choose to shoot at that" (point at something <u>acceptable</u>).

Notes (use back for additional notes):

_____
_____
_____
_____
_____
_____
_____
_____
_____
_____
_____
_____
_____
_____
_____
_____

<u>Note</u>: You may wish to explain to your child that you are having these special playtimes with him or her because "I am going to this special play class to learn some special ways to play with you!"

Homework Assignments:

1. Complete play session toy kit—get blanket/quilt and other materials. (see *Photograph of Toys Set Up for Play Session* in handouts) and confirm that the time and place you chose will work. Make arrangements for other children.

2. Give child appointment card and make "Special Playtime—Do Not Disturb" sign with child one to three days ahead (depending on child's age). See Template for Do Not Disturb Sign in handouts.

3. Read over handouts prior to play session:
   Play Session Do's & Don'ts
   Play Session Procedures Checklist

4. Play sessions begin at home this week—arrange to videotape your session and make notes about problems or questions you have about your sessions.

_____ ***I will bring my videotape for next week (if videotaping at clinic: my appt. day/time _____).***

CHILD-PARENT-RELATIONSHIP (C-P-R) TRAINING
Play Session Do's & Don'ts – Session 3

Parents: Your major task is to keenly show interest in your child's play and to communicate your interest in, and understanding of, your child's thoughts, feelings, and behavior through your words, actions, and undivided focus on your child.

<u>Do:</u>

1. Do set the stage.
- a. Prepare play area ahead of time (old blanket can be used to establish a visual boundary of the play area, as well as provide protection for flooring; a cookie sheet under the arts/crafts materials provides a hard surface for playdough, drawing, and gluing, and provides ease of clean up).
- b. Display the toys in a consistent manner around the perimeter of the play area.
- c. Convey freedom of the special playtime through your words: *"During our special playtime, <u>you</u> can play with the toys in lots of the ways you'd like to."*
- d. Allow your child to lead by <u>returning responsibility</u> to your child by responding, *"That's up to <u>you</u>," "You can decide,"* or *"That can be whatever <u>you</u> want it to be."*

2. Do let the child lead.
Allowing the child to lead during the playtime helps you to better understand your child's world and what your child needs from you. Convey your willingness to follow your child's lead through your responses: *"Show me what <u>you</u> want me to do," "<u>You</u> want me to put that on,"* "Hmmm…," or "I wonder…." Use whisper technique (co-conspirators) when child wants you to play a role: *"What should I say?"* or *"What happens next?"* (Modify responses for older kids: use conspiratorial tone, *"What happens now?" "What kind of teacher am I?"* etc.)

3. Do join in the child's play actively, as a follower.
Convey your willingness to follow your child's lead through your responses and your actions, by actively joining in the play (child is the director, parent is the actor): *"So I'm supposed to be the teacher," "<u>You</u> want me to be the robber, and I'm supposed to wear the black mask," "Now I'm supposed to pretend I'm locked up in jail, until <u>you</u> say I can get out,"* or *"<u>You</u> want me to stack these just as high as yours."* Use whisper technique in role-play: *"What should I say?" "What happens next?"*

4. Do verbally track the child's play (describe what you see).
Verbally tracking your child's play is a way of letting your child know that you are paying close attention and that you are interested and involved: *"<u>You're</u> filling that all the way to the top," "<u>You've</u> decided you want to paint next,"* or *"<u>You've</u> got 'em all lined up just how you want them."*

5. Do reflect the child's feelings.
Verbally reflecting children's feelings helps them feel understood and communicates your acceptance of their feelings and needs: *"<u>You're</u> proud of your picture," "That kind'a surprised <u>you</u>," "<u>You</u> really like how that feels on your hands," "<u>You</u> really wish that we could play longer," "<u>You</u> don't like the way that turned out,"* or *"<u>You</u> sound disappointed."* (<u>Hint: Look closely at your child's face to better identify how your child is feeling.</u>)

6. Do set firm and consistent limits.
Consistent limits create a structure for a safe and predictable environment for children. Children should never be permitted to hurt themselves or you. Limit setting provides an opportunity for your child to develop self-control and self-responsibility. Using a calm, patient, yet firm voice, say, *"The floor's not for putting playdough on; you can play with it on the tray"* or *"I know you'd like to shoot the gun at me, but I'm not for shooting. You can choose to shoot at that"*(point to something acceptable).

7. Do salute the child's power and encourage effort.
Verbally recognizing and encouraging your child's effort builds self-esteem and confidence and promotes self-motivation: *"<u>You</u> worked hard on that!" "<u>You</u> did it!" "<u>You</u> figured it out!" "<u>You've</u> got a plan for how you're gonna set those up," "<u>You</u> know just how you want that to be,"* or *"Sounds like <u>you</u> know lots about how to take care of babies."*

8. Do be verbally active.
Being verbally active communicates to your child that you are interested and involved in her play. If you are silent, your child will feel watched.
Note: Empathic grunts—"Hmm…"and so forth—also convey interest and involvement, when you are unsure of how to respond.

<u>Don't:</u>
1. Don't criticize any behavior.
2. Don't praise the child.
3. Don't ask leading questions.
4. Don't allow interruptions of the session.
5. Don't give information or teach.
6. Don't preach.
7. Don't initiate new activities.
8. Don't be passive or quiet.
   (Don'ts 1–7 are taken from Guerney, 1972)

Remember the "Be With" Attitudes: Your intent in your responses is what is most important. Convey to your child:
"I am here—I hear/see you—I understand—I care."

Reminder: These play session skills (the new skills you are applying) are relatively meaningless if applied mechanically and not as an attempt to be genuinely empathic and truly understanding of your child. **Your Intent & Attitude Are More Important Than Your Words!**

CHILD-PARENT-RELATIONSHIP (C-P-R) TRAINING
Play Session Procedures Checklist – Session 3

Depending on age of child, may need to remind him or her: "Today is the day for our special playtime!"

A. Prior to Session (Remember to "Set the Stage")
- ☐ Make arrangements for other family members (so that there will be no interruptions).
- ☐ Set up toys on old quilt—keep toy placement predictable.
- ☐ Have a clock visible in the room (or wear a watch).
- ☐ Put pets outside or in another room.
- ☐ Let the child use the bathroom prior to the play session.
- ☐ Switch on video recorder.

B. Beginning the Session
- ☐ Child and Parent: Hang "Do Not Disturb" sign (can also "unplug" phone if there is one in play session area). *Message to child: "This is so important that <u>No One</u> is allowed to interrupt this time together."*
- ☐ Tell Child: *"We will have 30 minutes of special playtime, and you can play with the toys in lots of the ways you want to."* (Voice needs to convey that parent is looking forward to this time with child.)
- ☐ <u>From this point, let the child lead.</u>

C. During the Session
- ☐ Sit on the same level as child, close enough to show interest but allowing enough space for child to move freely.
- ☐ Focus your eyes, ears, and body fully on child. (<u>Toes Follow Nose!</u>) Conveys full attention!
- ☐ Your voice should mostly be gentle and caring, but vary with the intensity and affect of child's play.
- ☐ Allow the child to identify the toys. [To promote make-believe play (i.e., what looks like a car to you might be a spaceship to your child), try to use nonspecific words ("this," "that," "it") if child hasn't named toy.]
- ☐ Play actively with the child, if the child requests your participation.
- ☐ Verbally reflect what you see and hear (child's play/activity, thoughts, feelings).
- ☐ Set limits on behaviors that make you feel uncomfortable.
- ☐ Give five-minute advance notice for session's end and then a one-minute notice.
  (**"Billy, we have five minutes left in our special playtime."**)

D. Ending the Session
- ☐ At 30 minutes, <u>stand</u> and announce, **"Our playtime is over for today."** Do not exceed time limit by more than two to three minutes.
- ☐ Parent does the cleaning up. If child chooses, child may help. (If child continues to play while "cleaning," set limit below.)
- ☐ <u>If child has difficulty leaving:</u>
  - Open the door or begin to put away toys.
  - Reflect child's feelings about not wanting to leave, but calmly and firmly restate that the playtime is over. (Restate limit as many times as needed—the goal is for child to be able to stop herself.)
    "I know you would like to stay and play with the toys, but our special playtime is over for today."
  - Adding a statement that gives child something to look forward to helps child see that, although she cannot continue to play with the special toys, there is something else she can do that is also enjoyable. For example:
    1. **"You can play with the toys next week during our special playtime."**
    2. **"It's time for snack; would you like grapes or cherries today?"**
    3. **"We can go outside and play on the trampoline."**

<u>Note</u>: *Patience is the order of the day when helping child to leave—OK to repeat limit calmly several times to allow child to struggle with leaving on her own. (Key is showing empathy and understanding in your voice tone and facial expressions as you state the limit). Younger children may need more time to 'hear' limit and respond.*

> *Never use Special Playtime for a reward or consequence—NO matter the child's behavior that day!*

CHILD-PARENT-RELATIONSHIP (C-P-R) TRAINING
Photograph of Toys Set Up for Play Session – Session 3

CHILD-PARENT-RELATIONSHIP (C-P-R) TRAINING
Parent Notes & Homework – Session 4

☞ RULES OF THUMB TO REMEMBER:

1. **"When a child is drowning, don't try to teach her to swim."** When a child is feeling upset or out of control, that is not the moment to impart a rule or teach a lesson.

2. **"During play sessions, limits are not needed until they are needed!"**

Basic Limit Setting:

Start by saying child's name: *"Sarah,"*

Reflect feeling: *"I know you'd like to shoot the gun at me…"*

Set limit: *"but I'm not for shooting."*

Give acceptable alternative: *"You can choose to shoot at that"* (point at something *acceptable*).

Notes (use back for additional notes):

_____
_____
_____
_____
_____
_____
_____
_____
_____
_____
_____
_____
_____
_____
_____
_____

Homework Assignments:

1. Complete *Limit Setting: A-C-T Practice Worksheet.*

2. Read over handouts prior to play session:
   Limit Setting: A-C-T Before It's Too Late!
   Play Session Do's & Don'ts
   Play Session Procedures Checklist

3. Conduct play session and complete *Parent Play Session Notes.*
   Notice one intense feeling in yourself during your play session this week.

   _____ **I will bring my videotape for next week (if videotaping at clinic: my appt. day/time _____).**

CHILD-PARENT-RELATIONSHIP (C-P-R) TRAINING
Limit Setting: A-C-T Before It's Too Late! - Session 4

<u>A</u>cknowledge the feeling
<u>C</u>ommunicate the limit
<u>T</u>arget alternatives

Three Step A-C-T Method of Limit Setting:

Scenario: Billy has been pretending that the bop bag is a bad guy and shooting him with the dart gun; he looks over at you and aims the dart gun at you, then laughs and says, "Now, you're one of the bad guys, too!"

1. **A**cknowledge your child's feeling or desire (*your voice must convey empathy and understanding*).
   "Billy, I know that you think that it would be fun to shoot me, too…"
      Child learns that his feelings, desires, and wishes are valid and accepted by parent (but not all behavior); just empathically reflecting your child's feeling often defuses the intensity of the feeling or need.

2. **C**ommunicate the limit (be specific and clear—and brief).
   "But I'm not for shooting."

3. **T**arget acceptable alternatives (provide one or more choices, depending on age of child).
   "You can pretend that the doll is me (pointing at the doll) and shoot at it."
      The goal is to provide your child with an acceptable outlet for expressing the feeling or the original action, while giving him an opportunity to exercise self-control. Note: Pointing helps redirect child's attention.

When to Set Limits?

✑ **RULE OF THUMB: "During play sessions, limits are not needed until they are needed!"**
Limits are set only when the need arises, and for four basic reasons:
- To protect child from hurting himself or parent
- To protect valuable property
- To maintain parent's acceptance of child
- To provide consistency in the play session by limiting child and toys to play area and ending on time

Before setting a limit in a play session, ask yourself:
- "Is this limit necessary?"
- "Can I consistently enforce this limit?"
- "If I don't' set a limit on this behavior, can I consistently allow this behavior and accept my child?"

Avoid conducting play sessions in areas of the house that require too many limits. Limits set during play sessions should allow for greater freedom of expression than would normally be allowed. The fewer the limits, the easier it is for you to be consistent—**consistency is very important.** Determine a few limits ahead of time (practice A-C-T): no hitting or shooting at parent; no playdough on carpet; no purposefully breaking toys, and so forth. *Hint: Children really do understand that playtimes are "special" and that the rules are different—they will <u>not</u> expect the same level of permissiveness during the rest of the week.*

How to Set Limits?

Limits are not punitive and should be stated firmly, but calmly and matter-of-factly. After empathically acknowledging your child's feeling or desire (very important step), you state, "The playdough is not for throwing at the table," just like you would state, "The sky is blue." Don't try to force your child to obey the limit. Remember to provide an acceptable alternative. In this method, it really is up to the child to decide to accept or break the limit; however, **it is your job, as the parent, to consistently enforce the limit.**

Why Establish Consistent Limits?

Providing children with consistent limits helps them feel safe and secure. This method of limiting children's behavior teaches them self-control and responsibility for their own behavior by allowing them to experience the consequences of their choices and decisions. Limits set in play sessions help children practice self-control and begin to learn to stop themselves in the real world.

CONSISTENT LIMITS → PREDICTABLE, SAFE ENVIRONMENT → SENSE OF SECURITY

CHILD-PARENT-RELATIONSHIP (C-P-R) TRAINING
Limit Setting: A-C-T Practice Worksheet - Session 4

<u>A</u>cknowledge the feeling
<u>C</u>ommunicate the limit
<u>T</u>arget alternatives

EXAMPLE # 1

Billy has been playing like the bop bag is the bad guy and hitting him; he picks up the scissors, looks at you, and then laughs and says, "I'm going to stab him, because he's bad!"

<u>A</u> "Billy, I know that you think that it would be fun to stab the bop bag (bobo)…"

<u>C</u> "but the bop bag (bobo) isn't for poking with the scissors."

<u>T</u> "You can use the rubber knife."

EXAMPLE # 2

The play session time is up and you have stated the limit two times. Your child becomes angry because you won't give in and let him play longer; he begins to hit you. Hitting is not allowed, so go immediately to second step of A-C-T, then follow with all three steps of A-C-T method of limit setting.

<u>C</u> (firmly) "Billy, I'm not for hitting."

<u>A</u> (empathically) "I know you're mad at me…"

<u>C</u> (firmly) "But people aren't for hitting."

<u>T</u> (neutral tone) "You can pretend the bop bag is me and hit it (pointing at bop bag)."

PRACTICE:

1. Your child begins to color on the dollhouse, saying, "It needs some red curtains!"

   (assuming you bought a dollhouse; however, it would be okay to color on a cardboard box/dollhouse)

<u>A</u> I know you really want to _____.

<u>C</u> But the dollhouse _____.

<u>T</u> You can _____.

2. Your child aims a loaded dart gun at you.

<u>A</u> _____.

<u>C</u> _____.

<u>T</u> _____.

3. After 15 minutes of the play session, your child announces that she wants to leave and go outside to play with her friends.

A _____.

C _____.

T _____.

4. Your child wants to play doctor and asks you to be the patient. Your child asks you to pull up your shirt so that she/he can listen to your heart.

A _____.

C _____.

T _____.

5. Describe a situation in which you think you might need to set a limit during the play session.
Situation: _____
_____

A _____.

C _____.

T _____.

CHILD-PARENT-RELATIONSHIP (C-P-R) TRAINING
Parent Play Session Notes - Session 4

Play Session #_____ Date: _____

Significant Happenings:

What I Learned About My Child:

Feelings Expressed:

Play Themes:

What I Learned About Myself:

My feelings during the play session:

What I think I was best at:

What was hardest or most challenging for me:

Questions or Concerns:

Skill I Want to Focus on in the Next Play Session: _____

CHILD-PARENT-RELATIONSHIP (C-P-R) TRAINING
Parent Notes & Homework – Session 5

👍 RULE OF THUMB TO REMEMBER:

"If you can't say it in 10 words or less, don't say it."
As parents, we have a tendency to overexplain to our children,
and our message gets lost in the words.

Notes (use back for additional notes):

_____

Homework Assignments:

1. Give each of your children a Sandwich Hug and Sandwich Kiss.

2. Read over handouts prior to play session:
   Limit Setting: A-C-T Before It's Too Late!
   Play Session Dos & Don'ts
   Play Session Procedures Checklist

3. Conduct play session (same time & place).
   a. Complete *Parent Play Session Notes*.
   b. Use *Play Session Skills Checklist* to note what you thought you did well, and select one skill you want to work on in your next play session.
   a. If you needed to set a limit during your playtime, describe on the checklist what happened and what you said or did.

   ___ **I will bring my videotape for next week (if videotaping at clinic: my appt. day/time___).**

4. Additional assignment:

CHILD-PARENT-RELATIONSHIP (C-P-R) TRAINING
Limit Setting: Why Use the Three-Step A-C-T Method - Session 5

<u>A</u>cknowledge the feeling

<u>C</u>ommunicate the limit

<u>T</u>arget alternatives

Discuss the different messages that are implied in the following typical parent responses to unacceptable behavior:

- It's probably not a good idea to paint the wall.

  Message: _____

- You can't paint the walls in here.

  Message: _____

- I can't let you paint the wall.

  Message: _____

- Maybe you could paint something else other than the wall.

  Message: _____

- The rule is you can't paint the wall.

  Message: _____

- The wall is not for painting on.

  Message: _____

CHILD-PARENT-RELATIONSHIP (C-P-R) TRAINING
In-Class Play Session Skills Checklist:
For Review of Videotaped (or Live) Play Session – Session 5

Directions: Indicate ✓ in blank when you observe a play session skill demonstrated in videotaped or live play session

1. ____ Set the Stage/Structured Play Session

2. ____ Conveyed "Be With" Attitudes
   Full attention/interested
   Toes followed nose

3. ____ Allowed Child to Lead
   Avoided giving suggestions
   Avoided asking questions
   Returned responsibility to child

4. ____ Followed Child's Lead
   Physically on child's level
   Moved closer when child was involved in play
   Joined in play when invited—took imaginary/pretend role when appropriate

5. ____ Reflective Responding Skills:

   ____ Reflected child's nonverbal play behavior (Tracking)

   ____ Reflected child's verbalizations (Content)

   ____ Reflected child's feelings/wants/wishes

   ____ Voice tone matched child's intensity/affect

   ____ Responses were brief and interactive

   ____ Facial expressions matched child's affect

6. ____ Used Encouragement/Self-Esteem-Building Responses

7. ____ Set Limits, As Needed, Using A-C-T

CHILD-PARENT-RELATIONSHIP (C-P-R) TRAINING
Parent Play Session Notes – Session 5

Play Session #_____ Date: _____

Significant Happenings:

What I Learned About My Child:

Feelings Expressed:

Play Themes:

What I Learned About Myself:

My feelings during the play session:

What I think I was best at:

What was hardest or most challenging for me:

Questions or Concerns:

Skill I Want to Focus on in the Next Play Session: _____

CHILD-PARENT-RELATIONSHIP (C-P-R) TRAINING
Play Session Skills Checklist - Session 5

Play Session #_____ Date: _____

(Note: Indicate ✓ in column if skill was used; — if skill was not used; and + if skill was a strength)

✓ — +	Skill	Notes/Comments
	Set the Stage/Structured Play Session	

	Conveyed "Be With" Attitudes
	  Full attention/interested
	  Toes followed nose	

	Allowed Child to Lead
	  Avoided giving suggestions
	  Avoided asking questions
	  Returned responsibility to child	

	Followed Child's Lead
	  Physically on child's level
	  Moved closer when child was involved in play
	  Joined in play when invited	

	Reflective Responding Skills:	
	Reflected child's nonverbal play (Tracking)	
	Reflected child's verbalizations (Content)	
	Reflected child's feelings/wants/wishes	
	Voice tone matched child's intensity/affect	
	Responses were brief and interactive	
	Facial expressions matched child's affect	
	Use of Encouragement/Self-Esteem-Building Responses	
	Set Limits, As Needed, Using A-C-T	

CHILD-PARENT-RELATIONSHIP (C-P-R) TRAINING
Parent Notes & Homework – Session 6

☝ RULES OF THUMB TO REMEMBER:

1. **"Grant in fantasy what you can't grant in reality."** In a play session, it is okay to act out feelings and wishes that in reality may require limits. For example, it's okay for the "baby sister" doll to be thrown out a window in playtime.

2. **"Big choices for big kids, little choices for little kids."** Choices given must be commensurate with child's developmental stage.

Notes (use back for additional notes):

_____
_____
_____
_____
_____
_____
_____
_____
_____
_____
_____

Homework Assignments:

1. Read *Choice-Giving 101: Teaching Responsibility & Decision-Making* and *Advanced Choice-Giving: Providing Choices as Consequences.*

2. Read *Common Problems in Play Sessions* and mark the top two to three issues you have questions about or write in an issue you are challenged by that is not on the worksheet.

3. Practice giving at least one kind of choice ("A" or "B") outside of the play session.
   A. Provide choices for the sole purpose of_empowering your child (two positive choices for child, where either choice is acceptable to you and either choice is desirable to child)
   What happened _____
   What you said _____
   How child responded _____

   B. Practice giving choices as a <u>method of discipline</u> (where choice-giving is used to provide a consequence for noncompliance of limit, family rule, or policy)
   What happened _____
   What you said _____
   How child responded _____

4. Conduct play session (same time & place)—review *Play Session Do's & Don'ts & Play Session Procedure Checklist*
   a. Complete *Parent Play Session Notes.*
   b. Use *Play Session Skills Checklist* to note what you thought you did well, and select one skill you want to work on in your next play session.
   _____ I will bring my videotape for next week (if videotaping at clinic: my appt. day/time _____).

5. Additional assignment:

CHILD-PARENT-RELATIONSHIP (C-P-R) TRAINING
Choice-Giving 101: Teaching Responsibility & Decision-Making – Session 6

- Providing children with <u>age-appropriate</u> **choices empowers children** by allowing them a measure of control over their circumstances. Children who feel more empowered and "in control" are more capable of regulating their own behavior, a prerequisite for self-control. Choices require that children tap into their inner resources, rather than relying on parents (external resources) to stop their behavior or solve the problem for them. If parents always intervene, the child learns that "Mom or Dad will stop me if I get out of hand" or "Mom or Dad will figure out a solution if I get in a jam."

- **Presenting children with choices provides opportunities for decision-making and problem-solving.** Through practice with choice-making, children learn to accept responsibility for their choices and actions and learn they are competent and capable. Choice-giving facilitates the development of the child's conscience; as children are allowed to learn from their mistakes, they learn to weigh decisions based on possible consequences.

- **Providing children with choices reduces power struggles** between parent and child and, importantly, preserves the child-parent relationship. Both parent and child are empowered; parent is responsible for, or in control of, providing parameters for choices, and the child is responsible for, or in control of, his decision (within parent-determined parameters).

Choice-Giving Strategies

- **Provide age-appropriate choices** that are <u>equally acceptable to the child and to you</u>. Remember that you must be willing to live with the choice the child makes. Do not use choices to try and manipulate the child to do what you want by presenting one choice that you want the child to choose and a second choice that you know the child won't like.

- **Provide little choices to little kids; big choices to big kids.** *Example: A 3-year-old can only handle choosing between two shirts or two food items.* **"Sarah, do you want to wear your red dress or your pink dress to school?" "Sarah, do you want an apple or orange with your lunch?"**

Choice-Giving to Avoid Potential Problem Behavior and Power Struggles

Choices can be used to avoid a potential problem. Similar to the example above, <u>choices given are equally acceptable to parent and child</u>. In this case, choices are planned in advance by the parent to avoid problems that the child has a history of struggling with. In the example above, if Sarah has trouble getting dressed in the morning, provide a choice of what to wear the evening before (to avoid a struggle the next morning); after she has made the choice, take the dress out of the closet, ready for morning. Children who are given the responsibility for making a decision are more likely to abide by the decision.

In selecting choices to prevent problems, it is very important that parents understand the real problem that their child is struggling with. If your child always comes home hungry and wants something sweet, but you want him to have a healthy snack, plan ahead by having on hand at least two choices of healthy snacks that <u>your child likes.</u> Before he heads for the ice cream, say:

   "Billy, I bought grapes and cherries for snack; which would you like?"
Or, if you made your child's favorite cookies, and it is acceptable for your 5-year-old to have one or two cookies, say:

   "Billy, I made your favorite cookies today; would you like one cookie or two?"

<u>Hint</u>: This is another place where "structuring for success" can be applied by eliminating the majority of unacceptable snack items and stocking up on healthy snack items! Structuring your home environment to minimize conflict allows both you and your child to feel more "in control." Remember: **Be a thermostat!**

Suggested Reading for Parents: "Teaching Your Child to Choose," Parenting, October, 2002.

CHILD-PARENT-RELATIONSHIP (C-P-R) TRAINING
Advance Choice-Giving: Providing Choices as Consequences – Session 6-7

Children need parental guidance and discipline. In many instances, parents must make decisions for children—decisions that children are not mature enough to take responsibility for—such as bedtime, other matters of health and safety, and compliance with household policies and rules. However, parents can provide their children with some measure of control in the situation by providing choices.

Oreo® Cookie Method of Choice-Giving (from "Choices, Cookies, & Kids" video by Dr. Garry Landreth)

Example 1: Three-year-old Sarah is clutching a handful of Oreo® cookies, ready to eat them all (it is right before bedtime, and the parent knows it would not be healthy for Sarah to have all the cookies. But Sarah does not know that—she just knows that she wants cookies!): **"Sarah, you can choose to keep one of the cookies to eat and put the rest back, or you can put all of the cookies back—which do you choose?"** Or, if it is permissible to the parent for Sarah to have two cookies: **"Sarah, you can have one cookie or two—which do you choose?"**

Example 2: Three-year-old Sarah does not want to take her medicine and adamantly tells you so! Taking the medicine is not a choice—that is a given. But the parent can provide the child with some control over the situation by saying, **"Sarah, you can choose to have apple juice or orange juice with your medicine—which do you choose?"**

Example 3: Seven-year-old Billy is tired and cranky and refuses to get in the car to go home from Grandma and Grandpa's house. **"Billy, you can choose to sit in the front seat with Daddy, or you can choose to sit in the back seat with Sarah—which do you choose?"**

Choice-Giving to Enforce Household Policies and Rules

Choice-giving can be used to enforce household policies/rules. Begin by working on one at a time. In general, provide two choices—one is phrased positively (consequence for complying with policy), and the other choice (consequence for not complying with policy) is stated as a consequence that you believe your child would not prefer (such as giving up favorite TV show). Consequence for noncompliance should be relevant and logical rather than punitive, and it must be **enforceable.**

Example: A household rule has been established that toys in the family room must be picked up off the floor before dinner (children cannot seem to remember without being told repeatedly, and parent is feeling frustrated with constant reminders and power struggles).

"We are about to institute a new and significant policy within the confines of this domicile" (big words get children's attention!). **"When you choose to pick up your toys before dinner, you choose to watch 30 minutes of television after dinner. When you choose not to pick up your toys before dinner, you choose not to watch television after dinner."** *Note: Be sure to let children know when there are 10–15 minutes before dinner, so they can have time to pick up their toys.*

Children may be able to comply the first time you announce this new policy, because you have just informed them. But what is important is that you begin to allow your children to use their internal resources and self-control to remember the new policy without constant reminders. (Remember that the new policy was implemented because you were frustrated and tired of nagging!) So, the second night, parent says, **"Billy and Sarah, dinner will be ready in 10 minutes; it is time to pick up your toys."** Parent walks out. When it is time for dinner, parent goes back into room to announce dinner:

a) The toys have not been picked up—say nothing at that moment. After dinner, go back into family room and announce to children, **"Looks like you decided to not watch television tonight."** Even if children get busy picking up the toys, they have already chosen not to watch TV for this night. **"Oh, you're thinking that if you pick your toys up now that you can watch TV, but the policy is that toys have to be put away before dinner."** After children plead for another chance, *follow through on the consequence,* calmly and empathically stating: **"I know that you wish you would have chosen to put your toys away before dinner, so you could choose to watch TV now. Tomorrow night, you can choose to put your toys away before dinner and choose to watch TV."** *Some children will choose not to watch TV for several nights in a row!*

b) The children are busy picking up toys and have put most of them away. Parent says (as she helps with the few remaining toys to demonstrate spirit of cooperation and prevent delay of dinner), **"It's time for dinner—looks like you've chosen to watch TV after dinner tonight."**

Guidelines for Choice-Giving in Relation to Limit Setting and Consequences

- Enforce consequence **without fail** and **without anger.**
- Consequence is for "today" only—each day (or play session) should be a chance for a fresh start; a chance to have learned from the previous decision and resulting consequence; a chance to use internal resources to control "self" and make a different decision.
- **Reflect** child's choice with empathy, but remain firm. Consistency and follow-through are critical!
- Communicate choices in a matter-of-fact voice—power struggles are likely to result if child hears frustration or anger in parent's voice and believes parent is invested in one choice over another. Child must be free to choose consequence for noncompliance.

Caution: *Once your child has reached the stage of "out of control," your child may not be able to hear and process a choice. Take a step back and focus on your child's feelings, reflecting her feelings empathically while limiting unacceptable behavior and holding her, if necessary, to prevent her from hurting herself or you.*

CHILD-PARENT-RELATIONSHIP (C-P-R) TRAINING
Common Problems in Play Sessions – Session 6

Q: My child notices that I talk differently in the play sessions and wants me to talk normally. What should I do?

A: Say, "I sound different to you. That's my way of letting you know I heard what you said. Remember, I'm going to that special class to learn how to play with you." (The child may be: saying he notices the parent is different; having a surprise reaction to the verbal attention; annoyed by too much reflection of words; or saying he notices the difference in the parent's reflective-type responses. The child may also be saying he doesn't want the parent to change, because that will mean he must then change and adjust to the parent's new way of responding.)

Q: My child asks many questions during the play sessions and resents my not answering them. What should I do?

A: We always begin by reflecting the child's feelings. "You're angry at me." Sometimes a child feels insecure when a parent changes typical ways of responding and is angry because he doesn't know how to react. Your child may feel insecure and be trying to get your attention the way he has done in the past. Your objective is to encourage your child's self-reliance and self-acceptance. "In our special playtime, the answer can be anything you want it to be." For example, your child might ask, "What should I draw?" You want your child to know he's in charge of his drawing during the special playtime, so you respond, "You've decided to draw, and in this special playtime, you can draw whatever you decide." Our objective is to empower the child, to enable the child to discover his own strengths.

Q: My child just plays and has fun. What am I doing wrong?

A: Nothing. Your child is supposed to use the time however she wants. The relationship you are building with your child during the special playtimes is more important than whether or not your child is working on a problem. As your relationship with your child is strengthened, your child's problem will diminish. Your child may be working on issues through her play that you are not aware of. Remember the lesson of the Band-Aid. What you are doing in the playtimes is working, even when you don't see any change. Children can change as a result of what they do in play sessions with parents or play therapists, even though we are not aware of what they are working on. Your job during the special playtimes is to follow your child's lead and be nonjudgmental, understanding, and accepting of your child. Your empathic responses will help your child focus on the issues that are important to her.

Q: I'm bored. What's the value of this?

A: Being bored in a playtime is not an unusual happening because parents have busy schedules, are on the go a lot, and are not used to sitting and interacting quietly for 30 minutes. You can increase your interest level and involvement in your child's play by responding to what you see in your child's face and asking yourself questions such as "What is he feeling?" "What is he trying to say in his play?" "What does he need from me?" or "What is so interesting to him about the toy or the play?" and by making more tracking responses and reflective responses. The most important thing you can do is continue to be patient with the process of the play sessions.

Q: My child doesn't respond to my comments. How do I know I'm on target?

A: Usually when you are on target, your child will let you know. If she doesn't respond to a reflection, you may want to explore other feelings she might be having or convey that you're trying to understand. For example, if you have reflected "You really are angry!" and your child doesn't respond, you might say, "... Or maybe it's not anger you're feeling, maybe you're just feeling really strong and powerful." If your child still doesn't respond, you might say, "Maybe that's not it either. I wonder what it could be that you're feeling."

Q: When is it okay for me to ask questions, and when is it not okay?

> **A:** Most of the time, questions can be rephrased as statements, for example, "I wonder if that's ever happened to you" instead of "Has that ever happened to you?" The only type of questions that are okay in play sessions are spoken as "stage whispers," as in "What should I say?"

Q: My child hates the play sessions. Should I discontinue them?

> **A:** Communicating understanding is always important. Say, "You don't want to have the special play-time. You would rather do something else. Let's have the special playtime for 10 minutes, then you can decide if you want to have the rest of the special playtime or do something else." This response helps your child to feel understood and to feel in control. A child in that position in a relationship is much more likely to compromise. In most cases, a child will get started playing and will decide to have the rest of the playtime.

Q: My child wants the playtime to be longer. Should I extend the session?

> **A:** Even though your child is having lots of fun, the time limit is adhered to because this promotes consistency, affords you an opportunity to be firm, and provides your child with an opportunity to bring himself under control and end a very desirable playtime. Use A-C-T limit setting, being sure to acknowledge your child's feelings. For example, you can say, "You're really having fun and would like to play a lot longer, but our special playtime is over for today. We will have another special playtime next Tuesday." If your child persists, you could say, "Joey, I wish we had more time, too, but our 30 minutes are up for today. We'll get to have another playtime next Tuesday."

Q: My child wants to play with the toys at other times during the week. Is that OK?

> **A:** Allowing your child to play with these toys only during the 30-minute playtimes helps to convey the message that this is a special time, a time just for the two of you, a fun time. Setting the toys apart makes the playtime unique and more desirable. Another reason is that this time with your child is an emotional relationship time; the toys become a part of that emotional relationship during which your child expresses and explores emotional messages through the toys because of the kinds of empathic responses you make. This same kind of emotional exploration cannot occur during other playtimes because you are not there to communicate understanding of your child's play. Additionally, being allowed to play with these toys only during the special playtimes helps your child learn to delay his need for gratification. If you are having trouble keeping your child from playing with the special toy kit, try storing it out of sight on the top shelf of your closet. If that doesn't work, lock it in the trunk of your car.

Q: My child wants me to shoot at him during the play session. What should I do?

> **A:** Set the limit. If your child says, "I'm the bad guy, shoot me," say, "I know you want me to shoot you, but you're not for shooting; I can pretend you're the bad guy getting away, and I'll catch you, or you can draw a picture of the bad guy getting shot."

Q: _____

_____

_____

_____

CHILD-PARENT-RELATIONSHIP (C-P-R) TRAINING
In-Class Play Session Skills Checklist:
For Review of Videotaped (or Live) Play Session – Session 6

Directions: Indicate ✓ in blank when you observe a play session skill demonstrated in videotaped or live play session

1. ____ Set the Stage/Structured Play Session

2. ____ Conveyed "Be With" Attitudes
   Full attention/interested
   Toes followed nose

3. ____ Allowed Child to Lead
   Avoided giving suggestions
   Avoided asking questions
   Returned responsibility to child

4. ____ Followed Child's Lead
   Physically on child's level
   Moved closer when child was involved in play
   Joined in play when invited—took imaginary/pretend role when appropriate

5. ____ Reflective Responding Skills:

   ____ Reflected child's nonverbal play behavior (Tracking)

   ____ Reflected child's verbalizations (Content)

   ____ Reflected child's feelings/wants/wishes

   ____ Voice tone matched child's intensity/affect

   ____ Responses were brief and interactive

   ____ Facial expressions matched child's affect

6. ____ Used Encouragement/Self-Esteem-Building Responses

7. ____ Set Limits, As Needed, Using A-C-T

CHILD-PARENT-RELATIONSHIP (C-P-R) TRAINING
Parent Play Session Notes – Session 6

Play Session #_____   Date: _____

Significant Happenings:

What I Learned About My Child:

Feelings Expressed:

Play Themes:

What I Learned About Myself:

My feelings during the play session:

What I think I was best at:

What was hardest or most challenging for me:

Questions or Concerns:

Skill I Want to Focus on in the Next Play Session: _____

CHILD-PARENT-RELATIONSHIP (C-P-R) TRAINING
Play Session Skills Checklist - Session 6

Play Session #_____ Date: _____

(Note: Indicate ✓ in column if skill was used; — if skill was not used; and + if skill was a strength)

✓ — +	Skill	Notes/Comments
	Set the Stage/Structured Play Session	
	Conveyed "Be With" Attitudes *Full attention/interested* *Toes followed nose*	
	Allowed Child to Lead *Avoided giving suggestions* *Avoided asking questions* *Returned responsibility to child*	
	Followed Child's Lead *Physically on child's level* *Moved closer when child was involved in play* *Joined in play when invited*	
	Reflective Responding Skills:	
	Reflected child's nonverbal play (Tracking)	
	Reflected child's verbalizations (Content)	
	Reflected child's feelings/wants/wishes	
	Voice tone matched child's intensity/affect	
	Responses were brief and interactive	
	Facial expressions matched child's affect	
	Use of Encouragement/Self-Esteem-Building Responses	
	Set Limits, As Needed, Using A-C-T	

CHILD-PARENT-RELATIONSHIP (C-P-R) TRAINING
Parent Notes & Homework – Session 7

☝ RULE OF THUMB TO REMEMBER:
"Never do for a child that which he can do for himself."
When you do, you rob your child of the joy of discovery and the opportunity to feel competent.
You will never know what your child is capable of unless you allow him to try!

Notes (use back for additional notes):

_____
_____
_____
_____
_____
_____
_____
_____
_____
_____
_____
_____
_____
_____
_____
_____

Homework Assignments:

1. Read *Esteem-Building Responses*—practice giving at least one esteem-building response <u>during</u> your play session (note on *Play Session Skills Checklist*). Also practice giving one esteem-building response <u>outside</u> of your play session.

   What happened outside of play session_____
   What you said _____
   How child responded (verbally or nonverbally)_____

2. Write a note to your child of focus, as well as other children in the family, pointing out a positive character quality you appreciate about the child (see *Positive Character Qualities* handout). Continue to write a note each week for three weeks (mail first note to child, if possible). Write down the following sentence:

   "Dear _____, I was just thinking about you, and what I was thinking is you are so _____ (thoughtful, responsible, considerate, loving, etc.). I love you, _____ (Mom, Dad)."

   Say to the child, in your own words, after the child reads the note (or you read it to the child), "That is such an important quality; we should put that note on the refrigerator (bulletin board, etc.)." <u>Reminder</u>: Don't expect a response from your child.

3. Conduct play session (same time & place)—review *Play Session Do's & Don'ts* & *Play Session Procedure Checklist*

   a. Complete *Parent Play Session Notes*.

   b. Use *Play Session Skills Checklist* to note what you thought you did well, <u>specifically focus on esteem-building responses</u>, and select one skill you want to work on in your next play session.

   _____ *I will bring my videotape for next week (if videotaping at clinic: my appt. day/time _____).*

4. Additional assignment:

CHILD-PARENT-RELATIONSHIP (C-P-R) TRAINING
Esteem Building Responses:
Developing Your Child's Sense of Competence - Session 7

👍 **Rule of Thumb: "Never do for a child that which he can do for himself."**

When you do, you rob your child of the joy of discovery and the opportunity to feel competent. You will never know what your child is capable of unless you allow him to try!

Parents help their child develop a positive view of "self," not only by providing their child with love and unconditional acceptance, but also by helping their child feel competent and capable. Parents help their child feel competent and capable by first allowing the child to **experience** what it is like to discover, figure out, and problem-solve. Parents show faith in their child and their child's capabilities by allowing him to struggle with a problem, all the while providing encouragement (encouragement vs. praise is covered in detail in Session 8). For most parents, allowing children to struggle is hard—but a necessary process for children to truly feel capable. The next step in helping children develop a positive view of self as competent and capable is learning to respond in ways that give children credit for ideas, effort, and accomplishments, without praising.

Esteem-Building Responses to Use in Play Sessions:

"You did it!"
"You figured it out."
"You like the way that turned out."
"You decided…"

"You decided that was the way that was supposed to fit together."
"You know just how you want that to look."
"You're not giving up—you're determined to figure that out."
"You've got a plan for how…"

Example 1: Child works and works to get the lid off the playdough and finally gets it off.
Parent response: **"You did it."**

Example 2: Child works and works to get the lid off the playdough, but can't get it off.
Parent response: **"You're determined to figure that out."**

Example 3: Child struggles to get the dart to fit into the gun and pushed in all the way and finally gets it in.
Parent response: **"You figured it out."**

Example 4: Child spends time drawing, cutting, and gluing a nondescript piece of "art" and shows you with a smile when he is finished.
Parent response: **"You really like the way that turned out."**

Example 5: Child is carefully setting up army soldiers and telling you all about a battle that is going to take place, what is going to happen, and how one side is going to sneak up, and so forth.
Parent response: **"You've got a plan for how that side is…"** or **"You've got that all planned out."**

Note: If your child tends to ask you to do things for him without trying first, ask the therapist to role-play how to return responsibility to your child to do things he is capable of figuring out for himself.

★★

The Struggle to Become a Butterfly: A True Story (Author Unknown)

A family in my neighborhood once brought in two cocoons that were just about to hatch. They watched as the first one began to open and the butterfly inside squeezed very slowly and painfully through a tiny hole that it chewed in one end of the cocoon. After lying exhausted for about 10 minutes following its agonizing emergence, the butterfly finally flew out the open window on its beautiful wings.

The family decided to help the second butterfly so that it would not have to go through such an excruciating ordeal. So, as it began to emerge, they carefully sliced open the cocoon with a razor blade, doing the equivalent of a Caesarean section. The second butterfly never did sprout wings, and in about 10 minutes, instead of flying away, it quietly died.

The family asked a biologist friend to explain what had happened. The scientist said that the difficult struggle to emerge from the small hole actually pushes liquids from deep inside the butterfly's body cavity into the tiny capillaries in the wings, where they harden to complete the healthy and beautiful adult butterfly.

Remember: WITHOUT THE STRUGGLE, THERE ARE NO WINGS!

CHILD-PARENT-RELATIONSHIP (C-P-R) TRAINING
Positive Character Qualities – Session 7

accountable	affectionate	appreciative	assertive
brave	careful	caring	clever
compassionate	confident	considerate	cooperative
courageous	courteous	creative	decisive
dependable	determined	direct	empathic
enjoyable	enthusiastic	energetic	feeling
forgiving	friendly	fun	generous
gentle	goal oriented	good sport	grateful
helpful	honest	humble	idealistic
insightful	intelligent	inventive	joyful
kind	loving	loyal	modest
neat	orderly	outgoing	patient
peaceful	persistent	polite	purposeful
punctual	quiet	reliable	resourceful
respectful	responsible	self-assured	self-controlled
self-disciplined	sensitive	sincere	smart
supportive	tactful	team player	tenacious
thoughtful	tolerant	trustworthy	truthful

CHILD-PARENT-RELATIONSHIP (C-P-R) TRAINING
In-Class Play Session Skills Checklist:

For Review of Videotaped (or Live) Play Session – Session 7

Directions: Indicate ✓ in blank when you observe a play session skill demonstrated in videotaped or live play session

1. ____ Set the Stage/Structured Play Session

2. ____ Conveyed "Be With" Attitudes
   Full attention/interested
   Toes followed nose

3. ____ Allowed Child to Lead
   Avoided giving suggestions
   Avoided asking questions
   Returned responsibility to child

4. ____ Followed Child's Lead
   Physically on child's level
   Moved closer when child was involved in play
   Joined in play when invited—took imaginary/pretend role when appropriate

5. ____ Reflective Responding Skills:

   ____ Reflected child's nonverbal play behavior (Tracking)

   ____ Reflected child's verbalizations (Content)

   ____ Reflected child's feelings/wants/wishes

   ____ Voice tone matched child's intensity/affect

   ____ Responses were brief and interactive

   ____ Facial expressions matched child's affect

6. ____ Used Encouragement/Self-Esteem-Building Responses

7. ____ Set Limits, As Needed, Using A-C-T

CHILD-PARENT-RELATIONSHIP (C-P-R) TRAINING
Parent Play Session Notes – Session 7

Play Session #_____ Date: _____

Significant Happenings:

What I Learned About My Child:

Feelings Expressed:

Play Themes:

What I Learned About Myself:

My feelings during the play session:

What I think I was best at:

What was hardest or most challenging for me:

Questions or Concerns:

Skill I Want to Focus on in the Next Play Session: _____

CHILD-PARENT-RELATIONSHIP (C-P-R) TRAINING
Play Session Skills Checklist - Session 7

Play Session #_____ Date: _____

(Note: Indicate ✓ in column if skill was used; — if skill was not used; and + if skill was a strength)

✓ — +	Skill	Notes/Comments
	Set the Stage/Structured Play Session	
	Conveyed "Be With" Attitudes *Full attention/interested* *Toes followed nose*	
	Allowed Child to Lead *Avoided giving suggestions* *Avoided asking questions* *Returned responsibility to child*	
	Followed Child's Lead *Physically on child's level* *Moved closer when child was involved in play* *Joined in play when invited*	
	Reflective Responding Skills:	
	Reflected child's nonverbal play (Tracking)	
	Reflected child's verbalizations (Content)	
	Reflected child's feelings/wants/wishes	
	Voice tone matched child's intensity/affect	
	Responses were brief and interactive	
	Facial expressions matched child's affect	
	Use of Encouragement/Self-Esteem-Building Responses	
	Set Limits, As Needed, Using A-C-T	

CHILD-PARENT-RELATIONSHIP (C-P-R) TRAINING
Parent Notes & Homework – Session 8

☝ RULE OF THUMB TO REMEMBER:
"Encourage the effort rather than praise the product!"
Children need encouragement like a plant needs water.

Notes (use back for additional notes):

_____
_____
_____
_____
_____
_____
_____
_____
_____
_____
_____
_____
_____
_____
_____
_____

Homework Assignments:

1. Read *Encouragement vs. Praise*—practice giving at least one encouragement response <u>during</u> your play session (note on *Play Session Skills Checklist*). Also practice giving at least one encouragement <u>outside</u> of your play session.

    What happend or what child said (outside of play session) _____
    What you said _____
    How child responded (verbally or nonverbally)_____

2. Write down one issue you are struggling with most <u>outside</u> of play session time.

    _____

3. Conduct play session (same time & place)—review *Play Session Do's & Don'ts & Play Session Procedure Checklist*

    a. Complete *Parent Play Session Notes*.

    b. Use *Play Session Skills Checklist* to note what you thought you did well, <u>specifically focus on encouragement responses</u>, and select one skill you want to work on in your next play session.

    _____ **I will bring my videotape for next week (if videotaping at clinic: my appt. day/time_____).**

4. Additional assignment:

Reminder: Write second note to your child of focus, as well as other children in the family, pointing out <u>another</u> positive character quality you appreciate about the child. (Vary how the note is delivered, for example, placing in child's lunchbox, taped to mirror in bathroom, on the child's pillow, under the child's dinner plate, etc.)

CHILD-PARENT-RELATIONSHIP (C-P-R) TRAINING
Encouragement vs. Praise – Session 8

👍 **Rule of Thumb:** "Encourage the effort rather than praise the product"

Praise: Although praise and encouragement both focus on positive behaviors and appear to be the same process, praise actually fosters dependence in children by teaching them to rely on an external source of control and motivation rather than on self-control and self-motivation. Praise is an attempt to motivate children with external rewards. In effect, the parent who praises is saying, "If you do something I consider good, you will have the reward of being recognized and valued by me." Overreliance on praise can produce crippling effects. Children come to believe that their worth depends upon the opinions of others. Praise employs words that place value judgments on children and focuses on external evaluation.

Examples: *"You're such a good boy/girl." The child may wonder, "Am I accepted only when I'm good?"*
"You got an A. That's great!" Are children to infer that they are worthwhile only when they make As?
"You did a good job." "I'm so proud of you." The message sent is that the parent's evaluation is more important than the child's.

Encouragement: Focuses on internal evaluation and the contributions children make—facilitates development of self-motivation and self-control. Encouraging parents teach their children to accept their own inadequacies, learn from mistakes (mistakes are wonderful opportunities for learning), have confidence in themselves, and feel useful through contribution. When commenting on children's efforts, be careful not to place value judgments on what they have done. Be alert to eliminate value-laden words (good, great, excellent, etc.) from your vocabulary at these times. Instead, substitute words of encouragement that help children believe in themselves. Encouragement focuses on effort and can always be given. Children who feel their efforts are encouraged, valued, and appreciated develop qualities of persistence and determination and tend to be good problem-solvers. *Note: Parent's voice should match child's level of affect; if child is excited about getting an "A" on a test, parent responds likewise with excitement in her voice, "You're really proud of that!" Use after-the-event celebrations (based on child's pride in achievement) instead of rewards (external motivators to get the child to achieve) to recognize achievement. In the above example, the parent could add "Sounds like something to celebrate; let's make a cake!" or "You choose the restaurant, my treat!"*

Encouraging Phrases That Recognize Effort and Improvement:
"You did it!" or "You got it!"
"You really worked hard on that."
"You didn't give up until you figured it out."
"Look at the progress you've made..." (Be specific)
"You've finished half of your worksheet and it's only 4 o'clock."

Encouraging Phrases That Show Confidence:
"I have confidence in you. You'll figure it out."
"That's a rough one, but I bet you'll figure it out."
"Sounds like you have a plan."
"Knowing you, I'm sure you will do fine."
"Sounds like you know a lot about_____."

Encouraging Phrases That Focus on Contributions, Assets, and Appreciation:
"Thanks, that was a big help."
"It was thoughtful of you to_____" or "I appreciate that you_____."
"You have a knack for _____. Can you give me a hand with that?"

In summary, encouragement is:
1. Valuing and accepting children as they are (not putting conditions on acceptance)
2. Pointing out the positive aspects of behavior
3. Showing faith in children, so that they can come to believe in themselves
4. Recognizing effort and improvement (rather than requiring achievement)
5. Showing appreciation for contributions

Adapted from Dinkmeyer, D., & McKay, G.D. The Parent's Handbook, (1982). Circle Pines, Minn: American Guidance Service.

CHILD-PARENT-RELATIONSHIP (C-P-R) TRAINING
In-Class Play Session Skills Checklist:
For Review of Videotaped (or Live) Play Session – Session 8

Directions: Indicate ✓ in blank when you observe a play session skill demonstrated in videotaped or live play session

1. ____ Set the Stage/Structured Play Session

2. ____ Conveyed "Be With" Attitudes
   Full attention/interested
   Toes followed nose

3. ____ Allowed Child to Lead
   Avoided giving suggestions
   Avoided asking questions
   Returned responsibility to child

4. ____ Followed Child's Lead
   Physically on child's level
   Moved closer when child was involved in play
   Joined in play when invited—took imaginary/pretend role when appropriate

5. ____ Reflective Responding Skills:

   ____ Reflected child's nonverbal play behavior (Tracking)

   ____ Reflected child's verbalizations (Content)

   ____ Reflected child's feelings/wants/wishes

   ____ Voice tone matched child's intensity/affect

   ____ Responses were brief and interactive

   ____ Facial expressions matched child's affect

6. ____ Used Encouragement/Self-Esteem-Building Responses

7. ____ Set Limits, As Needed, Using A-C-T

CHILD-PARENT-RELATIONSHIP (C-P-R) TRAINING
Parent Play Session Notes – Session 8

Play Session #_____ Date: _____

Significant Happenings:

What I Learned About My Child:

Feelings Expressed:

Play Themes:

What I Learned About Myself:

My feelings during the play session:

What I think I was best at:

What was hardest or most challenging for me:

Questions or Concerns:

Skill I Want to Focus on in the Next Play Session: _____

CHILD-PARENT-RELATIONSHIP (C-P-R) TRAINING
Play Session Skills Checklist - Session 8

Play Session #_____ Date: _____

(Note: Indicate ✓ in column if skill was used; — if skill was not used; and + if skill was a strength)

✓ — +	Skill	Notes/Comments
	Set the Stage/Structured Play Session	
	Conveyed "Be With" Attitudes *Full attention/interested* *Toes followed nose*	
	Allowed Child to Lead *Avoided giving suggestions* *Avoided asking questions* *Returned responsibility to child*	
	Followed Child's Lead *Physically on child's level* *Moved closer when child was involved in play* *Joined in play when invited*	
	Reflective Responding Skills:	
	Reflected child's nonverbal play (Tracking)	
	Reflected child's verbalizations (Content)	
	Reflected child's feelings/wants/wishes	
	Voice tone matched child's intensity/affect	
	Responses were brief and interactive	
	Facial expressions matched child's affect	
	Use of Encouragement/Self-Esteem-Building Responses	
	Set Limits, As Needed, Using A-C-T	

CHILD-PARENT-RELATIONSHIP (C-P-R) TRAINING
Parent Notes & Homework – Session 9

👍 RULES OF THUMB TO REMEMBER:

1. **"Where there are no limits, there is no security."** Consistent Limits = Security in the Relationship. When you don't follow through, you lose credibility and harm your relationship with your child.

2. **"Don't try to change everything at once!"** Focus on 'big' issues that ultimately will mean the most to your child's development of positive self-esteem and feelings of competence and usefulness.

Notes (use back for additional notes):

_____
_____
_____
_____
_____
_____
_____

Homework Assignments:

1. Review *Generalizing Limit Setting to Outside the Play Session*—if applicable, report on a time you used A-C-T outside of the play session.
   What happened _____
   What you said _____
   How child responded (verballly or nonbally)_____

2. Notice the number of times you touch your child in interactions outside the play session (hugging, patting on the head, a touch on the arm, etc.) and keep count this week. # of physical contacts: _____

3. A related assignment is to play-wrestle with your children. (Example: In a two-parent family with small children, Mom and kids can sneak up on Dad and try to get him down on the floor, accompanied by lots of fun and laughter.)

4. Choose one issue you are struggling with outside of the play session to focus on and report back next week on how you can use your play session skills to respond to the issue. _____
   _____

5. Conduct play session (same time & place)—review *Play Session Do's & Don'ts & Play Session Procedure Cheklist*
   a. Complete *Parent Play Session Notes*.
   b. Use *Play Session Skills Checklist* to note what you thought you did well, and select one skill you want to work on in your next play session.
   _____ **I will bring my videotape for next week (if videotaping at clinic: my appt. day/time _____).**

6. Additional assignment:

Reminder: Write third note to your child of focus, as well as other children in the family, pointing out <u>another</u> positive character quality you appreciate about the child. (Vary how the note is delivered.)

CHILD-PARENT-RELATIONSHIP (C-P-R) TRAINING
Advanced Limit Setting: Giving Choices as Consequences for Non-Compliance - Session 9

Play Session Example: After parent has stated that the playdough is for playing with on the tray, 5-year-old Billy dumps it on the floor. Next, parent follows the A-C-T method of limit setting: **"Billy, I know that you want to play with the playdough over there, but the floor (carpet, etc.) is not for putting playdough on; (pointing to tray) the tray is for putting the playdough on."** Billy continues to ignore parent and begins to smash the play-dough on the floor. Parent may patiently restate limit up to three times before beginning the next step of stating "If-Then" choices (consequences) for following or not following limit. Note: This example assumes that parent has chosen a location for the play session where the floor surface can be easily cleaned by parent after the session. (of child *begins* to put playdoh on carpet, parent can reach out and guide the playdoh can to the tray as the A-C-T limit is set)

Next step: <u>Begin "If-Then" choice-giving method to provide consequence for unacceptable behavior</u>. *Note the number of times the words "choose" or "choice" are used! Remember that the intent is for the child to bring himself under control; therefore, patience is the order of the day. Children need time and practice to learn self-control.*

Example: **"Billy, <u>If you choose</u> to play with the playdough on the tray (pointing to tray), <u>then you choose</u> to play with the playdough today. <u>If you choose</u> to continue to play with the playdough on the floor, <u>then you choose</u> not to play with the playdough for the rest of today."** (Pause.) Patiently restate if child does not make the choice to comply with the limit. (If no answer and Billy continues to play with playdough on floor, then he has made his choice.) **"Billy, looks like you've <u>chosen</u> to put the playdough up for today. You can <u>choose</u> to give me the playdough, or you can <u>choose</u> for me to put the playdough up for you; which do you <u>choose</u>?"** If child begins to cry and beg for the playdough, parent must be tough and follow through, acknowledging child's feelings and giving child hope that he will have a chance to make a different choice in the next play session. **"Billy, I understand that you're unhappy that you <u>chose</u> to have the playdough put up for today, but you can <u>choose</u> to play with it in our next play session."**

In the above example, if at any point the child took the playdough and put it on the tray to play with, the parent must be careful to respond matter-of-factly, **"Looks like you decided you wanted to play with it some more today."**

Practice:
1. Your child aims a loaded dart gun at you.

<u>A</u> _____.

<u>C</u> _____.

<u>T</u> _____.

Your child continues to aim the gun at you after you have set the limit using A-C-T three times.

If you choose to _aim the gun at me_
then you choose to _not to get to play with the gun._

If you choose to _aim the gun somewhere else_
then you choose to _get to play with the gun._

If your child aims and shoots the gun at you, you say:

I see you've chosen not to get to play with the gun.

If your child puts the gun down, you say:

I see you've chosen to play with the gun some more today

2. Describe a situation in which you think you might need to set a limit during the play session and you anticipate the child might not comply.
Situation:_____
_____
_____
_____

A   _____

C   _____

T   _____

If/Then: _____

_____
_____
_____
_____
_____

CHILD-PARENT-RELATIONSHIP (C-P-R) TRAINING
Generalizing Limit Setting to Outside the Play Session – Session 9

<u>A</u>cknowledge the feeling
<u>C</u>ommunicate the limit
<u>T</u>arget alternatives

Three-Step A-C-T Method of Limit Setting Followed by Choices (Consequences) for Non-compliance:

Scenario: *Child found your hidden stash of candy, has a piece in his hand, and is starting to unwrap it. (It is 30 minutes before dinner.)*

1. <u>A</u>cknowledge your child's feeling or desire *(your voice must convey empathy and understanding)*.
   (Empathically) **"Billy, I know you'd really like to have the candy…"**
   Child learns that his feelings, desires, and wishes are valid and accepted by parent (but not all behavior).
   Just empathically reflecting your child's feeling often defuses the intensity of the feeling or need.

2. <u>C</u>ommunicate the limit. (Be specific and clear—and brief.)
   "…but candy is not for eating before dinner."

3. <u>T</u>arget acceptable alternatives. (Provide one or more choices, depending on age of child.)
   "You can choose to have a piece of fruit now (pointing to bowl of fruit) **and choose to have the piece of candy after dinner."** (If you do not want your children to ever have candy, don't keep it around.)
   The goal is to provide your child with acceptable alternatives—ones that are acceptable to you, the parent, and ones that you believe will allow your child to get his need met (in this case, to have a piece of candy, but not until after dinner—and if he is hungry, to meet that need with an acceptable before-dinner snack).
   Note: Pointing helps redirect child's attention. If child chooses fruit, stop here.
   Patiently restate the limit up to three times, depending on the age of the child, to allow child to struggle with self-control before proceeding to the next step.

4. **Choice-Giving (consequences) as next step after noncompliance** (examples of possible responses):
   Billy continues to say that he doesn't want fruit; he wants the candy.
   — **"Billy, having candy now is not one of the <u>choices</u>. You can choose to give me the candy now and <u>choose</u> to eat it after dinner, or you can <u>choose</u> for me to put the candy up and <u>choose</u> not to have the candy after dinner. Which do you <u>choose</u>?** (Pause—Billy says nothing.) **"If you choose not to choose, you choose for me to choose for you."** (Pause.)
   a) (Billy gives you the candy.) **"I can tell that was a hard decision—I'll put it up here for you for after dinner."**
   b) (Billy continues to hold on to candy.) **"I see you've chosen for me to choose for you"** (as you reach for the candy to put it up). After dinner, if Billy comes to you and says "Now can I have the candy?" your response is, **"Remember when you chose not to give me the candy before dinner—at that very moment, you chose not to have candy after dinner."** Child may continue to plead and cry (because it has worked in the past). BE FIRM—don't give in!

Practice: It is a school night and 5-year-old Billy wants to watch just 30 more minutes of television before he goes to bed, because his favorite Charlie Brown special is coming on next.

<u>A</u>   _____ .

<u>C</u>   _____ .

<u>T</u>   _____ .
Patiently restate the limit up to three times; Billy doesn't comply. (It's important to remain empathic & calm, but ficm.)
You can choose to _____
_____
_____

What To Do Affect A-C-T

After you've followed the three-step A-C-T process with empathy and firmness:

1. If you are satisfied with your response to the child's question and the question or plea is repeated, DON'T DISCUSS.

2. If you think the child doesn't understand your response, say:
   — "I've already answered that question. You must have some question about my answer."

3. If you think the child understands, say:
   — "I can tell you'd like to discuss this some more, but I've already answered that question."

   OR

   — "I can tell you don't like my answer. If you are asking again because you want me to change my mind, I will not."

   OR

   — "Do you remember the answer I gave you a few minutes ago when you asked that same question?"
     If child answers, "No, I don't remember," say, "Go sit down in a quite place and think. I know you'll be able to remember."

4. If you are not satisfied with your response to the child's question:
   — If you are open to persuasion, say:
     "I don't know. Let's sit down and discuss it."
   — If you intend to answer the question later but are not prepared to answer now, say:
     "I can't answer that question now because (I want to talk it over with someone; I want to get more information; I want to think about it, etc.). I'll let you know (specific time)."
   — If child demands an answer now, say:
     "If you must have an answer now, the answer will have to be 'NO.'"

What To Do When Limit Setting Doesn't Work

You have been careful <u>several times</u> to calmly and empathically use **A-C-T and Choice-Giving**. Your child continues to deliberately disobey. What do you do?

1. <u>Look for natural causes for rebellion</u>: Fatigue, sickness, hunger, stress, and so forth. Take care of physical needs and crises before expecting cooperation.

2. <u>Remain in control, respecting yourself and the child</u>: You are not a failure if your child rebels, and your child is not bad. All kids need to "practice" rebelling. Remember: At this very moment, nothing is more important than your relationship with your child, so respond in a way that respects your child and yourself. *If you find yourself feeling angry at your child and losing control, walk outside or to another room.*

3. <u>Set reasonable consequences for disobedience</u>: *Let your child choose to obey or disobey*, but set a reasonable consequence for disobedience. Example: "If you choose to watch TV instead of going to bed, then you choose to give up TV all day tomorrow" (or whatever is a meaningful consequence for child).

4. <u>Never tolerate violence</u>: Physically restrain the child who becomes violent, without becoming aggressive yourself. Empathically and calmly **REFLECT** the child's anger and loneliness; provide compassionate control and alternatives as child begins to regain control.

5. <u>If the child refuses to choose, you choose for him</u>: The child's refusal to choose is also a choice. Set the consequences. Example: "If you choose not to (choice A or B), then you have chosen for me to choose for you."

6. <u>ENFORCE THE CONSEQUENCES</u>: Don't state consequences that you cannot enforce. If you crumble under your child's anger or tears, you have abdicated your role as parent and lost your power. **GET TOUGH!** When you <u>don't follow through</u>, you lose credibility and harm your relationship with your child.

7. <u>Recognize signs of more serious problems</u>: Depression, trauma (abuse/neglect/extreme grief/stress). The chronically angry or rebellious child is in emotional trouble and may need professional help. Share your concern with the child. Example: "John, I've noticed that you seem to be angry and unhappy most of the time. I love you, and I'm worried about you. We're going to get help so we can all be happier."

CHILD-PARENT-RELATIONSHIP (C-P-R) TRAINING
Structured Doll Play for Parents – Session 9

What is structured doll play?

Structured doll play is a lively way of storytelling for parents to help children who are feeling anxious or insecure. It provides a brief and specific experience for the children to prepare them for anxiety-provoking experiences, such as parents' divorce, going over to the babysitter, and so forth, or to help them regain a sense of normalcy and routine after a significant change in their life. It has a specific purpose and a clear message (e.g., Mom is going to come back at the end of the day to pick Lucy up).

Can my child benefit from structured doll play?

If your child is showing anxiety or fear, or has been through a traumatic experience, he/she can probably benefit from you using structured doll play with him/her. Structured doll play works best with children from ages 2–6. However, older or younger children can also benefit from it.

How do I do structured doll play?

1. Creating the story

   Structured doll play is basically creative storytelling about specific real life happenings. It is similar to reading a story from a storybook to your child; the major differences are:

   A. You create the story instead of reading out of a storybook.

   B. The story involves real life characters, such as Mom, Dad, Lucy (your child), babysitter Jane, Grandma, schoolteacher, dentist, and so forth.

   C. The story is about real life happenings, usually about future events that are coming up in the next day or two. It can also be a story of routine daily happenings.

   D. You have a specific purpose and a clear message. For example: Lucy is reluctant to go to the new day care. She would not let you leave when you dropped her off at day care. Your purpose is helping Lucy to feel more comfortable about going to day care. Your message may be, "Mom is going to return at the end of the day." (It's important that the message fit what the parent believes is of most concern to the child.)

   E. You use dolls to enhance the dramatic effect and help your child remember. You can also use sound effects to enrich the story and make it more powerful and fun. Remember, young children understand concrete things like dolls and scenes better than promises and reasons.

2. The making of a story (Think about a beginning, middle, and an end)

Beginning	Don't start off by saying Lucy is going to the babysitter. Start off by giving some background for the story (e.g., a predictable routine, like waking up in the morning).
Middle	Give content to the story by putting in details (e.g., putting on shoes or buckling seat belt). Remember to exaggerate and use sound effects (you'll probably feel silly at first, but children love it!).
End	Remember to end the story. Don't leave your child hanging. End the story with a big kiss. *"Mom drives to the babysitter's (Jane) house and rings the bell (ding-dong). Jane opens the door and Lucy sees Mom. Lucy jumps into Mom's lap. Mom gives Lucy a big hug and a kiss (make kissing noise). Mom and Lucy drive home together. They talk about the day on the way home."*

   Steps to making a story:
   A) Start with a title sentence (e.g., "This is a story about Lucy going to the babysitter").
   B) Introduce the characters by using real names of people.
   C) Tell the story (don't use "you" to refer to the doll representing your child. Use your child's name to stay objective, e.g., "Lucy is saying goodbye to Mom" rather than "You are saying goodbye to Mom").

3. Props and place

Remember: This is a creative business. So you need to decide on a comfortable time and place to do structured doll play and prepare your props (dolls) ahead of time. A good time might be in your child's bedroom in the evening before bedtime (to avoid disruptions and create a routine). You don't need to buy any special dolls—use your child's dolls and stuffed animals or puppets. (Save your money to give yourself a treat after telling a good story—it's a lot of work to tell a really good story!) You can also involve your child in picking out the dolls/stuffed animals by saying "I've got a special story to tell you tonight. It's about a little girl name Lucy who goes to Jane's (the babysitter). To tell the story, we need a Lucy doll, a Mommy doll, a Daddy doll, and a Jane doll. Can you help me pick out a doll (stuffed animal) for each character?" (Make sure you have a selection of your child's dolls/stuffed animals lined up to choose from.) *Note: You need to remember who is who, and the doll figures stay the same person thereafter (you can add new dolls as you use this method to tell different stories, like going to the dentist for the first time, etc.).*

4. How do I start?

You can start this new play experience by using nonthreatening, general daily life activities as the content of the story (e.g., going to the grocery store). This will help you practice and gain skills before plunging into more challenging themes. Focus your story on one theme and don't go beyond five minutes. You can think the story out in your head, or you can jot down brief notes to use as the script.

Helpful hints:

1. It may seem awkward to tell stories and act them out. Be patient with yourself—YOUR CHILD WILL THINK IT'S FUN AND WON'T NOTICE IF YOU MESS UP!

2. Include only those elements in the story that you have control over. Don't say how much fun Lucy is going to have (she may not be having much fun, if she's anxious). If you say something is going to happen at the babysitter's (going to the park, etc.), make sure you ask that the babysitter follow through on that activity the next day. The entire point of the story is to help the child feel more secure by being able to predict what will happen.

3. Don't build on your own feelings when you are telling the story. For example, "Mom is working in the office while Lucy is playing in day care. Mom is thinking of Lucy and she misses Lucy." (Take away the underlined phrase; including your own feelings in the story may make the child feel guilty for you missing her). Remember: The goal is to help Lucy go to day care without feeling anxious, so she can relax and have fun.

4. Make the story realistic and positive. You are the author of the story, so you can make it the way you want it to turn out in real life. Instead of focusing the story on how Lucy doesn't want to leave Mom, make the story go like this: "Lucy and Mom ring the doorbell together (ding-dong!). The door opens and Lucy smiles when she sees Jane. Lucy gives Mom a big hug, and she and Jane wave goodbye to Mom together…." (Remember to let Jane know about your story.)

5. Always end the story on a positive note THAT YOU CAN CONTROL. If the story involves the child not seeing you for several hours (especially if that is part of the concern), always include an "I'm so glad to see you!" reunion with kisses and hugs. The graphic representation of using dolls is more powerful than a verbal promise.

6. Your child may get distracted and interrupt the story. Briefly attend to the child, but be sure to finish the story. Telling the story after the child is already in bed helps with distractions. Parent can respond to requests to play with something else by saying, "You can play with your other dolls tomorrow; it's bedtime now." Or, if your child asks for a drink, "As soon as we've finished the story, I'll get you a drink."

234

CHILD-PARENT-RELATIONSHIP (C-P-R) TRAINING
In-Class Play Session Skills Checklist:
For Review of Videotaped (or Live) Play Session – Session 9

Directions: Indicate ✓ in blank when you observe a play session skill demonstrated in videotaped or live play session

1. ___ Set the Stage/Structured Play Session

2. ___ Conveyed "Be With" Attitudes
   Full attention/interested
   Toes followed nose

3. ___ Allowed Child to Lead
   Avoided giving suggestions
   Avoided asking questions
   Returned responsibility to child

4. ___ Followed Child's Lead
   Physically on child's level
   Moved closer when child was involved in play
   Joined in play when invited—took imaginary/pretend role when appropriate

5. ___ Reflective Responding Skills:

   ___ Reflected child's nonverbal play behavior (Tracking)

   ___ Reflected child's verbalizations (Content)

   ___ Reflected child's feelings/wants/wishes

   ___ Voice tone matched child's intensity/affect

   ___ Responses were brief and interactive

   ___ Facial expressions matched child's affect

6. ___ Used Encouragement/Self-Esteem-Building Responses

7. ___ Set Limits, As Needed, Using A-C-T

CHILD-PARENT-RELATIONSHIP (C-P-R) TRAINING
Parent Play Session Notes – Session 9

Play Session #_____ Date: _____

Significant Happenings:

What I Learned About My Child:

Feelings Expressed:

Play Themes:

What I Learned About Myself:

My feelings during the play session:

What I think I was best at:

What was hardest or most challenging for me:

Questions or Concerns:

Skill I Want to Focus on in the Next Play Session: _____

CHILD-PARENT-RELATIONSHIP (C-P-R) TRAINING
Play Session Skills Checklist - Session 9

Play Session #_____ Date: _____

(Note: Indicate ✓ in column if skill was used; — if skill was not used; and + if skill was a strength)

✓ — +	Skill	Notes/Comments
	Set the Stage/Structured Play Session	
	Conveyed "Be With" Attitudes *Full attention/interested* *Toes followed nose*	
	Allowed Child to Lead *Avoided giving suggestions* *Avoided asking questions* *Returned responsibility to child*	
	Followed Child's Lead *Physically on child's level* *Moved closer when child was involved in play* *Joined in play when invited*	
	Reflective Responding Skills:	
	Reflected child's nonverbal play (Tracking)	
	Reflected child's verbalizations (Content)	
	Reflected child's feelings/wants/wishes	
	Voice tone matched child's intensity/affect	
	Responses were brief and interactive	
	Facial expressions matched child's affect	
	Use of Encouragement/Self-Esteem-Building Responses	
	Set Limits, As Needed, Using A-C-T	

CHILD-PARENT-RELATIONSHIP (C-P-R) TRAINING
Parent Notes & Homework – Session 10

👍 RULES OF THUMB TO REMEMBER:

"Good things come in small packages."
Don't wait for big events to enter into your child's world—
the little ways are always with us. Hold onto precious moments!

Notes (use back for additional notes):

_____
_____
_____
_____
_____
_____
_____
_____
_____
_____
_____
_____

Homework Assignments:

<u>Continue play sessions</u>: If you stop now, the message is that you were playing with your child because you had to, not because you wanted to:

I agree to continue my play sessions with my child of focus for ___ weeks and/or begin sessions with _____ and do for ___ weeks.

Date and time for follow-up meetings: _____

Volunteer meeting coordinator: _____

<u>Recommended Reading</u>:

1. *Relational Parenting* (2000) and *How to Really Love Your Child* (1992), Ross Campbell

2. *Between Parent and Child* (1956), Haim Ginott

3. *Liberated Parents, Liberated Children* (1990), Adele Faber and Elaine Mazlish

4. *How to Talk So Kids Will Listen and Listen So Kids Will Talk* (2002), Adele Faber and Elaine Mazlish

5. *"SAY WHAT YOU SEE"* for Parents and Teachers (2005), Sandra Blackard (Free online resource available at www.languageoflistening.com)

CHILD-PARENT-RELATIONSHIP (C-P-R) TRAINING
Rules of Thumb & Other Things to Remember – Session 10

👍 Rules of Thumb

1. **Focus on the donut, not the hole!**
   Focus on the relationship (your strengths and your child's strengths), NOT the problem.

2. **Be a thermostat, not a thermometer!**
   Learn to RESPOND (reflect) rather than REACT. The child's feelings <u>are not</u> your feelings and needn't escalate with him/her.

3. **What's most important may not be what you do, but what you do after what you did!**
   We are certain to make mistakes, but we can recover. It is how we handle our mistakes that makes the difference.

4. **The parent's toes should follow his/her nose.**
   Body language conveys interest.

5. **You can't give away what you do not possess.**
   (Analogy: oxygen mask on airplane) You can't extend patience and acceptance to your child if you can't first offer it to yourself.

6. **When a child is drowning, don't try to teach her to swim.**
   When a child is feeling upset or out of control, that is not the moment to impart a rule or teach a lesson.

7. **During play sessions, limits are not needed until they are needed!**

8. **If you can't say it in 10 words or less, don't say it.**
   As parents, we tend to overexplain, and our message gets lost in the words.

9. **Grant in fantasy what you can't grant in reality.**
   In a play session, it is okay to act out feelings and wishes that in reality may require limits.

10. **Big choices for big kids, little choices for little kids.**
    Choices given must be commensurate with child's developmental stage.

11. **Never do for a child that which he can do for himself.**
    You will never know what your child is capable of unless you allow him to try!

12. **Encourage the effort rather than praise the product.**
    Children need encouragement like a plant needs water.

13. **Don't try to change everything at once!**
    Focus on 'big' issues that ultimately will mean the most to your child's development of positive self-esteem and feelings of competence and usefulness.

14. **Where there are no limits, there is no security. (Consistent Limits = Secure Relationship)**
    When you don't follow through, you lose credibility and harm your relationship with your child.

15. **Good things come in small packages.**
    Don't wait for big events to enter into your child's world—the little ways are always with us. Hold onto precious moments!

Other Things to Remember:

1. Reflective responses help children to feel understood and can lessen anger.

2. In play, children express what their lives are like now, what their needs are, or how they wish things could be.

3. In the playtimes, the parent is not the source of answers (reflect questions back to child: "Hmm—I wonder").

4. Don't ask questions you already know the answer to.

5. Questions imply non-understanding. Questions put children in their minds. Children live in their hearts.

6. What's important is not what the child knows, but what the child believes.

7. When you focus on the problem, you lose sight of the child.

8. Support the child's feeling, intent, or need, even if you can't support the child's behavior.

9. Noticing the child is a powerful builder of self-esteem.

10. Empower children by giving them credit for making decisions: "You decided to_____."

11. One of the best things we can communicate to our children is that they are competent. Tell children they are capable, and they will think they are capable. If you tell children enough times they can't do something, sure enough, they can't.

12. Encourage creativity and freedom—with freedom comes responsibility.

13. "We're about to institute a new and significant policy immediately effective within the confines of this domicile."

14. When we are flexible in our stance, we can handle anger much more easily. When parents are rigid in their approach, both parent and child can end up hurt (remember the stiff arm!).

15. When unsure of what to say to child or what to do, ask yourself, "What action or words will most preserve the relationship or do least harm?" Sometimes walking away and saying nothing, or telling the child, "I need to take a time-out to cool off, and then we can talk," is best. Always remember: "Nothing at this moment is more important than my relationship with my child."
(Also applies to spouses, significant others, etc.)

16. Live in the moment—today is enough. Don't push children toward the future.

CHILD PARENT RELATIONSHIP THERAPY (CPRT)

TRAINING RESOURCES

Using CPR Training Resources

The ***CPR Training Resources*** include a list of useful CPRT training resources. Resources are organized by videos, books, and manuals. Each of these categories is further divided into recommended and supplemental resources.

VIDEOS

Recommended Videos:

Center for Play Therapy (Producer), & Landreth, G. (Writer/Director). (1994). *Choices, cookies, & kids: A creative approach to discipline* [Video cassette-DVD]. Approximate length: 35 minutes. (Available in VHS and DVD from Center for Play Therapy, www.centerforplaytherapy.com, University of North Texas, P.O. Box 310829, Denton, TX 76203-1337, 940-565-3864).

Nova Presentation (Producer). *Life's first feelings* [Video cassette]. (Available on www.amazon.com, Item No. 4810. *The following two segments are used in CPRT Training Session 1 to help parents understand the importance of responding appropriately to children's feelings. Prior to showing to parents, filial therapists should view entire tape for helpful, research-based information on the universality of the development of emotions, as well as information on child temperament and child's innate internal locus of control*).

    Segment Info: 0:00   Tape Begins *(times listed are "real time," not "counter time")*
               5:14   Segment 1 Begins: Parent Responsive/Non-Responsive to Infant
               9:46   Segment 1 Ends *(Total time = 4min. 32 sec)*
            21:34   Segment 2 Begins: Universal Feelings/Facial Expressions
            27:01   Segment 2 Ends *(Total time = 5min. 27 sec)*

Supplemental Videos:

Center for Play Therapy (Producer), & Landreth, G. (Writer/Director). (1997). *Child-centered play therapy: A clinical session* [Video cassette-DVD]. (Available from Center for Play Therapy, www. centerforplaytherapy.com, University of North Texas, P.O. Box 310829, Denton, TX 76203-1337, 940-565-3864). 1) This video is useful for demonstration of play session skills for filial therapist that do not have their own video sessions (with permission to show parents). 2) This tape contains several "segments" that can be utilized to teach specific filial play skills. *The following 5 minute segment is particularly helpful in demonstrating "Being With" and allowing the child to lead as well as basic play session skills.*

    Segment Info: 0:00   Tape Begins
            42:11   Medical play segment begins
            47:12   Medical play segment ends

National Institute of Relationships Enhancement (Producer), & Guerney, L. (Writer/Director). (1989). *Filial therapy with Louise Guerney* [Video cassette]. (Available from 12500 Blake Road Silver Spring, MD 20904-2050). *Contains examples of parent-child play sessions).*

VanFleet, R. (Writer/Director). (1999). *Introduction to Filial Play Therapy* [Video cassette]. (Available from Family Enhancement & Play Therapy Center, P.O. Box 613, Boiling Springs, PA 17007).

VanFleet, R. (Writer/Director). *Overcoming resistance: Engaging parents in play therapy* [Video cassette]. (Available from Family Enhancement & Play Therapy Center, P.O. Box 613, Boiling Springs, PA 17007).

BOOKS AND MANUALS

Recommended Resources

Bratton, S., Landreth, G., Kellam, T., & Blackard, S. (2006). *Child Parent Relationship Therapy (CPRT) Treatment Manual: A 10-session filial therapy model.* New York, NY: Routledge. *The manual includes a CD-ROM of all training materials for ease of reproduction.*

Landreth, G., & Bratton, S. (2006). *Child Parent Relationship Therapy (CPRT): A 10-session filial therapy model.* New York: Routledge.

Supplemental Therapist Resources

Bailey, B. (2000). *I love you rituals.* New York, NY: HarperCollins.

Campbell, R. (1992). *How to really love your child.* Colorado Springs, CO: Chariot Victor.

Campbell, R. (2000). *Relational parenting.* Chicago, IL: Moody Press.

Faber, A., & Mazlish, E. (1990). *Liberated parents/Liberated children.* New York, NY: Avon Books.

Faber, A., & Mazlish, E. (2002). *How to talk so kids will listen & listen so kids will talk.* New York: Harper Collins.

Ginott, H. (1956). *Between parent and child.* New York, NY: Avon Books.

Guerney, L. (1987). *The parenting skills program: Leader's manual.* State College, PA: IDEALS.

Guerney, L. (1988). *Parenting: A skills training manual* (3rd ed.). State College, PA: IDEALS.

Guerney, L. (1990). *Parenting adolescents – A supplement to parenting: A skills training program.* Silver Spring, MD: IDEALS.

Kraft, A., & Landreth, G. (1998). *Parents as therapeutic partners: Listening to your child's play.* Muncie, IN: Jason Aronson.

Landreth, G. (2002). *Play therapy: The art of the relationship.* New York, NY: Routledge.

Nelson, J. (1996). *Positive discipline.* New York, NY: Ballantine Books.

Ortwein, M. C. (1997). *Mastering the magic of play: A training manual for parents in filial therapy.* Silver Spring, MD: IDEALS.

VanFleet, R. (1994). *Filial therapy: Strengthening parent-child relationships through play.* Sarasota, FL: Professional Resources.

VanFleet, R. (2000). *A parent's handbook of filial play therapy.* Boiling Springs, PA: Play Therapy Press.

VanFleet, R., & Guerney, L. (2003). *Casebook of filial therapy.* Boiling Springs, PA: Play Therapy Press.

Supplemental Children's Literature That Can Be Used in CPRT Training

Hausman, B., & Fellman, S. (1999). *A to Z: Do you ever feel like me?* New York, NY: Dutton Children's Books.

Manning-Ramirez, L., & Salcines, M. (2001). *Playtime for Molly*. McAllen, TX: Marlin Books.

McBratney, S. (1994). *Guess how much I love you.* Cambridge, MA: Candlewick Press.

Melmed, L. (1993). *I love you as much...* New York, NY: Lothrop, Lee & Shepard Books.

Munsch, R. (1986). *Love you forever.* Willowdale, Ontario, Canada: Firefly Books. ***Authors strongly recommend this book for parents*** .

Supplemental Articles for Parents That Can Be Used in CPRT Training *(Note: Filial therapist can also use additional resources, as needed, on special topics related to the needs of parents, i.e., adoptive parent group, parents of chronically ill children, parents of preadolescents, etc.)*

Critzer, D. (1996). Children's feelings. *Positive Parenting Newsletter, (1)*10. Retrieved February 28, 2003, from www.positiveparenting.com/newletter/news_july_1996.html

Dreisbach, S. (1997). My child's nothing like me. *Working Mother, 61*, 53, 60–61.

Gibbs, N. (1995). The EQ factor. *Time, 146,* 60–68.

Hitz, R. & Driscoll, A. (1988). Praise or encouragement? New insights into praise: Implications for early childhood teachers. *Young Children, 43*(5): 6–13.

Hitz, R., & Driscoll, A. (1994, Spring). Encouragement, not praise. *Texas Child Care Quarterly,* 3–10.

Hormann, E. (1983, November). Explaining death to children. *Single Parent, 25,* 27.

Klein, M. (2003). Teaching your child to choose. *Parenting,* 116–123.

Melvin, A. (1987, December 11). Let's not forget how to play. *Dallas Morning News, p. 30A.*

Pickhardt, C. (1984, September). Self-care: Insurance against abusing others. *Single Parent,* 6.

Thompkins, M. (1991). In praise of praising less. *Extensions, 6(1),* 1–4.

Vaughn, L. (1985, January). Are you an enslaved parent? *Prevention,* 60–65.

Supplemental Resources for Inspirational Poems/Stories About Parenting and Children

Canfield, J., & Hansen, M. (1993). *Chicken soup for the soul.* Deerfield Beach, FL: Health Communications.

Rogers, F. (2005) Life's Journey According to Mister Rogers: Things to Remember Along The Way. New York, NY: Hypercion.

Rogers, F. (2003) The World According to Mister Rogers: Important things to Remember. New York, NY: Hypercion.

Supplemental Resources for Feelings Lists/Charts

Boulden Publishing. www.bouldenpublishing.com. *"Children's Poster" (of feelings), and "Feelings & Faces" products, are available for purchase.*

Self Esteem Shop. www.selfesteemshop.com *"Feelings" poster and additional resources are available in Spanish and English. Versions are available for purchase.*

Additional Resources for Professional Development

Note: The World of Play Therapy Literature (Landreth et al., 2003) contains a listing of over 250 publications on filial therapy, including all research on filial therapy. (Available for purchase from the Center for Play Therapy, www.centerforplaytherapy.com. The Center houses the majority of these publications. An online bibliographic and ordering service is also available.)

Bratton, S. (1997).Training parents to facilitate their child's adjustment to divorce using the filial/family play therapy approach. In E. Schaefer & J. M. Briesmeister (Eds.), *Handbook of parent training* (2nd ed., pp. 549–572). New York: John Wiley & Sons.

Bratton, S., & Crane, J. (2003). Filial/family play therapy with single parents. In VanFleet, R. & Guerney, L. (Eds.), *Casebook of filial therapy.* Boiling Springs, PA: Play Therapy Press.

Fuchs, N. (1957). Play therapy at home. *Merrill-Palmer Quarterly, 3,* 87–95.

Ginsberg, B. (1989). Training parents as therapeutic agents with foster/adoptive children using the filial approach. In E.Schaefer & J. M. Briesmeister (Eds.), *Handbook of parent training: Parents as co-therapists for children's behavior problems* (pp. 442–478). New York: John Wiley & Sons.

Greenberg, P. (1989). Learning self-esteem and self-discipline through play. *Young Children,* 29–31.

Greenspan, S., & Greenspan, N. (1985). First Feelings: Milestones in The Emotional Development of Your Baby and Child. New York, NY: Penguin Books.

Guerney, L., & Guerney, B. (1989). Child relationship enhancement: Family therapy and parent education. Special issue: Person-centered approaches with families. *Person Centered Review, 4(3),* 344–357.

Guerney, B., Guerney, L., & Andronico, M. (1966). Filial therapy. *Yale Scientific Magazine, 40,* 6–14.

Guerney, L. (1976). Filial therapy program. In D. H. Olson (Ed.), *Treating Relationships* (pp. 67–91). Lake Mills, IA: Graphic Publishing.

Guerney, L. (2000). Filial therapy into the 21st century. *International Journal of Play Therapy, 9(2),* 1–17.

Landreth, G., Schumann, B., Hilpl, K., Kale-Fraites, A., Bratton, S., & Homeyer, L. (Eds.). (2003). *The world of play therapy literature: A definitive guide to authors and subject in the field* (4th ed.). Denton, TX: Center for Play Therapy. *Filial therapy resources begin on p. 172, with over 250 citations.* (Available for purchase from the Center for Play Therapy, www.centerforplaytherapy.com, University of North Texas, P.O. Box 310829, Denton, TX 76203-1337, 940-565-3864). To purchase the online searchable bibliography database of play therapy, go to http://www.coe.unt.edu/cpt/prosindex.html.

Moustakas, C. (1959). The therapeutic approach of parents. *Psychotherapy with children: The living relationship* (pp. 271–277). New York: Harper & Row.

Ortwein, M.C. (1997). Mastering the magic of play: A training manual for parents in filial therapy. Silver Spacing. MD: Ideals.

Strom, R. (1975). Parents and teachers as play observers. *Childhood Education,* 139–141.

Swick, K. (1989). Parental efficacy and social competence in young children. *Dimensions,* 25–26.

Additional Resources for Parents *(Therapist should be familiar with all books recommended to parents.)*

Axline, V. (1964). *Dibs in search of self.* New York: Ballantine Books.

Bailey, B. (2000). *I love you rituals.* New York: HarperCollins.

Blackard, S. *"SAY WHAT YOU SEE" for Parents and Teachers* (2005)—(Free online resource available at *www.languageoflistening.com*)

Brazelton, T. B., & Greenspan, S. I. (2000). *The irreducible needs of children.* Cambridge, MA: Perseus.

Campbell, R. (1992). *How to really love your child.* Colorado Springs, CO: Chariot Victor.

Campbell, R. (2000). *Relational parenting.* Chicago: Moody Press.

Faber, A., & Mazlish, E. (1990). *Liberated parents/Liberated children.* New York: Avon Books.

Faber, A., & Mazlish, E. (1998). *Siblings without rivalry: How to help your children live together so you can live too.* New York: Avon.

Faber, A., & Mazlish, E. (2002). *How to talk so kids will listen & listen so kids will talk.* New York: Harper Collins.

Ginott, H. (1956). *Between parent and child.* New York: Avon Books.

Glenn, H. S., & Nelsen, J. (1988). *Raising self-reliant children in a self-indulgent world.* Rocklin, CA: Prima Publishing & Communications.

Greenspan, S., & Greenspan, N. (1985). First Feelings Milestones in The Emotional Development of Your Baby and Child. New York, NY: Penguin Books.

Guerney, L. (1987). *The parenting skills program: Leader's manual.* State College, PA: IDEALS.

Guerney, L. (1988). *Parenting: A skills training manual* (3rd ed.). State College, PA: IDEALS.

Illg, F. L., Ames, L. B. A., & Baker, S. M. (1981). *Child behavior: Specific advice on problems of child behavior.* New York: Barnes & Noble.

Nelson, J. (1996). *Positive discipline.* New York: Ballantine Books.

Schaefer, C. (1984). *How to talk to children about really important things.* New York: Harper & Row.

Schaefer, C. E., & Digeronimo, T. F. (2000). *Ages and Stages: A parent's guide to normal childhood development.* NY: John Wiley & Sons.

Additional Professional Resources

Association for Filial and Relationship Enhancement Method (AFREM). www.afrem.org. Membership dues are: $20.00/yr. individual, $30.00/yr. couple, $10.00/yr. student. Membership form is available on the website.

MEASUREMENTS Used in CPRT and Filial Therapy Research

Published Instruments

The following published instruments are included because they have been used to measure CPRT/filial therapy effectiveness. Examples of published instruments that have been used to examine changes in parental behavior as a result of filial training include the Parenting Stress Index (PSI) and the Family Environment Scale (FES). Changes in children as a result of filial training have been quantified through the use of measurements such as the Child Behavior Checklist (CBCL) and the Joseph Preschool and Primary Self-Concept Scale (JPPSCS).

Abidin, R. (1983). *Parenting stress index*. Charlottesville, VA: Pediatric Psychology Press. (The PSI can be ordered from Psychological Assessment Resources at 1-800-331-8378 or via e-mail at www. parinc.com or www.custserv@parinc.com.)

Achenbach, T. M., & Edlebrock, C.S. (1983/2001). *Manual for the child behavior checklist and revised behavioral profile*. Burlington, VT: University of Vermont. (The CBC is available for purchase at www.aseba.org.)

Joseph, J. (1979). *Joseph pre-school and primary self-concept screening instructional manual*. Chicago: Stoelting. The JPPSST is available for purchase at http://www.stoeltingco.com/tests/store/view-level3.asp?keyword1=38&keyword3=956.

Moos, R. H. (1974). *Family environment scale*. Palo Alto, CA: Consulting Psychologists Press, Inc. (The FES is available for purchase at http://www.mindgarden.com/products/fescs.htm.)

Muller, D. G., & Leonetti, R. (1972). *Primary self-concept inventory test manual*. Austin, TX: Urban Research Group, Inc.

Pino, C., Simons, N., & Slawinowski, M. (1984). *The children's version of the family environmental scale manual*. New York: Slosson Educational Publications, Inc. (The CVFES is available for purchase at http://www.slosson.com/productCat6206.ctlg.)

Reynolds, C. R., & Kamphaus, R. W. (1992). *Behavior assessment system for children (BASC)*. Circle Pines, MN: American Guidance Service, Inc.

Unpublished Instruments

The Measurement of Empathy in Adult-Child Interaction (MEACI), the Porter Parental Acceptance Scale (PPAS), and the Filial Problem Checklist (FPC) have been used frequently in filial therapy research to assess child behavior problems and to more specifically measure parent (and teacher) skills and attitudes consistent with the goals of filial therapy. With the permission of their authors, these instruments, along with administration and scoring directions, are included in Appendix E on the accompanying CD to facilitate ease of reproduction. We gratefully acknowledge Dr. Louise Guerney and Dr. Blaine Porter for allowing us to include these instruments to facilitate their use by CPRT/filial therapy researchers.

Measurement of Empathy in Adult-Child Interactions Scale (MEACI). The MEACI measures the ability of parents or teachers to demonstrate empathic behaviors in adult-child play sessions. The MEACI has its origins in the work of Guerney, Stover, and DeMeritt's (1968) untitled assessment that measured mothers' empathy in mother-child interactions during spontaneous play with their children. Stover, Guerney, and O'Connell (1971) revised the scale and established acceptable reliability and validity scores. Bratton (1993) developed the current MEACI rating form (included below) from information obtained from Stover, L., Guerney, B., & O'Connell, M. (1971) and personal communication with Louise Guerney (April 12, 1992). Specifically, the MEACI examines three major aspects of empathic behaviors: communication of acceptance, allowing the child self-direction, and involvement with the child. Empathic behaviors are rated at three-minute intervals during the observed parent-child play sessions.

Porter Parental Acceptance Scale (PPAS). The PPAS was originally developed by Dr. Blaine Porter in 1954 and recently revised by the author (Porter, 2005). The PPAS measures parental acceptance of child, a core element in the communication of empathy and a fundamental condition needed to facilitate a child's development of positive self-worth (Bratton & Landreth, 1995). Specifically, the four subscales of the PPAS measure respect for the child's feelings and the child's right to express them, appreciation of the child's uniqueness, recognition of the child's need for autonomy and independence, and a parent's experience of unconditional love for a child.

Filial Problem Checklist (FPC). The FPC was developed at the individual and Family Consultation Center, Pennsylvania State University in 1974 by Peter Horner MS to measure the effectiveness of filial therapy in reducing problematic behaviors. The FPC is a parent self-report instrument that contains 108 problematic child behaviors that parents rate, to indicate the severity of the problem. A total score is obtained and used pre-treatment and post-treatment to compare parents' perception of change in their child's behavior.

References

Bratton, S., Landreth, G., & Homeyer, L. (1993). An intensive three-day play therapy supervision/training model. *International Journal of Play Therapy, 2(s)*, 61–79.

Bratton, S., & Landreth, G. (1995). Filial therapy with single parents: Effects on parental acceptance, empathy, and stress. *International Journal of Play Therapy, (4)1*, 61–88.

Guerney, B., Stover, L., & DeMeritt, S. (1968). A measurement of empathy for parent-child interaction. *Journal of Genetic Psychology, 112*, 49–55.

Stover, L. Guerney, B., & O'Connell, M. (1971). Measurements of acceptance, allowing self-direction, involvement, and empathy in adult-child interaction. *Journal of Psychology, 77*, 261–269.

APPENDICES

Using the Appendices

Appendix A includes helpful organizational and practical materials for CPRT training. These materials are prepared for ease of reprinting for each new group and include a *Parent Information Form* to complete prior to Session 1 and to note important information about group participants (this form should be brought to every session; therefore we suggest inserting it in the front of the *Therapist Notebook*); the *Materials Checklist* for Sessions 1–10 to help keep track of what the therapist needs to bring to each session (the therapist is advised to bring a few extras of all printed materials that parents will need for each session, in the likely case a parent forgets the notebook); *CPRT Progress Notes* to assess the clinical progress of individual group members throughout Sessions 1–10; and the *Therapist Skills Checklist* for the novice CPRT therapist or student intern to self-assess important CPRT skills. This appendix also contains items for parents that are to be handed out separately from the *Parent Notebook* materials, including *Playtime Appointment Cards, Do Not Disturb Template,* and *Certificates of Completion*.

Appendix B includes a poster format of the most frequently used handout, *Play Session Dos and Don'ts*, formatted so that the therapist can print it out on three sheets of 8 ½" x 11" paper, tape it together, and laminate it as a poster to provide a handy visual for referencing these important skills during Sessions 3–10.

Appendix C includes supplemental parent worksheets and therapist versions with example answers. These supplemental handouts provide opportunities for additional practice of CPRT skills and are used at the discretion of the therapist's assessment of the parents' needs. The session numbers on each worksheet corresponds to when that particular skill is generally introduced or practiced. Worksheets include: *Feelings Response Worksheet* for Session 2, *Choice-Giving Worksheet* for Session 6, *Esteem-Building Responses Worksheet* for Session 7, *Encouragement vs. Praise Worksheet* for Session 8, and *Advanced Limit Setting: Giving Choices as Consequences Worksheet* for Session 9. References to these optional worksheets are included in the *Study Guide* in the sessions we recommend their use; however, they may be used flexibly, depending on the needs of a particular group of parents. Although these supplemental worksheets are provided as additional practice for CPRT skills that a particular groups of parents may be having difficulty with, the therapist is cautioned to avoid overwhelming parents with too much information or homework. Again, it is expected that the therapist will exercise clinical judgment in determining when and if to use supplemental materials.

Appendix D includes information for successful marketing of C-P-R Training to parents. A sample brochure, a sample newspaper ad, and two sample flyers are included. These materials may be electronically adapted for therapist use.

Appendix E includes three unpublished assessments that have been used for research in CPRT and filial therapy: *Porter Parental Acceptance Scale* (PPAS), and *Filial Problems Checklist* (FPC), and *Measurement of Empathy in Adult-Child Interaction* (MEACI). All three measures are designed to be administered pre and post treatment. The PPAS and FPC are self-report instruments administered to parents; the PPAS measures parent's attitude of acceptance toward the child of focus, while the FPC measures the parent's perception of the child of focus's behavior. The MEACI is a direct observational measure of parental empathy that requires pre and post videotaping of parents (the use of this instrument requires substantial training and inter-rater reliability). Instruments and scoring are included in separate files for ease of printing. We gratefully acknowledge Dr. Louise Guerney and Dr. Blaine Porter for generously allowing us to include these materials for use by CPRT/filial therapists.

Appendices

Note: The appendices listed below are found only on the accompanying CD-ROM.

When appropriate, the Study Guide and Materials Checklist for each treatment session refer to the materials contained in each appendix.

Appendix A: Required Materials

- Parent Information Form (For Therapist—Complete prior to Session 1; Bring to all sessions)
- Materials Checklists (For Therapist—Sessions 1–10)
- CPRT Progress Notes for Sessions 1–10
- CPRT Progress Notes–blank form (for use in adapting filial format)
- CPRT–Therapist Skill Checklist (Sessions 1–10)
- Template for Do Not Disturb Sign
- Appointment Cards for Parents–Young Child (Sessions 3 & 10)
- Appointment Cards for Parents–Older Child (Sessions 3 & 10)
- Certificate of Completion for Parents (Session 10)

Appendix B: Poster

- Play Session Do's & Don'ts (Sessions 3–10)

Appendix C: Supplemental Parent Worksheets (and Answer Sheets)

- Feelings Response Practice Worksheet (Session 2)
- Feelings Response Practice Answersheet (for Therapist—Session 2)
- Choice-Giving Practice Worksheet (Session 6)
- Choice-Giving Practice Answersheet (for Therapist—Session 6)
- Esteem-Building Responses Worksheet (Session 7)
- Esteem-Building Responses Answersheet (for Therapist—Session 7)
- Encouragement vs. Praise Worksheet (Session 8)
- Encouragement vs. Praise Answersheet (for Therapist—Session 8)
- Advanced Limit Setting: Giving Choices as Consequences Worksheet (Session 9)
- Advanced Limit Setting: Giving Choices as Consequences Answersheet (for Therapist—Session 9)

Appendix D: Marketing CPRT Training

- Sample Brochure
- Sample Newspaper Ad

- Sample CPRT Flyer #1: Parenting Can Be Difficult
- Sample CPRT Flyer #2: Give Your Children What They Need Most: **YOU**

Appendix E: CPRT/Filial Therapy Assessment Instruments

Measurement of Empathy in Adult-Child Interaction (MEACI)
- Instrument
- Directions for Scoring

Porter Parental Acceptance Scale (PPAS)
- Instrument
- Directions for Scoring

Filial Problems Checklist (FPC)
- Instrument
- Directions for Scoring

CONTENTS OF COMPANION
CD-ROM

Using the CD-ROM

The **CD-ROM** allows the therapist to print the required CPRT training materials (*Therapist Notebook* and *Parent Notebook*) for ease of reproduction and enhanced usability for parents and therapists.

We strongly urge therapists to print *Parent Notebooks* from the CD-ROM for correct pagination. The CD-ROM version is formatted to be printed double-sided to save paper and to ensure each CPRT Session begins on a new page, further allowing the use of divider tabs to organize the *Parent Notebook* by Session number. Similarly, we recommend that therapists print the *Therapist Notebook* from the CD-ROM, which allows for customizing the Treatment Outlines as needed.

The CD-ROM also includes several useful appendices not found in the manual. The appendices contain organizational materials, clinical forms, marketing materials, assessments, and supplemental skill practice worksheets for parents.

Note: Permission to copy the materials is granted to the therapist in conjunction with the purchase of this training. The copyright statement should be printed out and included on all copied materials.

Companion CD-ROM

📁 Therapist Notebook: Treatment Outlines & Handouts for Sessions 1–10

📁 Parent Notebook: Handouts, Notes, & Homework for Sessions 1–10

📁 CPRT Training Resources

📁 Appendix A: Required Materials

- Parent Information Form (For Therapist—Session 1)
- Materials Checklist (For Therapist—Sessions 1–10)
- CPRT Progress Notes for Sessions 1–10
- CPRT Progress Notes–blank form
- CPRT–Therapist Skill Checklist (for novice CPRT therapist or intern)
- Template for "Do Not Disturb" sign
- Appointment Cards for Parents–Young Child (Sessions 3 and 10)
- Appointment Cards for Parents–Older Child (Sessions 3 and 10)
- Certificate of Completion for Parents (Session 10)

📁 Appendix B: Poster

- Play Session Do's & Don'ts (Sessions 3–10)

📁 Appendix C: Supplemental Parent Worksheets (and Answer Sheets)

- Feelings Response Practice Worksheet (Session 2)
- Feelings Response Practice Answersheet (for Therapist—Session 2)
- Choice-Giving Practice Worksheet (Session 6)
- Choice-Giving Practice Answersheet (for Therapist—Session 6)
- Esteem-Building Responses Worksheet (Session 7)
- Esteem-Building Responses Answersheet (for Therapist—Session 7)
- Encouragement vs. Praise Worksheet (Session 8)
- Encouragement vs. Praise Answersheet (for Therapist—Session 8)
- Advanced Limit Setting: Giving Choices as Consequences Worksheet (Session 9)
- Advanced Limit Setting: Giving Choices as Consequences Answersheet (for Therapist—Session 9)

Appendix D: Marketing CPRT Training

- Sample Brochure
- Sample Newspaper Article
- Sample CPRT Flyer #1: Parenting Can Be Difficult
- Sample CPRT Flyer #2: Give Your Children What They Need Most: **YOU**

Appendix E: CPRT/Filial Therapy Assessments

Measurement of Empathy in Adult-Child Interaction (MEACI)
- Instrument
- Directions for Scoring

Porter Parental Acceptance Scale (PPAS)
- Instrument
- Directions for Scoring

Filial Problems Checklist (FPC)
- Instrument
- Directions for Scoring